Beyond the Crisis in
US American Studies:
Scandinavian Perspectives

Beyond the Crisis in US American Studies: Scandinavian Perspectives

Edited by David E. Nye

UNIVERSITY PRESS OF SOUTERN DENMARK · 2007

© The authors and University Press of Southern Denmark 2007
Set and printed by Narayana Press
ISBN 978-87-7674-252-2

Cover illustration: Main Street Shop Facades in Selma, Alabama, 1935.
Photo: Walker Evans / Corbis

University of Southern Denmark Studies in History and Social Sciences vol. 348

University Press of Southern Denmark
Campusvej 55
DK-5230 Odense M
Phone: +45 6615 7999
Fax: +45 6615 8126
Press@forlag.sdu.dk
www.universitypress.dk

Distribution in the United States and Canada:
International Specialized Book Services
5804 NE Hassalo Street
Portland, OR 97213-3644 USA
www.isbs.com

Distribution in the United Kingdom:
Gazelle
White Cross Mills
Hightown
Lancaster
LA1 4 XS
U.K.
www.gazellebooks.co.uk

"In the end, the future of American Studies in Europe will ... depend on the ability of European scholars ... to establish their American work according to their own methods and standards, learning from each other as much as from the Americans ...". – Sigmund Skard, 1958

Contents

Preface 9
ROB KROES   Coming in from the Cold: American
                  Studies from the Periphery · 11

The Institutionalized Crisis of American Studies 23
ROLF LUNDÉN   The Eternal, Irresoluble Tensions in
                  American Studies · 25
DAVID E. NYE   American Studies as a Contested
                  Crossroads · 59

American Studies from the Outside In 83
DAVID E. NYE   American Studies in Stereo · 85
MARK LUCCARELLI   Re-thinking American Studies for the 21st
                  Century · 107

Research Trajectories 123
JØRN BRØNDAL   Who Were They? Writing Scandinavian-
                  American History · 125
ORM ØVERLAND   Studying Myself in the United States
                  – Studying the United States in
                  Myself · 165
DAVID E. NYE   Absent Native Son · 199

Bibliography 227

Index 253

Contributors 257

This book is dedicated to the memory of **Niels Thorsen**, who enlivened many a NAAS conference. He taught at Copenhagen University, where for a decade he served as editor of *American Studies in Scandinavia*.

Preface

The present volume is part of the 40th anniversary celebration of *American Studies in Scandinavia*, which began publication in 1967. It is the first of a series of books that will bring together the distinctive scholarship of the community of Americanists who are members of the Nordic Association of American Studies. Each future volume, like this one, will focus on a single topic, combining several new essays with a selection of articles from previous issues of the journal. This inaugural work in the series contains three articles from *American Studies in Scandinavia* (those by Rolf Lundén, Orm Øverland, and Mark Luccarelli), one essay published earlier in Danish (that by Jørn Brøndal), and four that have not been published before. They have been edited so that they speak to one another, and arranged to present a common argument.

It seemed appropriate to begin this series by situating Scandinavian practice in relationship to the current difficulties of American Studies in the United States, where for a decade scholars have been attacking one another. Is this a crisis in American Studies as a whole? Or is the problem largely confined to the United States? How is this interdisciplinary field different, when practiced in Scandinavia? These questions ultimately are about the direction and the international coherence of American Studies. As Rob Kroes notes in his introduction, for too long European scholars have watched Americanists in the United States as though looking through a one-way window, invisible to those arguing on the other side of the glass. For too long US Americanists have scarcely realized that what appeared a mirror could be a window.

Coming in from the Cold: American Studies from the Periphery

ROB KROES

In his contribution to a 1986 collection of essays – *Anti-Americanism in Europe* – Dutch sociologist Johan Goudsblom (1986) used the metaphor of the one-way mirror to describe the situation of Dutch intellectuals studying the outside world. The one-way mirror, as psychologists use it in their research, allows observers to watch, unobserved, what is going on in an adjacent room. Those on the other side of the glass cannot see through it. To them it looks like an ordinary mirror, reflecting their own image back at them. Had Goudsblom been from Scandinavia, he would more likely have used the image of Andersen's little match girl, looking in from the cold at a happy family at Christmas time, while being ignored by those on the inside, feasting. The latter image is probably the more poignant one when it comes to describing the situation of American Studies scholars studying America from abroad. Pertinent as their observations may be, whether or not they take their cues from heated debate among the insiders, as a rule they are left out in the cold to fend for themselves.

In twentieth-century European narratives about European-American cultural encounters variations on the little match girl theme have become a recurring trope. A classic example is Jacques Tati's *Jour de fête*. At one point the central character, a postman in a French small town – an amiable bungler as only Tati can invent them – is shown peeking through an opening in the canvas of a large circus tent. On the inside a documentary film is being shown on the mail delivery system in the United States. Mail delivery men are shown on motorbikes, jumping through hoops of fire, and at full speed catching mailbags dropped from airplanes. To Tati's postman it has the power of an epiphany, an eye-opening encounter with American modernity. In a parody of cultural appropriation the postman adapts his delivery act, mounting his bike with quasi-American zest and pluck, in a self-styled new mail (male?) identity. The documentary footage itself must have been Tati's parody of the many film shorts shown across Europe under Marshall Plan auspices to introduce Europeans to American-style modernity and efficiency.

I have argued for a fuller exploration by European American Studies scholars of this narrative trope (Kroes, 1999). Each instance represents a formative moment in the larger process of what we may summarily call the Americanization of Europe. In each, it is America that provides the impetus for the revelation, the model to be emulated. Dramatically these moments serve as epic concentrations, condensing into a single moment what in fact has been the continuing process of the transformation of identities in Europe. An entire list could be composed of such moments, all of them variations on the theme of Europeans looking in from the outside, undergoing a culture shock, and experiencing it as a moment of conversion. In European film as well as literature a range of vignettes can be found illustrating these moments of encounter and appropriation in a number of settings and configurations. There is Pascal Quignard's *L'occupation américaine* (1994) giving the encounter the form and flavor of a cultural romance. In the story America is represented by an army base in France, like a spaceship from Mars sitting in the midst of the French countryside, utterly alien yet endlessly intriguing in the radiance it exerts on two French children who in their early explorations go through the rubble and refuse from the base with its discarded bits of an American consumption culture. They are like anthropologists trying to read sense into the material fragments of a way of life that otherwise is self-enclosed and inaccessible to them. As the story unfolds, access is slowly gained and a friendship develops around the shared language of jazz music. The story reminds us of similar vignettes in Bertrand Tavernier's 1986 film *Round Midnight* or Alan Parker's 1991 film *The Commitments*. Tavernier shows us a French jazz aficionado out in the street, unable to afford the price of admission, listening in to a French Jazz club to hear one of his cultural heroes play. Again, the film tells the story of a French-American friendship developing around the language of jazz, imported from the United States and appropriated by young French people as a meaningful expression of their cultural desires. In Alan Parker's film the setting for the encounter with a form of American culture – the blues as represented in James Brown's high-adrenalin primal scream – is typically mediated, literally so. A group of young working-class Dubliners, in an urgent quest for a musical form that will allow them to give voice to their sense of self, watches James Brown do his thing on TV. In an instant act of cultural translation their leader tells his friends that they have to become like James Brown. "He is like us. The Irish are the blacks of Europe, the Dubliners are the blacks of Ireland, and we Northenders are the blacks of Dublin. Say it once and say it loud: we are black and we are proud." In disbelief his friends silently repeat the last words, their lips moving to form the words of the punch line, "We are black and we are proud." Slowly the message sinks in. Yet another appropriation of American culture has taken place before our eyes, affecting the sense of identity of these youngsters. They are cast in the role of celebrants in a ritual of cultural conversion.

These are stories that all have a special resonance among European publics. They call forth a repertoire of recollections of meaningful moments in their lives, growing up in a Europe exposed to a veritable flood of American cultural messages and cultural practices, all equally suggestive of cultural alternatives to what European parental cultural models had to offer. Throughout the twentieth century the American way with culture, through a variety of ways of mediation, has developed into a potent cultural vector orienting the collective gaze of Europeans across the Atlantic. It has added to the range of cultural options for Europeans, facilitating forms of selective appropriation, or causing cultural resistance and culture wars within the various national settings in Europe. Yet, as a shared point of reference, helping Europeans define who they are, America to all Europeans has become the presence on the other side of the one-way mirror, supremely unaware of the impact of its cultural doings on those observing it. When Americans look around, the mirror reflects their own image back to them and suggests a world increasingly cast in an American image.

In my years as President of the European Association for American Studies (from 1992 to 1996), at the behest of Paul Lauter, the then President of the US American Studies Association, I wrote a piece for the ASA Newsletter on the state of American Studies outside the United States. Lauter's invitation in itself was the sign of a growing readiness to acknowledge the existence of a community of scholars studying the United States from outside its national borders. Yet at the same time it was an acknowledgement that way too little attention had been paid to their work, that American Studies as it had developed in the United States was mostly a self-referential community, sharing concerns as defined by American scholars. In ASA circles at the time, as well as more generally among American scholars, historians in particular, whose research had focused on America, there was a growing sense of intellectual parochialism, translating into a felt need for, as it was called then, the internationalization of the study of America.

In my piece, trying to take stock of the situation as it had prevailed until then, I remember using the metaphor of phototropism in my description of much American Studies work done outside America. Like phototropic organisms foreign American Studies scholars had collectively oriented their gaze toward the guiding light of American Studies as done in the US. They tended to take their intellectual cues and research interests from the ruling fashions in the field in the US, seeking recognition of their work on an equal footing with their American colleagues. Yet, in whatever way one measures the success of their efforts, through publications in the US or through citations of their work, they hardly ever managed to penetrate into the inner circles of the discipline. Much of their work, particularly when done in languages other than English, went unnoticed in the US. Yet, as I argued, the very fact that so many of these outsiders studying America held their gaze focused on the American Studies community in the US prevented them from developing peripheral vision, from taking note themselves of work done by fellow outsiders, preventing them from a sense of community, more than that: a sense of mission that it was for them to develop rival forms of American Studies, and to bring other perspectives and concerns to bear on the construction of America as a force and presence in the world. It was typically for them to internationalize the study of America.

Yet, over the years, slowly a sense of community began to take shape among the outsiders. Ever since the 1950s non-American associations for American Studies had been founded, as national, regional, or in the case of the European Association for American Studies (founded in 1954) transnational associations. But in the early years many footprints were left testifying to the American auspices of these organizational ventures. Often money was provided through the United

States Information Agency (U.S.I.A.), keynote speakers were often American, and much of the work presented by members of such associations was hard to tell apart from work done by Americans. At the same time, though, the very existence of such independent non-American associations for American Studies provided the impetus for exploring an agenda for research typically to be done by non-Americans, an agenda that could expand the range of research questions guiding the work of American Americanists. Early publications by the EAAS, for instance, based on its biennial conventions, did explore the history of European attitudes vis-à-vis the United States.[1] As Arie N.J. den Hollander, the then President of EAAS put it in the introduction to one of the two volumes of collected essays he edited for EAAS: "The themes of the study conferences organized by the European Association for American Studies have always been chosen with an eye to the possibility of a specific European contribution to the understanding of American phenomena. American civilization, like any other culture, is an interdependent system of countless elements, based upon linked premises and categories whose importance is in no way the less because they are so seldom verbally expressed: they are taken for granted. It was the aim of the EAAS conferences in Rome (24-27 September 1967) and in Brussels (13-16 October 1970) to explore some of these tacit assumptions and make them explicit. We have tried to do so by a method of comparison, by demonstrating that Americans and Europeans frequently do the same thing in very different ways, ways that are culturally determined." (1991, 2). If the thrust of these words is toward internationalizing American Studies, toward "exporting internationalism" in Hans Bungert's words (cf. note 4), EAAS may well have contributed to the later sense of need for precisely such internationalization among American communities of scholars as organized in the American Studies Association (ASA) and the Organization of American Historians (OAH).

Also, by bringing together European scholars to reflect on such themes, organizations like EAAS may well have fostered a sense of community and shared intellectual interests among non-American Americanists. It may have helped them develop their peripheral vision, weaning them off their fixation on the leading light of American Studies done the American way, and become aware of work done by their non-American colleagues. Collectively, they began to stake out a claim for the relevance and significance of their work and for the difference it made compared to mainstream work done by their American colleagues. In a striking parallel to what Orm Øverland in his recent work, as well as in his contribution to this volume, has called "home-making myths" of immigrants in America, laying claim to the difference they collectively had made to the history of America, non-American Americanists developed their own claim-making narratives. Ironically, early American sponsorship of American Studies in Europe may well have spawned this intellectual emancipation of Americanists abroad. A prime example is Sigmund Skard, who in a survey of American Studies in Europe facilitated by USIA and the Rockefeller Foundation, argued provocatively that Europe, while largely unaware of the fact, may well have a history of reflection on American civilization and the cultural difference it represented in the eyes of Europeans that long predates the American Studies movement in the United States. Yet he was well aware of the daunting project he was facing. As he put it in his introduction: "These tentative samplings made it clear that interest in the study of American Civilization in the widest sense was much more general than was commonly known. Since the recent war discussion had been going on in almost every European country about the definition and scope, character and purpose of the new subject; and the problems were the same everywhere. But there was little coordination. Schools, universities and individuals were often ignorant of the work that was being done in other countries, in their own country, and even in neighboring institutions or faculties, and forged ahead on their own with a pioneering pride which was the supreme sign of their isolation." (1958, 7) Again, in words I used before, there was insufficient peripheral vision among students of America in Europe.

But things have changed significantly. Former lines of compartmentalization have been breached, collegial communities of non-American Americanists transcending nations and regions of the world have formed. There is an increasing amount of work done internationally. International meetings now regularly bring together scholars who previously, in Skard's words, may have worked in isolation. What is more, vibrant links have now been established with the community of American scholars in the field. It is no longer exceptional to see volumes produced on crucial subjects of American Studies where non-Americans bring their comparative expertise to bear. With time, the one-way mirror effect has weakened, it seems. American Americanists now can look through the window, and to their surprise they can discover that Europeans are talking about similar things, but the conversations are not merely echoes or repetitions of their own ideas. The years of isolation have produced a new discourse.

Thus, on the occasion of the fiftieth anniversary of American Studies at the University of Amsterdam an international group of scholars was brought together, including colleagues from European countries, Japan, South-Africa, and the United States to report on what to them had been the formative voices in their intellectual growth as American Studies scholars within their various national settings. The perspective arising from these many reflections was one of a truly international web of intellectual exchange, being locally appropriated and transformed and reflected back internationally.[2] Admittedly, and perhaps not surprisingly, many of the essays by non-Americans still showed the vectorial force of leading

American voices and views, as these had helped form the perspectives of non-American colleagues in the field. It is better perhaps to conceive of the relevance of the volume as a step in the emerging awareness of a web of international intellectual exchange. Other recent volumes in the Amsterdam series bring out more prominently the voices and perspectives of non-American Americanists, such as *Within the US Orbit: Small National Cultures vis-á-vis the United States* or *Straddling Borders: The American Resonance in Transnational Identities*. The former volume brings together scholars from Belgium, Canada, Denmark, Hungary, the Netherlands and Sweden, reporting on the radiance of American culture as experienced in their various national settings, all characterized by their concerns of smallness and fragility in the face of an overbearing American cultural presence. The latter volume takes the analysis a logical step further, exploring the ways in which the appropriation of American cultural forms elsewhere may have worked to widen and open up people's sense of their identity and place in the world, adding to their repertoires for self-definition and cultural reference.[3]

Much in my argument so far suggests a view of American Studies as basically a variant of cultural studies or cultural history, focusing on problems of cultural reception, selective appropriation and resistance, and ultimately problems of identity formation and meaningful self-definition, by individuals or collectively by nations. The latter aspect is particularly prominent in studies of anti-Americanism, as recently in a book by Philippe Roger (2005) on the long history of French anti-Americanism. As he tells the story, French anti-Americanism is an ingrained feature of French national culture, gaining layers in almost sedimentary fashion as time proceeds. Yet many other studies of anti-Americanism highlight the political rather than the cultural dimensions of the phenomenon, focusing on subjects such as power and national interest, subjects neglected in much self-styled American Studies work. Normally the area is covered by scholars, working in history or political science, who would not conceive of themselves as being engaged in American Studies. Diplomatic history on both sides of the Atlantic may have renewed itself in suggesting new paradigms for the study of America as empire, in American Studies as currently defined in ASA circles – or in the newly founded International Association of American Studies (IASA) – the trend seems to be in the opposite direction, away from organizing concepts such as the state or the nation. The so-called linguistic turn in American Studies does not help, in the way it has come to conceive of its deconstruction of entrenched linguistic categories as so many victories won over entrenched power relations. Exploding the names language has given to America's population of African descent, from Negroes, to Blacks, to Afro-Americans, has done nothing to improve their social condition. Nor does a plea to remove the nation-state referent from American Studies help us much at a time when the American nation-state unilaterally asserts itself in its worldwide claim to pursue first and foremost America's national interest. Such intellectual moves leave us empty-handed when it comes to understanding the driving forces behind America's most recent appearance as an imperial raging bull.

Let us return once again to Johan Goudsblom's piece that I quoted earlier. Referring to the way that in the 1950s Dutch social scientists increasingly oriented themselves toward the model of American sociology he has this to say: "Yet these (American) theories were in some respects strangely deficient. Thus, to mention some of the most noteworthy omissions, sociology as it was practiced in America in the fifties offered no theory of the state, and in particular no theory of inter-state relations and of state formation; as a consequence, it also lacked a theory of long-term social processes. ... The primary emphasis was on values." (116-117) This may remind us that in American American Studies, not just in its current fashion but more generally, the emphasis has been on ideals, ideas and values such as those that inspired the formation of American Civilization.

There seems to be a continuing need for European American Studies people, with their more catholic view of who constitute the community of scholars and what are the various intellectual lineages informing their work, to produce oppositional readings of American power, seen comprehensively as cultural, political, economic, and military power, with all the feed-back loops between these various manifestations. If there are worries about the diminishing bandwidth of American public debate concerning the state of the American Republic, there is a need for Europeans to fill in the gaps and voids. If Americans don't do it themselves Europeans need to remind them of Machiavelli's dictum that the preservation of a republican order consists in "redurre le leggi i suoi principii" – the constant return to the principles undergirding their republican order. I felt the need to do precisely this at the time of my farewell to a university career in American Studies, trying to gauge the recent changes in my views of America. That address was subsequently published in a special section of the *Journal of American History*.[4]

Let me add a final autobiographical note. In my farewell address I already felt more strongly than ever before in my work that I spoke with a European voice. This leads me to making a more general point. My long-time involvement with the American Studies community in Europe, the exchanges over the years with colleagues in the one language we had in common – English – increasingly felt like a proto-European experience, turning me into a European while studying America. It is an unintended outcome of my work as an Americanist, yet something for which I have to thank America.

Notes

1 See, e.g., some early EAAS publications such as: Max Silberschmidt, ed., *Amerika-Europa: Freund und Rivale*, Arie N.J. den Hollander, ed. *Diverging Parallels: America As Compared With European Thought and Action*, and Arie N.J. den Hollander, ed., *Contagious Conflict: The Impact of American Dissent on European Life*. See also Hans Bungert, "Importing the United States, Exporting Internationalism: The First Forty Years of the EAAS, 1954-1994."

2 Rob Kroes, ed., *Predecessors: Intellectual Lineages in American Studies*

3 Rob Kroes, ed., *Within the US Orbit: Small National Cultures vis-à-vis the United States*; Rob Kroes, ed., *Straddling Borders: The American Resonance in Transnational Identities*

4 Rob Kroes, "European Anti-Americanism: What's New?" (2006).

The Institutionalized Crisis of American Studies

The Eternal, Irresoluble Tensions in American Studies

ROLF LUNDÉN

There are two central tensions within American Studies, the first between the disciplines and interdisciplinarity, the second between national and transnational orientations. These tensions have characterized American Studies from its inception, and they are still awaiting their resolution. Recent controversies between representatives of the myth-and-symbol school and the "New" American Studies can be understood in the light of the discipline-interdisciplinarity tension which has tended to dominate discussions inside the United States. In contrast, European Amercanists have been more concerned with Transnational American Studies, and have accordingly taken a different theoretical and research trajectory. These interlinked tensions have characterized but also troubled American Studies since its emergence some one hundred years ago: on the one hand, the tension between the conviction that the individual discipline is the basis for American Studies vs. the belief that true interdisciplinarity is possible; on the other, the tension between a national focus and an inter/transnational orientation. This essay addresses these contending approaches from a historical perspective, while contrasting US American Studies with non-American, particularly European, American Studies.[1]

The first part of my discussion will be devoted to the academic discipline vs. interdisciplinarity, to the tension between specialization and integration, tradition and renewal, or, to use the terms of Sigmund Skard, the grand old man of Nordic American Studies, to the relationship between American Studies and American Studies "Proper." The confrontation between these two ways of dealing with the study of America has existed since the beginning of this field of study, and it is still an unresolved issue. The pivotal texts I will use for this discussion are Skard's "The American Studies Movement," delivered as a lecture at the second Nordic Association for American Studies Conference in 1964 and printed in the proceedings *USA in Focus,* on the one hand, and three articles from the Spring 2005 issue of *American Literary History*, on the other. In analyzing these texts I will put the searchlight on the particular question of discipline and interdisciplinarity.

The second half of the article will focus on an equally troubling tension in American Studies, the one based on geographical criteria, whether American Studies should restrict itself to study the specificity of culture within the borders of the United States or whether is should have a cross-cultural, international, comparative orientation. I will trace how the tradition in Europe as well as the United States of these contending directions, with a special emphasis on Transnational American Studies now launched as a "new" development in US American Studies, goes back to at least the 1950s.

I. American Studies vs. American Studies "Proper"

In his 1964 article, "The American Studies Movement," Sigmund Skard gives an overview of American Studies on both sides of the Atlantic from the eighteenth century up to the 1960s. He draws a picture of the meandering development in American Studies, at times favoring the individual discipline, at other times advocating an approach of integrated, interdisciplinary studies. First of all, Skard makes it clear that American Studies is a European invention. The first real scholarship on American culture was produced by people like Filippo Mazzei (1788) and de Tocqueville. Up until the end of the nineteenth century these studies were generalizations, syntheses of American civilization as a whole, often seen in comparison with world developments. In the 1860s and 1870s American studies starts to become an academic subject. In the 1870s a chair in the study of America is established in Strasbourg; the first American Institute is set up in Berlin in 1910.

Simultaneously with the academization of the subject in Germany in the late 1800s, a general shift takes place from a synthetic/holistic approach toward an increased emphasis on specialization. Disciplines are defined, departments and institutes are established, separated from each other. As a consequence, a deep suspicion of generalizations becomes common. The German tradition of specialization, of constructing disciplines, spreads to the United States, where each specialty tends to isolate itself from its neighboring disciplines.

But soon enough, in the decades around the turn of the century, a reaction against specialization occurred in Europe. Initiatives to further a more synthetic, integrated American Studies were taken in France and Germany. In France, the subject "Literature et Civilisation Americaines" was established, and in Germany, to protest against the atomistic approach of historians, a synthetic and speculative *Kulturkunde* came into existence. Around 1912, Skard writes, "Karl Lamprecht's interdepartmental Institute of World Civilization proclaimed as part of its program to see America as well as other nations from the aspects of social mass movements and the morphology of cultures" ("The American Studies Movement" 144). Lamprecht's initiative sounds to me like one of the precursors of presentday transnational American Studies.

After WWI, American Studies continued to grow in France and Germany. In 1918 Charles Cestre was appointed by Sorbonne to the first permanent European chair in "American literature and civilization." He insisted on the idea of manysidedness as distinctive of American Studies. Several other chairs with the same designation appeared, and Collège de

France established a full professorship in American Civilization. In Germany in the 1920s *Geistesgeschichte* and comparative research became common in order to study the soul of a nation, and demands for *Auslandskunde* were raised. In 1921, a program for *Amerikakunde* was formulated, a new, interdisciplinary study of American civilization integrating history, literature, and economics.

However, the resistance to this newfangledness was strong from the established disciplines. In their harsh objections the critics held that "all *Kulturkunde*, whether German or foreign, runs the risk of dilettantism" (146). The advocates of the specialized disciplines were unsuccessful, however, and *Kulturkunde* was appropriated with a twist in 1933 by the Nazi government. In the years to follow, making use of *Auslandkunde*, Hitler could generalize about races and nations, not least the Americans. American Studies, Skard points out, thus became thoroughly discredited. In the Soviet Union a similar manipulation of American Studies took place, in which America was one part of a coherent study of the entire Capitalist world.

If we cross the Atlantic, the same picture of opposition between disciplinary and interdisciplinary American Studies is repeated. In the period after WWI and up to and past WWII, American universities, according to Skard, were characterized by "the traditional emphasis on foreign and past civilizations, particularly British, at the expense of America itself; the academic departmentalism with its formal narrowness; the worship of facts and details; and the fear of large views and value judgments" (147). Gradually a reaction grew; there was a need and urge to emphasize the unity of the nation, to redefine its heritage and give a sense of direction to its culture. There was thus a reform movement for a new synthesis of knowledge. The beginnings were very modest. By the end of the 1920s there were no more than three American Studies programs in the United States. One of the reasons for this slow start was that advocates of American literature were involved in establishing their own subject as a separate discipline. The rest of this story is well-known, how the American Studies Association was started in 1951 and how the myth-and-symbol school grew strong and influential; I will have reason to return to this form of holistic American Studies below.

The catchword of the American Studies of the 1950s was "integration," designating a fusion of disciplines and a fusion of the various aspects of American society; the goal was to study the United States as a whole, to search for the essential "American" identity. And now we are entering Sigmund Skard's own time of writing, the late 1950s and early 1960s. Skard draws a picture of internal as well as external criticism and opposition. He points to the cultural conservatism, not least in the English departments, which looked at "the motley, incoherent and 'pluralistic' civilization of modern USA with aversion and concern" (151). But he also questions the practical results of the new scholarly field. The overwhelming majority of the 1900 institutions of higher learning in the United States taught American Studies in some discipline or other, but only 120 of them had some form of integrated arrangement for American Studies. Relatively few American universities had established graduate departments in American Studies "proper." The tension, then, between disciplinary and interdisciplinary studies must have been considerable at the beginning of the 1960s.

A third problem, according to Skard, and which will be further addressed in the second half of my discussion, was the parochialism and narrowness of American Studies in the United States. The lack of comparative studies was striking; the students knew, for instance, nothing of their European roots. Nor were American scholars aware of American Studies research going on outside America. Voices were raised demanding that all American Studies should by definition be comparative. Another fear uttered by critics was that the somewhat limitless scope of American Studies may lead to intellectual looseness or cheap popularity, allowing the students to know less and less about more and more. It is easy to guess where such criticism came from. These critics held that the "crossdepartmental study of widely divergent fields may lead to an amateurish toying with methods and knowledge within disciplines which, each in itself, requires a lifetime of concentrated study" (153). Still other critics, or maybe the same ones, argued that American Studies was merely a façade, that integration existed only on paper, that programs consisted of lectures and courses given by scholars in specialized disciplines. A final reservation was that American civilization is too complex to be synthesized.

Skard's own remedy to some of these problems was the following: "The undoubted danger of dilettantism involved in such a transgression of boundaries can only be countered by a sharpened critical attitude within each individual field concerned" (159). This sounds somewhat like what a disillusioned Daniel Aaron said to me when I happened to meet him in the late 1980s: "Back to the disciplines."

Let us now take a giant leap forward – 41 years to be more precise, to the Spring 2005 issue of *American Literary History*. What has happened during those four decades? Skard ended his survey by calling the debate over American Studies a "long and inconclusive bickering" whose "outcome remains ambiguous and is bound to continue to be so" (170). Are we now any closer to a resolution to the tension between discipline and interdisciplinarity? Chameleonlike, the issues have shifted color, but basically, it seems to me they are the same. Before we turn to the three articles in *American Literary History*, a few general words may be needed about American Studies between 1968, which Leo Marx has called the Great Divide, and the present situation, with a particular focus on the opposition between discipline and American Studies "proper."

The questioning of integrated American Studies from c. 1940 until the 1960s by members of established disciplines has obviously continued in the period when American Studies shifted towards an interrogation of gender, race, sexuality, ethnicity and has become even more heated, it seems to me, in the present-day age when American Studies has moved closer to cultural studies and into transnational and postnational American Studies. But there has also been a tension among those who represent integrated American Studies, between members of the myth-and-symbol school and the two later inflections of American Studies, a confrontation that could very well be analyzed in terms of specialization and integration.

In the Spring 2005 issue of *American Literary History*, Leo Marx, in "On Recovering the 'Ur' Theory of American Studies," divides American Studies into BD and AD – Before the Divide, 1968, and After the Divide – and gives his perspective on the development. He depicts BD American Studies as an "essentially holistic, affirmative, nationalistic project." Its scholars believed in both the project and in America. But he also acknowledges that American Studies never found an interdisciplinary method, and self-ironically admits that he and his colleagues "managed to ignore, in keeping with the nationalistic, patriarchal, racialist, hegemonic master narrative to which they subscribed, the sharp differences of gender, class, race, ethnicity, and sexual preference that divided Americans into virtually separate groups" (123). In the 1970s, he says, this holistic unifying view was denounced and repudiated, and AD Americanists turned their attention to "concrete particulars, to the precise, close-up, empirical, often quasi-ethnographic study of the beliefs and behavior of clearly defined, relatively small, even face-to-face local groups with shared identities" (124). He claims that it became far more important to the AD Americanists to study the dividing than the cohering forces at work in America.

It may sound as if Marx is accusing the AD Americanists of having run back to their respective disciplines, back to specialization, abandoning their commitment to interdisciplinary studies. This is obviously not true, nor does Marx level such a critique. The work of the Americanists focusing on gender, sexuality, race, ethnicity was still interdisciplinary but giving attention not to American society as a whole but to distinct smaller aspects of it. Race, gender, etc. are obviously best studied with an interdisciplinary approach. What Marx questions is rather that the AD scholars disregarded the search for a unified "American" specificity.

Without making a distinction between the Americanists of the 1970s and 1980s, on the one hand, and the development in the 1990s in American Studies, on the other – they are all AD Americanists to Marx – Marx launches an attack on the latter group, which he defines as "an energetic cohort of vocal, theoretically inclined, ultra-Left Americanists" (130). He strongly opposes the attempts to delete or redefine the "American" in American Studies, and counts Alan Wolfe, after his review in *The New Republic,* as a brother in arms. Marx agrees with Wolfe's extreme views: "[Wolfe] concludes that many of these scholars, in particular those who write in the unintelligible jargon of critical theory, have 'developed a hatred for America so visceral that it makes one wonder why they bother studying America at all'" (130).

American Literary History invited two scholars, George Lipsitz and Amy Kaplan, to respond to Marx's piece, and it becomes clear from these three contributions how ideologically inflamed the issue of American Studies has become. Lipsitz claims in his article "Our America" that Marx's "'America' is an America of white male propertied power, of imperial ambition, of collectivist coercion disguised as the defense of individual freedom…. In the name of unity, our leaders seek unanimity. They seek to foster through fear what they cannot inspire by faith. When they cannot lead us, they lie to us. They insist that the story of America must be a unified narrative told from one point of view. They want a land where we dance to their tune, not our land of a thousand dances" (136).

So, while Marx implies that the New Americanists are unpatriotic America-haters, Lipsitz counters by implying that Marx is George W. Bush's errand-boy. It is time, Lipsitz holds, for American Studies to assume "our moral responsibility to engage with the concerns, injuries, and aspirations of a world wider than any one nation" (139). "Our America," he concludes, "and our American Studies should be one that hears [the cries of the poor and desperate], no matter what theoretical or epistemological form they take" (140).

Amy Kaplan's response is titled "A Call for a Truce," but it turns out, as she starts countering Marx's arguments, that she herself has difficulties accepting a truce – which she finally admits. Kaplan holds that Marx caricatures and demeans the work of the AD scholars. According to Kaplan, Marx laments the loss of the original belief in America and the ur-theory of American Studies, a loss he attributes to "disillusionment ensuing upon the US war in Vietnam, the importation of European theory, a focus on social conflict and divisions, and the fragmentation of scholarship into smaller subdivisions of race, gender, ethnicity, class, and sexuality" (142). Kaplan herself sees the same development entirely differently: "Looking back at the last thirty years of scholarship, I see a breath-taking proliferation of innovative work about the structures and institutions of social oppression; about the vitality of different social groups, individuals and alliances to struggle against and transform those institutions; and about the creativity to invent and express alternative forms of belonging to different local and global communities, of which the nation is only one. Where I find a rich, complex, and multivalent portrait of America emerging from this work, Marx finds a diminishment of the original project" (142-43).

I do not want to disregard the ideological differences of this battle of the Americanists, but it seems to me that one aspect of the debate concerns the age-old tension between discipline and the interdisciplinary. Seemingly, part of the problem is that Marx has, retrospectively and maybe nostalgically, started to regard the holistic American Studies of the 1940s up to the 1960s as a discipline, a discipline which has later, after the Great Divide, been betrayed, fragmented, subdivided by an even more interdisciplinary form of American Studies which has abandoned the study of America as a whole. And his argument with the ultra-Left Americanists of the 1990s may in part stem from his irritation with their foregrounding of "the transnational and *post-disciplinary* critical impulse in contemporary American Studies," (my emphasis) as the brochure advertizing the 2005 Summer Institute at Dartmouth phrases it. What "post-disciplinary" means, exactly, is difficult to know, apart from the term expressing a critique of earlier forms of integrated, interdisciplinary American Studies for having been too dependent on individual disciplines. I would not be surprised if Marx would repeat what Aaron said: "Back to the disciplines." Nor would I be surprised if he regarded the old school of Americanists as doing in-depth research in comparison to the dilettantism of the New Americanists.

To return to the situation in Europe, I also want to return to Sigmund Skard's picture of American Studies in Europe after WWII. There were attempts after the war, Skard writes, to introduce "integrated" or "cross-departmental" American Studies in Germany. These attempts were complete failures. Interest in American Studies as such was strong, but there was a "stern determination" to establish such studies within the established disciplines. There was, naturally enough, great suspicion of all kinds of area studies, or *Auslandkunde*, because of its previous connection with Nazism. But that was not the only reason. Skard points perceptively to the main reason for the difference between the United States and Europe on this issue – that the national conditions were different. Americans are born into their civilization and language, Europeans are outsiders to that civilization. Skard says: "Outside of the English-speaking nations even an elementary knowledge of this background has to be acquired with sweat and tears, and always imperfectly, within the framework of the established disciplines; there is no 'integrated' approach to English intonation" ("The American Studies Movement" 163). As a consequence, in Germany the study of American civilization took place within the existing disciplines, primarily English and History, and, as Skard says, "'integration' in the American sense does not enter into the picture at all" (164). Separate courses on American culture were offered together in a study program, but, as Hans Galinsky, one of the important European Americanists of the 1960s, pointed out, "integration between the subjects is hopefully supposed to take place within the mind of the ideal student who attends all these heterogeneous courses" (165).

Concerning the Nordic countries Skard gives the following picture of the 1960s. In Denmark and Iceland American Studies were in their infancy. "In Finland, Norway, and Sweden the subject is now firmly entrenched in the traditional departments… but so far, there has been hardly any time to spare for organized integrated work" (166). As an example of Skard's impression, one may mention the fact that in 1962 two positions in American Studies were established at Uppsala university, one in history, one in literature, both financed by ACLS money. As far as I remember, no co-operation existed between the two fields. However, and this is a curious piece of information, in the conference volume from the second NAAS conference in 1964, there is a report from Sweden which says that an "entirely new subject," American Civilization, is being inaugurated at Uppsala university: "The aim is to concentrate on five areas of study: American history, American literature, sociology, art, and geography or music. The plans have been accepted by the university but await final approval from the Chancellor" (Skard, *USA in Focus* 200). However, this new subject never materialized.[2]

II. Transnational American Studies: Old Wine in New Bottles, or New Wine in Old?

Both Skard's overview and the debate summarized above between Marx and Lipsitz and Kaplan not only concern the tension between discipline and interdisciplinarity, but, equally so, the tension between the national and transnational orientations within American Studies. Marx clearly feels that the AD scholars have betrayed the nationalistic project, and Lipsitz and Kaplan, equally explicitly, demonstrate their commitment to American Studies that include a "world wider than any one nation" and "global communities, of which the nation is only one." So let me now shift the searchlight and deal more in detail with the history of the tension between the national and the transnational. As I will show, this doubleness has existed from the inception of American Studies; transnational American Studies has been practiced for decades in the United States, but primarily in Europe, albeit in slightly different forms and with a shifting theoretical framework.

In the 1990s, "New" American Studies started deconstructing traditional models of nationalist synthesis; the search for some essential "American" identity has now been abandoned and has been "shown to be as impossible as the old chimera of the 'Great American Novel'" (Giles 525). In his 1998 article "Circling the Spheres: A Dialogue," Laurence Buell lets professor B say: "In the nineties there's been a striking push in African American studies to go beyond stressing the internal teleology... to develop a comparative approach or scene of negotiation across ethnic or national borders. I'm thinking of Gilroy's Black Atlantic, Sollors on interracialism, Douglas on Manhattan in the twenties" (471). Professor B here draws attention to a general shift in US American Studies of the 1990s – the development toward what has been termed transnational, trans-Atlantic, hemispheric, pan-American American Studies, depending on which geographical constellation one has in mind. Numerous manifestations of this shift may be mentioned. In 1993, Cathy Davidson described how Duke University had started a cross-disciplinary, multinational, multilingual "Seminar on the Americas" program "that has me reading everything from Belizean fiction to political analyses of Cree land and resource rights in Quebec" (134). In 1995, Eric Cheyfiz proposed the creation of "Americas Cultural Studies," a social project combining theory and practice (843). In 1998, Janice Radway discussed the possibility of changing the name of ASA to either the International Association for the Study of the United States or the Inter-American Studies Association, suggestions she herself rejected (18, 20). A few years ago the International Association of American Studies was formed, with the aim of studying the Americas.

Various combinations of Pan-American studies have been suggested: North-American studies, i.e. studies that also include Canada, Mexico, the Caribbean and the near Latin American countries (Pease 7); studies of both the Americas (Radway 20, Porter 504); Pacific Rim Studies and Cross-Atlantic Studies. Concerning the latter, Buell lets professor C express the view that "a modest… first step that would test Americanists' powers of stretchability would be for US literary studies to make the 'Atlantic culture' move more than it does. Even if it were just a matter of doing a little more by way of Anglo-American comparative work" (478).

While many Americanists have enthusiastically embraced this new development within their field, others, both American and European – like J. Gerald Kennedy, Heinz Ickstadt and David Nye – have voiced their concern as to the dangers involved in such transnational studies. Kennedy has pointed out that "transnational studies by Paul Gilroy, Paul Giles, and Kirsten Silva Gruesz have indeed redefined 'American' literary studies by problematizing its boundaries. But we neglect national myths and foundational narratives at the risk of exempting nationalism itself from certain forms of interrogation" (2). Ickstadt has warned that such vast and culturally diversified studies run the risk of "promoting academic dilettantism, however well-intended and progressive [they] may be" (14). In his paper, "American Studies in an Age of Globalization,"[3] Ickstadt referred to Spivak who sees the danger that studies of such global scope "become so diluted that all linguistic specificity or scholarly depth in the study of culture is [...] ignored" (Ickstadt 15, from Spivak, *A Critique of Postcolonial Reason: Toward a History of the Vanishing Present* [1999] 170). Another danger, apart from neglect of the national perspective and scholarly dilettantism, is the one of imperialism. If US Americanists only look outward from the United States and refuse to see the reciprocal nature of the exchanges involved, such studies may mean appropriation of other cultures and, as Radway puts it, a "troublesome imperialist gesture" (21). Similarly, Gregory Jay has expressed his fear that the introduction of transnational American Studies "could end up repeating the history of colonial imperialism at the level of academic study" (in Porter 499). A fourth limitation is the danger that transnational American Studies may study non-American cultures only as they affect life in the United States. Desmond and Dominguez claim, for instance, that the study of the relationship between Latin America and the United States "is usually limited to analyses of migration of people from Latin America to the United States, the historical contests over the US border, the theorization of cultural borderlands, and the development of a Hispanic population in the United States" (476). Doris Friedensohn expresses similar reservations: "For many United States Americanists, the possibility of doing comparative work is a welcome corrective to our parochialism. However, we rarely have the grounding in a foreign culture which foreign Americanists possess" (79). Leo Marx would surely agree with all these critics in their objections to taking the "American" out of American Studies.

As an example of transnational American Studies, let me quote a somewhat long passage:

> Current interpreters repudiate the previous notion of consensus, and stress the discords and perplexities of America's evolution. A growing number of scholars in the United States are attracted by the comparative approach, which seeks to relate American life and thought to that of other nations. In a way, every interpretation of American identity has done this. The novelty is that past interpretations dwelt upon the *difference* of the United States from other nations. The new approach is ready to stress the *similarities*... Instead of looking for the unique, quintessentially *American* aspect of a particular theme, the new challenge – amazingly obvious once it is stated, and yet amazingly neglected in recent decades – is to see the Unites States in a wider context, with its own peculiarities... but also with its persistent involvement in a wider, Euro-American and world realm. (Walker 52)

Judging by the main drift of this quotation – if not its discourse – one might suspect that it was written in the 1990s. However, it was written in 1971, by Marcus Cunliffe, the British scholar, in an article called "American Studies in Europe." The article appeared in *American Studies Abroad*, edited by Robert H. Walker, a volume that gathered articles previously published in *American Studies International*. Cunliffe's article is one of self-criticism. He comes to the conclusion that in 1971 European Americanists had on the whole not yet "said startingly fresh things about the United States." Referring to what Henry Adams wrote to Henry James about their generation being a set of "improvised Europeans," Cunliffe suggests that European Americanists are "improvised Americans" who have "so successfully acclimated ourselves that we have ceased to possess a distinctive, European viewpoint." (51) As a remedy to this scholarly provincialism, he points out that European Americanists enjoy special advantages in that they can take a larger, binocular view of the United States. More specifically he suggests the comparative approach referred to above, which for the first time gives European Americanists the prospect of "joining the dialogue on at least equal terms, of presenting revised interpretations, and of examining the United States in a wide perspective." Down that path lies, according to Cunliffe, "the possibility of a new consciousness" (52).

Walker's volume consists of numerous articles reporting on the status of American Studies in countries around the world. Several of these reports emphasize the existence of or the desire to implement a comparative approach. The report from Argentina, "American Studies in Argentina" by Rolando Costa Picazo, points out that Domingo Faustino Sarmiento, before he became President of Argentina in 1868, founded a periodical, *Ambas Américas* (Both Americas), whose aim was, as he wrote in the first issue, the following: "For reciprocal convenience, the two Americas must engage in intellectual dialogue and establish means of communication" (Walker 40). In that spirit of reciprocity and comparison, American Studies in Argentina was later founded, according to Picazo. The Argentine Association of American Studies was founded in 1966, stressing the need for a comparative approach, carrying out a program of activities that would "contribute to the scientific study of the United States in Argentina and Argentina in the United States." The association organized conferences with themes like "Historical and Cultural Processes in the United States and Argentina, 1880-1940," with workshops like "Land Occupation in Both Countries" and "Humor in American and Argentine Literature."

In the article on American Studies in Great Britain, J. E. Morpurgo laments that British scholars had written far too many studies on the "use of the semi-colon in the novels of Thomas Wolfe" and not enough pondered a comparative approach. He writes that he is convinced that in the next few years "the prime emphasis of British-based American Studies must be on comparison and the consideration of interaction…. At all levels the future strength of American Studies in Britain is likely to be based," he asserts, "upon the rich possibilities of American-British Studies. Happily for us the frontier between American Studies and American-British Studies is not clearly drawn" (Walker 57). Peter Buitenhuis, director of the North American Studies Programme at McGill University, Montreal, gives in the same book a survey of American Studies in Canada. The Canadian Association for American Studies came into existence in 1964, and its members soon realized that a "pure" study of the United States was impossible, and, as Buitenhuis writes, "that, of necessity, the comparatist approach was implicit in our activities." "At one general meeting it was even suggested," he continues, "that the name of the Association be changed to the Canadian Association for Canadian and American Studies….The word American is, of course, an umbrella large enough to shelter anything going on within North America – or South for that matter, although questions about the latter have not yet arisen" (Walker 36). The CAAS organized in the latter part of the 1960s conferences and published proceedings with themes like *Canada and the United States in the Great Depression*, *War and Society in North America*, and "Art and Nature in North America." However, in the nationalist Canada of the late 1960s, such a comparative approach was not always applauded; as one critic put it: "attempts to homogenize the two countries... condescends [sic] to Canadian problems and is blind to Canadian needs" (37).

As a contrast to all the foreign perspectives in the volume, there is one article on "Recent Trends in American Studies in the United States" by David W. Marcell. Here nothing is said of the advantage of comparing United States culture to that of other nations. To illustrate the "recent trends" in US American Studies, Marcell describes courses and programs in the field at various American universities. He offers us as an example a "core course" at the University of Denver on "Individualism in America" which is "designed to examine and evaluate the ways in which Americans have defined themselves as persons and as a people... Its central theme is individualism and its manifestations as a social value, in social behavior, national myths, and self-identification. During the past year the course focused on the writings of Jefferson, Thoreau, Emerson, Whitman, Lincoln, Andrew Carnegie, William Graham Sumner, and John Dewey" (Walker 27-28). Marcell lists other courses like "American Personality and the Creative Arts" at Wisconsin State which intends to illustrate the "distinctive features of the American personality" through, again, the works of white males like Franklin, Frank Lloyd Wright, Charles Ives, Albert Ryder, Melville, William Whyte, Whitman, Sandburg, and Aaron Copeland. The focus on national specificity here seems total, but, as we know, also in the United States there existed comparatist, international initiatives in American Studies.

I have devoted much time to Walker's *American Studies Abroad* because, to me, it raises the question whether the new developments in US American Studies towards a transnational perspective are so new after all. In his self-criticism, Marcus Cunliffe not only called European Americanists "improvised Americans," he also proclaimed that if they did not assume a comparative approach, they would be "doomed to scholarly provincialism" (Walker 51). Questions we might ask ourselves are: What happened to the desire for and the attempts at transnational American Studies that obviously existed in 1971 in both the United States and other parts of the world? And, who ended up in scholarly provincialism, the Americans or the non-Americans?

Transnational American Studies thus seems to have a longer history than what is commonly held, going back to at least the 1950s, and there are strong indications that American Studies in the United States in the 1960s and 1970s contemplated moving in the direction of an internationalized perspective, which did not come about. If not the majority, at least a substantial number of non-American, particularly European, Americanists seem to have invested early in comparative, trans-Atlantic studies, more so than their colleagues in the United States. It also seems clear that, when it comes to comparative studies, communication was for a very long time more or less non-existent between Europe and the United States.

One may draw attention to three examples of the early awareness among US Americanists of the need for a comparative method and of the hegemony at the time of national(istic) American Studies. The first example comes from 1948, when Tremaine McDowell in his *American Studies* speaks strongly in favor of comparative courses on the United States and Foreign Civilizations as being the "perhaps most profitable" for American Studies, deploring the lack of such courses in the country. He holds that

> we and the world outside rarely meet in the same classroom; America is disastrously isolated from Europe and from Asia by the oceans of departmentalism. No additions to college and university curriculums can contribute more to world understanding and likewise to American Studies than courses which in themselves bridge the Atlantic and the Pacific. (65)

In 1961, at the first conference organized by the Nordic Association for American Studies (founded in 1959), Kenneth B. Murdock, who had spent much time at the universities of Uppsala, Oslo, and Copenhagen, gave a lecture in which he, having stated that he was proud to have been part of establishing an American Studies program at Harvard in 1939, gave voice to a certain anxiety that parallels Skard's fears, discussed above, concerning the growing parochialism and chauvinism of US American Studies:

> But I have grave misgivings as to some of the results in some American institutions. In spite of the efforts of the leaders of the American Studies Association, there has been an alarming tendency toward chauvinism, toward a fanatic devotion to every American subject, toward the exaltation of every American book or every American notion as good because American, and a terrifying disposition to act as if to know the work of Jefferson or Hamilton, Emerson or Melville, Hemingway or Faulkner, William James or John Dewey, the painter Cole or the architect Sullivan, were an excuse for forgetting Bacon or Milton, Machiavelli or Voltaire, Coleridge or Goethe, Proust or Baudelaire, Strindberg or Ibsen. Too many scholars have proceeded as if comprehension of American writers and thinkers could be fully realized without sound knowledge of those of Europe or of classical antiquity….We discourse in scholarly fashion on American romanticism and know little of English, German or French romantics….; we talk of the "American Way," of "American know-how," as if we could define them, although in most cases we cannot, largely because we have nothing to compare them with, no points of reference with which

to measure them, no broad horizon against which to judge their true stature in proper perspective. (Åhnebrink, ed., *Amerika och Norden* 191)

Here one may point not only to the fact that the dominant American Studies at the time, according to Murdock, seems to have been chauvinistic, but also to the fact that, in the listing of only white males, it was thoroughly gender and color blind.

In the volume *American Studies in Transition* from 1964, similar voices are heard. One is that of Lawrence W. Chisolm from Yale, who in his contribution, "Cosmotopian Possibilities," argues that to avoid ethnocentric error American Studies should adopt cross-cultural thinking. We should learn, he holds, "to think habitually in comparative cultural terms," to engage a "systematic study of and experience in several cultures, our own and at least two others." He, interestingly enough, mentions a Swedish example: "The clarity of Myrdal's *An American Dilemma* owed much, clearly, to comparative cultural perspective." He also holds that "a reorientation of American Studies toward comparative cultural history should develop new kinds of questions and some new areas of study as part of a collaborative international enterprise" (Fishwick, ed., 307-11).

What happened to the comparative approach that Cunliffe, Murdock, and others testified existed in the 1960s and early 1970s? There are no ready answers, but it seems to me that Europeans continued being both "improvised Americans" and comparatists, while American Studies in the United States developed away from a transnational perspective – if it ever had one. One explanation for the resistance among US Americanists to cross-Atlantic studies could be the fact that US American Studies was founded on the premise of the uniqueness of American culture, in opposition to the common view that the United States was a mere extension of Europe (cf May 182-83). In the historiography of American Studies in the United States a picture emerges of the gradual shift occurring around 1970 that I have already referred to above. The historical surveys of this development do not speak of a budding movement toward a comparatist approach, the way Cunliffe does. The shift around 1970 is rather described as one towards the study of ethnicity, race, gender, sexuality – and, to a degree, class – in a national perspective. This reaction against the myth-and-symbol school was undoubtedly a salutary one, but it may have prevented the development of an international perspective. American Studies still remained, basically, a nationalist project. Yetman and Katzman, looking back in 2000, saw the following development: "the shifts in American studies over the last twenty-five years to focus on race, ethnicity, class, gender, and sexuality... have led away from macro perspectives" (8). However, the dominance of national American Studies was not complete; as Gene Wise pointed to in 1979, during the 1970s the comparatist, cross-cultural approach lived on, even if it was a life in the shadows (205).

Numerous European Americanists, on the other hand, being outsiders, based in their own culture and at a distance from American culture, more naturally assumed a transnational outlook. As David Nye puts it: "Abroad, American Studies scholars inhabit two cultural and linguistic universes, which sometimes intersect, but more often run parallel to or contradict one another." Nye holds that such scholars experience what he calls "stereo cultural vision" (8). And Dale Carter has pointed to the fact that thirty years ago the University of Warwick, England, established a Joint School of Comparative American Studies (Carter 12). Simultaneously, however, many European contributions were not of a comparatist kind but in the tradition of national US American Studies. The shift taking place in the United States around 1970 also happened in Europe. This "national" work is not what concerns me here, but rather the comparatist studies that were produced from the 1950s and onwards but which were not quite accepted at the time as a form of American Studies. I would like to draw attention to three forms of research that may be defined as transnational and that have been pursued in Europe for decades before internationalism in the 1990s became such a central concern in US American Studies: Emigration/immigration, ethnic culture, and Americanization/the Image of America abroad. Such studies all involve more than one culture and they all employ a comparatist approach. My focus here will be on Sweden, but obviously the picture is similar concerning relations between the United States and other European, and also non-European, countries.

Emigration/Immigration Research

In his 1999 article "American Civilization as a Discipline?" Murray Murphey draws attention to the frequent lack of a cross-cultural perspective when he says that the study of immigrants should include "the study of the cultures from which they came." "Further," he continues, "we need to know not only about those who came but about those who came and went back, and about those who never came at all. Relations between immigrants here and their relatives in the homeland often continued through two or three generations, and in some cases even longer, with resources flowing in both directions, yet we know relatively little about these extended relationships" (16).

If Murphey had had access to, or made himself familiar with, the extensive research on, for instance, Swedish emigration to the U.S., he would have found it unnecessary to write as he did. Much of the research he is asking for has already been done, even though, obviously, much more could be accomplished. It is true that some of this European research on transnational relations is in Swedish, German, French etc., but certainly not all. And one might even argue that much of this work in other languages than English is worth translating.

The first studies on Scandinavian immigration to the US were produced in the 1930s and 1940s by American historians of Scandinavian descent: George Stephenson, Theodore Blegen, and Marcus Lee Hansen. Not only did they write on Scandinavian immigration, but two of them, Stephenson and Hansen, also wrote general histories on immigration; the latter published in 1940 *The Immigrant in American History*. It is interesting to note that both Stephenson and Blegen were professors of history at the University of Minnesota; Stephenson gave courses on immigration in the 1930s and Blegen wrote, for instance, *Norwegian Migration: The American Transition* in 1940. As is well known, one of the first American Studies programs was started at the University of Minnesota in the 1940s. Leo Marx, Tremaine McDowell, and others have told the story of the inception and growth of that program. Marx mentions in his 1999 recollection numerous colleagues who contributed to the American Studies program there from the departments of English, Art, Political Science, and from History – David Noble and Clark Chambers – but there is no mention of Stephenson and Blegen. The conclusion is close at hand that immigration history was not considered part of American Studies. Leo Marx has confirmed to me that he knew Blegen and Stephenson at Minnesota and that they were not considered part of American Studies. He said: "They were down the hall. They were in Scandinavian Studies." McDowell, however, gives a slightly different picture of the Minnesota program. In their summer program occasional courses were given on "Influence of Europe on American Culture" and "Anglo-American Cultural Relations to 1860," and a few afternoon lectures on "The Germans of Minnesota" and "The Orient and America." At one of the one-week, non-credit American Studies summer institutes, Theodore Blegen gave a lecture on "Immigrant Songs and Ballads" (77-80).

In Sweden, the first studies of emigration history also appeared in the 1930s and 1940s (Westin, Nelson), but it was not until around 1960 that the large-scale research on emigration was established through a major project at Uppsala University, which eventually produced some twenty books and numerous articles on various aspects of the Swedish emigration to the United States and on Swedish-American culture. "Much of the work of the Uppsala project," Dag Blanck writes in his survey, "Five Decades of Research of Swedish Immigration to North America," "exhibits a clear demographic and statistical bent." In addition, Blanck continues, "much of the Uppsala work put an emphasis on the situation in Sweden, and was less concerned with the New World" (188). A few studies, however, dealt with the situation of the Swedish immigrants in the U.S., followed them from the homeland to the new settlements, and, in a study or two, back to Sweden again. Many of these studies were written in English, and others, originally in Swedish, were later described and discussed in Norman and Runblom's *Transatlantic Connections* from 1987. Among later important works devoted to the trans-Atlantic relations between Sweden and the United States one may mention two books, written by American scholars and published in Sweden, Robert C. Ostergren's *A Community Transplanted: The Trans-Atlantic Experience of a Swedish Immigrant Settlement in the Upper Middle West, 1835-1915* (1988) and H. Arnold Barton's *A Folk Divided: Homeland Swedes and Swedish Americans, 1840-1940* (1994). So, Murray Murphey could very well have learned more about the issues he thought were missing from the agenda.

Scandinavian emigration historiography was, however, rather provincial, as the American historian Kathleen Conzen has pointed out. It was certainly impressive in scope and width, but it was "a historiography content to talk only to itself and debate only within its own context" (Blanck 192). It is obvious that Swedish historians would have benefited from co-operation with American colleagues in this field, but, even if they had tried to do so, there would probably have been very little interest at that time, in the 1970s, in reciprocal exchanges among American historians or Americanists. In 1977, historians Robert Swierenga and Charlotte Erickson separately pointed out that American immigration scholars would be well advised to read the work of Swedish historians (Blanck 190). The cross-Atlantic exchange in this field had not yet developed, it seems, but comparative research was being done on both sides of the Atlantic.

Ethnicity Studies
The shift in American Studies in the 1970s included the study of ethnicity and ethnic culture in America. However, it seems to me, the interest in ethnic culture was selective: it concerned mostly certain ethnic groups and it never became cross-cultural to any significant extent. The scholarly emphasis was put on the cultures of Asian-Americans, Mexican-Americans, Caribbean-Americans, and a few other groups like Mediterranean-Americans. Few US Americanists, however, did work on the culture of Scandinavian-Americans, Finnish-Americans, German-Americans, etc. More or less, these cultures remained outside US American Studies. Why did Americanists privilege certain ethnic groups over others? To again use the Swedish example, is the explanation for their marginalization the fact that Swedes immigrated so long ago, that they are white, that they assimilated so well into mainstream Anglo culture? But not even their culture in the past – when they were newly immigrated and unassimilated – has attracted much interest among US Americanists.

There was a shift from the early interest among Swedish emigration historians from quantification and social structure to issues of ethnicity such as assimilation, cultural persistence, organizational and religious life, literary and artistic activities, the role of women, radicalism in the Swedish-American communities. A source of inspiration for this change was the research on ethnicity done in the 1970s and 1980s by American scholars. Swedish studies appeared on how a "Swedish ethnic consciousness was established in that cultural construct that became known as Swedish-America" (Blanck 191). The American work, by Sollors and others, on the invention of ethnicity was also applied to Swedish research in this area.

Numerous important studies appeared by Swedish, and also American, scholars on the social, cultural, and religious life of the Swedish immigrants, on internal migration and social mobility, on their religious commitment, political involvement, and union activities, on language maintenance, on art, music, and literature in the new settlements. Much of this new European and American research counter-balanced Oscar Handlin's ideas of the immigrants as the "uprooted," showing how they rather managed to mix the Old and New World cultures, to integrate the old habits into the new surroundings. In addition to Ostergren's and Barton's studies mentioned above, John Bodnar's *The Transplanted* (1985) describes in sharp contrast to Handlin, the immigrants' experience as one heavily based on maintained links to the Old World (Norman and Runblom 142).

As examples of recent research two books may be mentioned, one Swedish and one Norwegian-American. First, Hans Norman and Harald Runblom's *Transatlantic Connections*, which succinctly builds on new developments in immigration and ethnicity research concerning the Nordic countries and which, in a historical perspective, compares the situation of Nordic immigrants in Latin America, the United States, and Canada. In his article Murray Murphey also asked for studies that would compare immigration of one certain ethnic group into the United States with immigration of members of the same group into another country to "make it possible to sort out what is due to the ethnic group and what to the host culture, something that cannot be done by looking only at the US case." (16) Norman and Runblom did just that, among other things, more than a decade before Murphey asked for it.

The other exemplary text is Jon Gjerde's *The Minds of the West: Ethnocultural Evolution in the Rural Middle West 1830-1917* (1997), which in a highly interesting fashion deals with mainly three themes: community formation, the farming economy and community, and the political and cultural factors and obstacles which faced the immigrants. He discusses what one reviewer called "a *Kulturkampf* between immigrants and Yankees over public schools, temperance, and women's suffrage" (Blanck 2000, 117). Gjerde makes use of the concept of "complementary identities," the possession of which made it possible for the immigrants to "pledge… allegiance to both American citizenship and ethnic adherence" (Gjerde 8).

In the past two decades, European and American scholars of ethnicity in America have increasingly started to learn from each other. As one Swedish historian puts it: "Bridges have been built between the earlier separated worlds of migration researchers in America and Europe and this has affected the interpretations of immigrant life" (Norman and Runblom 142).

Americanization/The Image of America Abroad

At most American Studies conferences in Europe there have for decades been lectures, panels, and workshops on such themes as Americanization, the American influence, the impact of America on smaller nations, and the Image of America abroad. At the first NAAS conference in 1961, at which Murdock expressed his discontent with some institutions of US American Studies, the theme was "America and the Nordic countries," and the lectures were comparisons between the five Nordic countries and the United States, many of them devoted to the "American Impact on Scandinavia" and the Image of America in Scandinavia. In the conference, lecture after lecture explored numerous aspects of the relations between the Nordic countries and the United States. They recorded the fact that the European interest in, and fear of, the American impact on Europe had a long history – for instance, that the Dane E. C. van Haven wrote in 1792 a book with the title *What Influence Has the Birth of America Had on the People of Europe?* – and spoke insightfully on such topics as the image of America in Scandinavia, the influence of American literature on the indigenous literatures, the dependence of Scandinavian literary critics on American New Criticism, and the influence of American sociology on the way Scandinavian sociology was formed (Åhnebrink 221-22).

Even though such studies have not been spoken of as examples of transnational American studies, both of these forms of comparative research – the American influence on Europe and the European Image of America – have over the past fifty years produced extensive results. The research on the American influence is now burgeoning, not only in Europe; scholars in the US and elsewhere in the world have also, particularly in the past fifteen years, increasingly given attention to this field of study. Let me just mention four rather recent studies: Rob Kroes' *If You've Seen One, You've Seen the Mall* (1996), which deals with Europeans and American mass culture; Richard Kuisel's *Seducing the French: The Dilemma of Americanization* (1993); and *"Here, There and Everywhere": The Foreign Politics of American Popular Culture* (2000), edited by Reinhold Wagnleitner and Elaine Tyler May. And finally, Richard Pells' *NOT LIKE US: How Europeans Have Loved, Hated, and Transformed American Culture since World War II* (1997), a broad discussion of economic and social life, of mass culture, of American Studies in Europe, but also the Europeanization of America.[4]

Scandinavian scholars have also been active in this field of study. Halvdan Koht wrote, in 1949, *The American Spirit in Europe: A Survey of Transatlantic Influences*, and several books on the American influence in the individual Nordic countries have appeared. In Sweden, the research has changed from one emphasizing the character and scope of the American values and material objects imported, i. e. the specifically *American* contribution to, or intrusion into, e.g., Swedish culture, towards looking at the process of transculturation, at Swedish society as a contact zone, or a borderland, where the encounter between the incoming American culture and the indigenous culture creates a culture of hybridity. One phenomenon that received special attention is the distinction between what has been termed *manifest* and *latent* influence. The enormous influx of films, toys, books, holidays like Halloween and Valentine's Day, sports like American football, etc., is, to all Swedes, obviously of American origin. But most of the influence is rather invisible and enters the culture in the form of the school system, university disciplines, election campaigns, and such phenomena as positive thinking and creative writing courses.

Conclusion
So, what is the situation like today in the Nordic countries and what has happened since the 1960s? It seems to me, and of course I am generalizing, that the picture Skard gives is more or less still true. There is no doubt that American Studies has changed since the 1960s. The shift after Marx's Great Divide has also taken place in Europe and in the Nordic Countries. Looking, for instance, at the programs for EAAS and NAAS conferences over the past two decades, it is obvious that the focus on ethnicity, race, sexuality, gender, and class has also been embraced by European scholars. And new disciplines have been added to the conference programs, like politics and film studies. But, it seems to me, interdisciplinary, integrated American Studies has not been embraced. Scholars from different disciplines come together in conference workshops, we produce scholarly books together, we establish area studies

programs at our universities, but these efforts and achievements are *multi*disciplinary in nature rather than *inter*disciplinary. We are trained in specialized disciplines and come together in projects and programs to make our specialized contributions. I think Paul Lauter's description of American Studies outside the United States is more or less correct. In many places abroad, he writes,

> American Studies "belongs" to one or another largely self-contained discipline, like history or English, and these are heavily the fields within which American Studies students actually labor. Thus work in American Studies is less likely to take interdisciplinary form or by itself to challenge existing structures of knowledge. In many areas one remains not an Americanist but a historian or an economist who happens to study the United States. (34)

When it comes to the latest development in American Studies, transnational and postnational American Studies, it seems to me that that particular inflection has had, so far, little impact on actual research or teaching in the Nordic countries. In spite of the fact that both the NAAS conferences in Copenhagen in 2001 and Trondheim in 2003 had the conference themes of "Trading Cultures" and "Transnational Dimensions of Life and Culture in the US," respectively, the resistance to this form of American Studies seems rather extensive, maybe because we feel as Europeans that we for decades, although somewhat differently, have actually practiced comparative, transnational American Studies – such as emigration, ethnicity, American influence research – but primarily because we have a very strong tradition – for better or for worse – of working within established disciplines.

Finally, let me ask the question: Does it really matter whether we pursue truly interdisciplinary work or do our research within the disciplines, whether we are disciplinary, multidisciplinary, interdisciplinary or post-disciplinary American Studies scholars, whether we are located in American Studies or in American Studies "Proper"? Skard refers to the Constitution of the Canadian Association for American Studies, adopted in 1964. The association declared that it wished to "include among its members both those who favor the newer interdisciplinary approach and those who see American Studies as a number of separate but related studies within the framework of the traditional disciplines" (170). It seems to me that this is also what the Nordic Association for American Studies has done since 1961 and what it should continue to do.

Notes

1. The present article is one of several that have appeared in the past few years in *American Studies in Scandinavia* analyzing and debating the development of US and European American Studies. Two are reprinted in this volume: Luccarelli, (2004) and Øverland (2005). See also Brøndal and Blanck, "The Concept of Being Scandinavian-American," (2002); and Johannessen, "'The Insincere Embrace': Canons and the Market," (2004). Two related special issues of *American Studies in Scandinavia* have also appeared: "Redefining American Studies: Not English Only," ed. Øverland, (Spring 2000) and one on Americanization, eds. Erik Åsard and Herion Sarafidis, (Autumn 2003).
2. The minutes from the University Board, the Humanities Faculty Board, and the Language Section Board between 1962 and 1968 contain no reference to such a discipline or area study having been proposed.
3. Lecture delivered at the EAAS conference in Bordeaux, March 22-25, 2002.
4. Pells' *Not Like Us* contains an excellent bibliography on various aspects of the American influence on Europe. However, its

focus is primarily on Great Britain, Germany, France, and Italy, leaving out works on the Nordic countries. Books and anthologies devoted to the American influence on the latter countries include: Åhnebrink, (1964), which contains several articles on the American impact on the Nordic countries; Lundén and Åsard, eds., *Networks of Americanization: Aspects of the American Influence in Sweden* (1992); Åsard and Herion Sarafidis, eds., Special Issue on Americanization in *American Studies in Scandinavia* 35:2 (Autumn 2003); Erickson, ed., *American Religious Influences in Sweden* (1996); Bryn (1992); Eero Kuparinen and Keijo Virtanen, eds., *The Impact of American Culture* (1982).

American Studies as a Contested Crossroads

DAVID E. NYE

The American Studies Association (ASA) appears to be one of the most successful interdisciplinary projects of the last half-century. Beginning with a handful of scholars at the end of the Second World War, it grew with each succeeding decade, spreading from a few American universities to all parts of the Untied States and to nations around the world. In Europe alone there are associations within every country, thousands of members, and many successful journals. In the United States, the ASA has more than 5,000 members, and more than 30 committees, staffed by eager volunteers. About 100 doctoral dissertations are completed each year in the 26 graduate programs that give American Studies Ph.D.s,[1] as well as many more doctorates in American history and American literature.

Yet the field today is an embattled discipline, with a deep split among its members. As Rolf Lundén explained in the preceding chapter, this conflict has appeared not only in scholarly journals but also in forums like *The New Republic*, where Alan Wolfe wrote a particularly pointed attack on the current leadership.[2] There are three common explanations for this crisis: (1) generational conflict, (2) incompatible ideology, and (3) methodological differences. I will explore each of these explanations in turn, and then add a fourth explanation based on the changing structure and organization of the ASA itself.

One might view this as essentially a generational conflict between, on the one hand, scholars who came of age before

1970 and on the other, the generation that entered the university after the Civil Rights Movement, during the Vietnam War and the Counterculture. But even a brief examination of the people involved shows that there is no clear age profile for either group. The supposedly "older" group does include such figures as Leo Marx, emeritus but still teaching at MIT and Alan Trachtenberg, emeritus at Yale. But it also includes many of their students and some younger scholars who are just starting out. Indeed, I understand that in the fall of 2006 many new graduate students at the University of Texas, Austin, were sympathetic to the "myth and symbol" approach.[3] The other side in the conflict includes Janice Radway (Duke), Amy Kaplan (University of Pennsylvania), George Lipsitz (University of San Diego), and Donald Pease (Dartmouth), but it also includes some emeritus scholars, notably David W. Noble.[4] As these names might suggest, the battle is not simply a generational conflict, nor is it being fought out primarily by scholars in their 30s and 40s. The most vocal figures all are over 50, and prominent figures in both camps are over 70.[5]

If generational conflict is an unsatisfactory explanation, ideological differences seem to be a stronger one. The distinction here is not between the political right and left, but closer to that between the so-called 'Old Left' and 'New Left.' The first tradition in American studies scholars was not overtly political or ideological in their publications, but most were at least liberal, if not further to the left. When Leo Marx got to Harvard as an undergraduate, one of the first things he did was join a demonstration against American neutrality in the Spanish Civil War. His teacher, F. O. Matthiesen, whose *American Renaissance* literally changed the curriculum of American literature at colleges and universities all over the United States, was a socialist. He was also gay, and hardly an apologist for the status quo. Such scholars looked for sources of potential transformation in earlier American history and literature. Children of the New Deal, they saw America as a society that was evolving toward an inclusive, democratic society. They were almost always supporters of the early Civil Rights Movement, and they called upon Americans to live up to the promise of the Declaration of Independence. Marx tells the story of the young Fulbright lecturer who found it difficult to explain American Studies to his English hosts. Finally, after a good deal of theoretical talk, in exasperation, he exclaimed, "You don't understand. I *believe* in America."[6] This declaration of faith was not a naïve belief that the American government of the McCarthy period was always virtuous and good. Nor was it an affirmation of the class structure or racial hierarchies of the time. Rather, it was a faith in the democratic project. That generation believed in the long-term trajectory of American history toward an egalitarian society.

I know this generation well, for my parents were part of it. This generation was born c. 1920 and went to university in the late 1930s and 1940s. They personally knew Civil War veterans, who were still alive in the 1920s and 1930s. Many scholars of this first tradition fought in World War II, like Leo Marx, who served in the Navy. Most felt that their lives were part of a democratic process that had begun with the American Revolution and that had continued in the Civil War and World War II. The American Studies they created during the 1950s and 1960s attempted to delineate the essentially democratic roots of the nation. They looked for the common symbols and shared narratives that Americans had used to invent themselves as a single people, and which they were still using to complete the process. Courses in these years often focused on topics such as "American Individualism," "American Nationalism," and "The American Character." Important books explored the emergence of national symbols, such as Brooklyn Bridge, or national heroes, such as Andrew Jackson or Charles Lindberg. The assumption was not that the United States was entirely coherent, not that its values were perfectly realized, but that the experiment in democracy on the whole was succeeding, and that the nation was evolving in the right direction. Scholars in American Studies from c. 1945 until at least 1965 saw a surface of national unity beneath which lay many contradictions and tensions that were resolved through symbols, myths, and rituals of democracy. They were acutely aware of the inconsistencies between ideals and practices, but on the whole they remained optimistic. In short, they "believed" in America.

Then an ideological split emerged as a result of the turbulence of the late 1960s and early 1970s, which distanced scholars, some young and some old, from the nation. Survivors of the Counterculture, scarred by Vietnam and Watergate, they no longer believed in the older *conception* of the United States. They remained egalitarians. They were still on the Left. But they no longer believed that a national character existed or was even desirable. They no longer thought there were shared, common symbols. Instead, they focused on multicultural differences, on gendered differences, on class conflicts, on racial divides. The break in American Studies, in this perspective, was a fissure between worldviews. To many (though not all) younger scholars it seemed absurd to imagine that Brooklyn Bridge or the Statue of Liberty could be a common symbol for all Americans. To them it seemed obvious that there never has been and never will be an 'American character.' Likewise, they no longer believed that a complex painting, novel, or poem could represent, or speak for, the nation as a whole. The first generation of American Studies scholars had rediscovered and celebrated *Moby Dick* as a masterwork that helped one to understand American society. They had confidently quoted Walt Whitman as a spokesperson for the culture. In contrast, many in the current generation tell me that they have never read *Leaves of Grass* or *Moby Dick,* and feel no need to do so.

This ideological divide was further reinforced by changes in methods. The early American studies only began to be called 'the myth and symbol school' in about 1970, by those who rejected the approach. The so-called myth and symbol approach had never been extensively theorized, in part because theory was far less fashionable in the humanities during the 1950s, and to some degree because publishers discouraged methodological introductions. For example, John William Ward had an introductory chapter on method in his *Andrew Jackson: Symbol for an Age*, but Oxford University Press made him take it out. Yet one can safely make a few generalizations. Ward, Marx, Trachtenberg, and others of this group relied on an anthropological view of culture. This was anthropology before Claude Levi-Strauss, when it was still a relatively new field and "culture" was still a fresh and exciting term. The myth and symbol scholars assumed that every culture has common styles, values, ideas, and aesthetic concerns, which reappear in many contexts. For example, gender relations could be expressed in the physical layout of a house or institution, or a set of religious ideas might be expressed in poetry, in architecture, or in annual rituals. The fundamental notion was that cultures have coherent patterns, and that an interdisciplinary approach could discover these common elements. The goal of American studies, it followed, was to locate the patterns, to express the larger design, and thereby to understand the nation.

An influential article by John Kouwenhoven, "What's American about American Culture?" exemplifies this early approach.[7] Kouwenhoven was a professor at Columbia University who found Americanness in such things as the grid pattern imposed everywhere on the landscape, or in the idea of interchangeable parts that can be found in the credit system of higher education or on the assembly line. He found Americanness in skyscrapers, in the poetry of Walt Whitman, and in the structure of jazz. Kouwenhoven's essay still is read today in some courses, and students still find it useful to explain some aspects of American culture. However, students now feel uncomfortable to see that Kouwenhoven scarcely mentions African Americans or gender. He defines American-ness too much from a white, male, middle-class perspective. Are these defects insurmountable? Perhaps not. Such work can be a starting point, a draft requiring correction. The theory is salvageable if one argues that Kouwenhoven has articulated the cultural patterns of the dominant culture, which in turn provoked minority responses, creating a distinctive American dialogue. (This is the kind of project I later took up in *America as Second Creation* (2003), in which alternating chapters present narratives and counter-narratives.)

As late as 1970, it briefly seemed possible that the 'myth and symbol' tradition might evolve into a more highly self-conscious methodology. For example, Cecil Tate wrote a short theoretical book, *The Search for Method in American Studies* (1973), showing a convergence between the ideas of Levi-Strauss and the actual practices of the 'myth and symbol' school. In the same years, Richard Slotkin published *Regeneration Through Violence* (1975), the first of three heavily researched empirical studies of the intertwining mythologies of the frontier, American expansion, and confrontation with Native Americans and other avatars of "the other." Alternately, David W. Noble (1965), Anthony F. C. Wallace (1980), and others amalgamated the first tradition of American Studies with the work of Thomas Kuhn, whose *The Structure of Scientific Revolutions*, was extremely influential during the 1970s. Working along parallel lines, Gene Wise wrote an influential article and book (1979, 1980) organizing previous scholarship into paradigms. My dissertation (1974) also reworked the 'myth and symbol school', but by the time it had become a book (1979), the tide had decisively turned against all such efforts to recuperate the first tradition.

Instead, many American Studies scholars drew inspiration from European debates. The sharpness of this break with the field's own past could illustrate Michel Foucault's concept of the epistemic shift. Scholars simply walked away from the earlier discussion and began a new debate. Some followed the turn toward deconstruction. Jacques Derrida's critique of Levi-Strauss seemed to invalidate the myth and symbol approach or any other approach that looked for closure or synthesis. However, deconstruction was not acceptable to other Americanists, who read neo-Marxists and sought to use Critical Theory to make sense of what they then always termed "late capitalism." (I have not, however, heard anyone use the term "late socialism.") Still others attempted to graft semiotics onto American studies, looking to the work of Roland Barthes and Umberto Eco.[8]

My second book (1983), the Edison anti-biography discussed elsewhere in this volume, also attempted to combine these traditions. Its first lines announced: "This study rejects the existence of its subject, Thomas Alva Edison, and will not attempt to recapture him in language. He once existed, but neither he nor any other figure can be recreated." Modify this opening statement slightly – to eliminate Edison as the subject – and one can see the problem that deconstruction posed for American Studies. Imagine a course syllabus that announced: "This course on US history rejects the existence of American culture, and will not attempt to recapture it in language." If one thoroughly embraced deconstruction, the subject of American Studies disappeared, for by its tenets it would be impossible to define one individual, much less to look for an American character or national symbols.[9] If deconstruction did not become the basis for a new American Studies methodology, however, it served as a wrecking ball against the 'myth and symbol school' and cleared the ground for other approaches.

To see how the field changed, contrast two influential books, one from each era: Leo Marx's *The Machine in the Garden* (1965) and Janice Radway's *Reading the Romance* (1985). Marx developed a sweeping synthesis of American literature, tracing a major theme through 300 years. He defined the literary genre of the pastoral, and discussed its classical origins, but he did not give much place to theory. He dealt with some popular literature, political speeches, essays, and even advertising, but his book primarily concerned canonical writers. Marx anchored his argument in readings of Cooper, Thoreau, Emerson, Whitman, Melville, Twain, James, and Fitzgerald. Marx provided a blueprint that teachers found well suited to the introductory course of American literature.

Radway also wrote a study of one genre, the Romance, but she focused almost entirely on recent popular novels read by women. She first analyzed the romance's formal structure (based on the work of Vladimir Propp), and then became a participant observer in a group of avid romance novel readers. Radway argued that the meaning of Romance texts emerged from such collective reading. She treated the books not only as a genre but also as a part of their readers' lives. Radway did not simply report their collective interpretations; she surrounded it with a complex methodological meditation. The effect of her work, as her reliance on Stanley Fish suggests, was to relativize American Studies. She concluded: "our contention that good books are 'serious', critical of American culture, complex, and difficult is nothing more than an assumption peculiar to our interpretive community of literary academics." (1985, 46) Radway became the editor of the *American Quarterly,* giving added weight to her opinions. Later, she became President of the ASA, two decades after Leo Marx had been president during the 1970s. Radway explicitly rejected both the earlier American Studies project and any canon of "great books" or other ideal representation of American culture. She had moved from texts to interpretive communities, from national symbols to varying cultural practices, from high culture to popular culture.

With only peripheral reference to deconstruction, scholars such as Radway pushed American Studies toward a focus on gender, race, and ethnicity. Indeed, in her Presidential address (1998), Radway suggested that American Studies might change its name. It was not just that the designation "America" belonged to all the regions of the New World, but also that the whole idea of a nation implied a solidity and permanence and identity that Radway did not wish to endorse. In part, she argued that the United States was expanding its power and influence throughout the globe, and that whether regarded as cultural imperialism or globalization, the incontestable fact was that American Studies no longer was simply defined by a geographical boundary. Radway followed recent work in Chicano studies, which attacked the whole idea of frontiers, or cultural borders, suggesting instead that these were zones of multicultural contact, where creative forces were set free of cultural constraints. She further suggested that American Studies might seriously consider merging with the National Ethnic Studies Association, a successful organization that had grown rapidly since being organized in 1972. Her proposals met heated objection, split the association and launched the debate that still continues.[10]

It might seem that, taken together, the generational, ideological, and methodological explanations of the conflict in American Studies are more than sufficient. They explain how the field could move from a belief in national character to rejecting the very possibility that a national character existed, or was even desirable. But all three explanations are based on the erroneous idea that American Studies is autonomous and that it is a discipline. It is neither; not autonomous because it has always fed off other departments, not a discipline because no method or approach has ever won widespread acceptance for long. Rather than think of American Studies as a discipline, where one might then find consensus on methods, followed by conflicts, generational divides, new paradigms, and so forth, it is more accurate to see American Studies as a crossroads, or meeting point between disciplines.

Indeed, it often functioned as an escape from orthodoxies in departments. For example, in the 1950s, when the New Critics reigned supreme in English departments, they demanded that scholars look at the literary text, and only the text, ignoring the author's life, the history that surrounded its composition, and its cultural context. The orthodoxy of most English departments was strongly opposed to the first tradition of American Studies, which saw literary texts as the expression of the myths and values of the society where they were produced. Such literary scholars escaped to the crossroads of American Studies, which welcomed them, published them, and legitimized their work. However, by 1980 at the latest, English departments in the US had abandoned the New Criticism, and all sorts of cultural approaches were becoming acceptable. As a result, such scholars no longer *needed* American Studies. They could get tenure in English departments, and they could publish papers elsewhere. They might come to American Studies meetings, they might participate in their own university's American Studies programs, but they no longer needed the field in order to establish themselves, or to prosper.

If the field provided this service for American literature in the 1950s and 1960s, during the same period it did something similar for American historians interested in cultural and social history. In c. 1950 American history remained focused on politics, wars, and foreign affairs, and it told a story of the powerful and the brilliant that was almost entirely male. To look at a program from the American Historical Association in the middle of the 1950s is to look at a narrow, hierarchical discipline. Traditional American historians disliked the new American Studies approach. One famous incident can serve as a representative example. John William Ward's *Andrew Jackson: Symbol for an Age* was almost turned down as a dissertation.[11] He wrote it at one of the leading American Studies programs, Minnesota, but the dissertation committee also contained historians, one of whom refused to approve it. He almost succeeded in getting another committee member to oppose it as well. Thus, even a leading center for American Studies faced strong opposition in the early 1950s. Ward did get his Ph.D., and he went on to a distinguished career. But such a dissertation was unacceptable in many US history departments at the time.

Thus, early American Studies provided an escape hatch, an unorthodox meeting place, for historians as well as literary scholars. And, again, by 1980 at the latest, American historians no longer needed to escape from their own professional meetings to do interdisciplinary cultural and social history. The annual programs of the American Historical Association and Organization of American Historians took on many themes from the American Studies Association.

In short, by looking at American Studies as a crossroads, one can see that people came to this meeting point from different disciplinary homes, arriving with different needs. During the 1950s and 1960s, the ASA encouraged innovators from English and history departments, and their work was so successful that the home disciplines were transformed. But the irony of this success soon became evident, as scholars from these disciplines no longer needed validation or publication through American Studies. Even chairs of American Studies programs might not go to ASA meetings as often as they went to one in their home discipline.

There is one telling fact about the 1950s and 1960s in American Studies, which in some ways was such a successful period that it is sometimes thought to have been a "golden era" when the field won acceptance and became influential in the academy, namely that there were few meetings. The ASA held its first convention as late as 1967, and for more than a decade meetings were only held biennially. Thus, most of what are now regarded as classic works in the field were written before there were annual conventions, indeed, before there were any conventions at all. Even when biannual meetings began the ASA could not be the core discipline for any of its members. History and literature associations met annually, and there were several to choose between. A young scholar, who was just starting out in the 1970s, could at most attend three ASA conventions before going up for tenure in the sixth year. Failure to get on the program for just one of these three meetings could undermine a career. In contrast, a scholar could attend as many as six conventions of the larger associations of American literature or American history.

Such annual conventions were extremely important in forming a professional identity, and they were also far larger than the ASA's meetings. The Modern Language Association (MLA), the OAH and the AHA attracted thousands of scholars and all the major publishers, whose editors could make or break a new Ph.D.'s career. In contrast, the biannual ASA never attracted as many as 1000 scholars in these years. The ASA was innovative and interdisciplinary, but the young scholar quickly realized that, in career terms, it was a sideshow. Notably, the ASA then was almost never the venue for job interviews. The convention was in October, early in the academic year, well before new jobs were advertised. Universities still hold interviews just after Christmas at the MLA or AHA or in the early spring at the OAH. In short, at least until the 1980s, the American Studies Association was a minor crossroads and not on the main highway to a job, to publication, or to tenure. A crossroads only open every other year, the American Studies meeting was pleasant because no tension-producing job interviews took place, and because it encouraged unorthodox papers. However, as new approaches to literary and cultural history won acceptance at major, annual, academic meetings, the ASA became less necessary to those who had started it.

The partial remigration of scholars back to their home

disciplines did not mean, however, that American Studies died out. Rather, starting in the 1970s but particularly the 1980s, it became the crossroads for new groups of scholars seeking their place in academia. Many were women and from minority groups. As the focus shifted to race, ethnicity, and gender, the ASA became an attractive venue for a 'rainbow coalition' of minorities who soon were highly visible in the formal organization. Officers and committee members of the ASA, once a white, largely male organization, were chosen with the goal of achieving better racial and gender balance. Minorities and women thereafter dominated an organization whose presidents had all been white males from 1951 until 1985. On the whole, this was undoubtedly a good thing. Many aspects of American history were rediscovered; many authors who had been forgotten were reclaimed. However, many of the new members did not have degrees in American Studies and had not made a scholarly commitment to interdisciplinarity. Instead, as American Studies evolved into a multicultural crossroads, it moved toward becoming an ethnic studies organization. Indeed, it began to resemble something like a discipline. This partly explains Radway's call for American Studies to merge with ethnic studies. By 1998 the organization had changed. At that conference, the only item on the agenda the first night was an open meeting with prominent members of ethnic studies departments and of the National Ethnic Studies Association. The possible merger did not occur, but it was a clear sign that the ASA was narrowing its focus (even if it did so in the name of inclusion) and becoming a much different crossroads than it had been. Significantly, the Seattle conference program paid no attention at all to either Microsoft or Boeing, both headquartered there, which arguably ought to be part of the subject matter of American Studies, no matter how one defined it, but they were not mentioned in Radway's talk. Nor, judging from the conference of that year, could a future historian learn that the US was experiencing feverish stock market speculation in good part driven by high-tech expectations.

Perhaps every interdisciplinary organization eventually is tempted to narrow down and convert itself into a discipline. The first generation, with its biannual meetings, seemed keen to avoid this. But when the ASA started to meet annually in the 1980s, it then had the potential to become a discipline. In theory, any number of subjects might have been included. But in practice, the ASA had already made its choice to focus on race, gender, and ethnicity. The new emphasis did not come without a cost, however, for as these new groups entered conference programs, there was less room for others who had once been there.

Nor was this the only shift. In the same years, research presented at the conventions also tended to become more contemporary in focus. Scholars interested in the Colonial period or the first half of the nineteenth century began to attend other meetings. There were additional casualties of this shift. The early ASA fostered both environmental history and the history of technology. However, neither subject figures prominently in the programs today. Instead, such scholars gradually left the American Studies crossroads for the Society for the History of Technology and the Association for Environmental History. In short, as the ASA narrowed its focus, it ceded subject areas and members to other organizations.[12]

Americanists with broad interdisciplinary interests did not desert American Studies. Rather, the ASA deserted them as it moved its crossroads to a new location. It left to political scientists the study of US elections and foreign affairs. It left to economic and business historians the study of the US economy. Its annual program tends to ignore American history before 1900, except for topics that include race, class, and gender, and it gives little or no attention to American technology or environmental history. The interdisciplinary quest of the first generation has been abandoned in many programs. The result resembles rather uncannily the way a multinational corporation sheds older divisions and throws senior employees out of work, in order to develop new, high-growth areas. No doubt the analogy is unfair, but the executive committee of the ASA, over the years, has presided over a transformation so profound that senior people trained in the field may find little of interest at the national meetings.

At the same time, some new Ph.D.s find that some departments of American Studies will not hire them but prefer sociologists and anthropologists, notably at Minnesota. Its three recent appointments together illustrate this tendency. Each specializes in areas that would need to be broadened considerably to accommodate a European university setting or to be part of the wider vision of American studies embraced in the earlier generation. Individually, I have no quarrel with the research or interests of any of these three scholars. But taken as a group, they suggest a decisive shift. One offers a seminar on how American workplaces structure gender and racial inequalities through seemingly benign and neutral practices (i.e. not a broad course on labor history, where gender and race would be themes). Another offers a seminar focusing on the diaspora of Filipino sailors (i.e. not a broad course on immigration and/or on maritime history). The third has a course on the history of Native American education (not the history of US education, or even the narrower but still large topic of education of minorities). Two decades ago these subjects would have been judged too narrow for American Studies, which emphasized interdisciplinary synthesis. Such scholars, who appear to have excellent credentials, would then likely have been hired in departments of sociology, anthropology, and education, as indeed these are the departments where they received their doctorates. In hiring them Minnesota's American Studies chose – three times – not to hire those with degrees in American Studies.

Nor is Minnesota entirely unusual in this respect. American Studies national meetings are much concerned with similar subjects. But scholars in the history of business, diplomacy, the environment, technology, law, formal political institutions, the Colonial period, and so on have largely disappeared from ASA meetings, including some who are active as American Studies faculty at their home universities. What was conceived of as a broadly interdisciplinary field in the 1950s and 1960s has reached out to scholars interested in Asian Americans, African Americans, women, Hispanics, and Native Americans, but in the process the ASA has had less and less space on the program for other topics. The ASA convention no longer represents anything close to the full range of US subject matter offered at American universities. The organization has abandoned some of the goals it had until c. 1965. In some ways this has been heuristic, notably the shift from canonical high culture to popular culture or the shift from seeing the frontier as the moving line between "savagery and civilization" to viewing it as the *"frontera,"* a space of cultural encounters and creolization. But the field has also moved from an interdisciplinary combination of history and literature to the social sciences, from study of the United States as a whole to privileging certain groups. Given such a state of affairs, should the ASA disappear in a merger with ethnic studies, as Radway suggested in 1998? Or should it reconnect with its earlier goals and find common ground with sister organizations in other countries?

As Rolf Lundén showed in the previous chapter, half a century of calls for a more comparative American Studies have not lead to much engagement with work done outside the US. Rather, the narrowing of focus at home seems to have matched a declining interest in the rest of the world. As a former Fulbrighter in Spain and later as a member of the board of the Fulbright Selection Committee in Denmark, I have always urged young scholars to seize this opportunity, for reasons outlined in the following chapter. However, the interest in going abroad for a year palpably declined as the ASA changed. I have seen the lists of applicants for many years, not only for Denmark but to some extent for other nations as well. In the 1990s the size of this applicant pool began to shrink, even for the best-paid, prestigious senior Fulbright positions. This is not merely a personal impression, as I discussed these matters with administrators in other Fulbright Commissions and with administrators in the United States. Strangely, although the ASA was growing rapidly, its members were not prominent among the applicants. In particular, despite considerable efforts at recruitment, few minority candidates came forward. My university tried every year for a decade without succeeding in attracting even one minority applicant.

Another way to measure how international the ASA really is would be to look at whether its presidents have taken a full year abroad on academic exchange or devoted a meaningful part of their scholarly life to engagement with other cultures. The presidents of the 1950s and 1960s almost all went abroad on Fulbrights or other grants at some point in their career. But this appears to be less often the case with more recent presidents. In many cases, the cvs posted on their home pages say nothing about living or teaching overseas. Since presidents are elected by the membership, it seems that such experience is not thought particularly important, as long as all presidents rhetorically embrace internationalism. As a final example, consider how many of the ASA's institutional members are located outside the United States. In 2006 the *American Quarterly* listed c. 120 institutional members of the ASA. None were from Latin America. None were from Asia. None were from Africa. None were even from Europe, with the sole exception of the British Library. Make no mistake, despite occasional bursts of internationalist rhetoric, from the outside the ASA can seem more narrow and provincial now than it did forty years ago.

The 'New Americanist' project, ironically, seems to flourish in a hothouse of academic isolationism. Perhaps this is because any comparison of the United States with other nations would immediately foreground the importance of the very elements that are largely lacking from the ASA program and lacking in many university curricula: study of formal politics, interest in foreign relations, engagement with American business, and comparison of the United States with other cultures. Furthermore, once overseas, the American Studies scholar dedicated to the idea that there is no national character might be disconcerted to discover that foreigners can immediately see that they are Americans. They might be unhappy to discover that, regardless or race or gender, they happen to walk, eat, and converse in ways that are recognizably American, even at a distance of 100 meters. It is far easier to think that there is no national character at an ASA meeting in San Diego or Boston than to do so after six months at a small university in Poland or Indonesia. This does not mean that the postmodern ASA scholar refuses to lecture abroad. On the contrary, a trip abroad in exchange for a lecture or two is always attractive. But to go away long enough to master a foreign language, to rethink the questions of American Studies in light of this experience, to do comparative research, to work together with a non-American on a common project? Much of the ASA membership seems less ready to do these things now than they were forty years ago.

In conclusion, the ASA has grown into a large organization that is successful, if measured in terms of growth. Yet its focus has become less inclusive and more contemporary. The subject matter, once capacious, tends to focus on race, gender, and ethnicity. The early goal of an interdisciplinary synthesis of literature, history and the social sciences has given way to an increasing emphasis on the social sciences, to the point where people who have degrees in sociology and anthropology and who work on race, gender, and ethnicity often fill new positions in American Studies. Any organization that radically changes in this way will experience conflict. It is not a generational conflict, although in a few cases senior scholars have left the enterprise after dedicating themselves to it for thirty years or more. Nor is it simply an ideological or methodological conflict. Rather, it is a debate about whether the ASA should have be inclusive and interdisciplinary or more narrowly focused, about whether it is to represent the idea of a national culture or the idea of post-national diversity, about whether to accept a transnational (and thereby comparative) perspective or to embrace the idea of the dissolution of nationality in a globalizing world culture, heavily inflected by the United States.

For New Americanists, the ASA is still a worthwhile crossroads. But for many others, the ASA has all but lost Walt Whitman's ambition to be vast, to contain multitudes. There was another alternative. The ASA might have become a more inclusive, umbrella organization like the MLA. It could have been far larger, with sub-divisions that focused on particular interdisciplinary areas. But if the ASA in the United States once aspired to study everything American, in recent decades, it has largely abandoned that project. This is not just one more case of the triumph of academic specialization, for in such cases each sub-specialty talks largely to itself. In contrast, the battle in the ASA is over who speaks for (and defines the meaning of) an interdisciplinary study. It has become a sectarian struggle, in which each side tends to exaggerate the other's position. Thus Alan Wolfe describes the New Americanists as hating the nation and denying its identity. New Americanists, in turn, call their opponents liberal dupes or stooges of the State Department.

This unfortunate tactic has been adopted by Donald Pease, who proclaims himself to be post-national. He has argued that the romance genre, identified by some critics since the 1950s as a characteristic form of American literature, became an instrumental part of the political unconscious of the Cold War (1997). In his largely theoretical essay, there are no close readings of individual works by any of the critics who are vilified in this manner. Nor does Pease consider the cultural politics of English Departments in the early Cold War. It would be far more accurate to argue that the New Criticism was central to the de-politicization of literature in the 1940s and 1950s, compared to the self-consciously political literary criticism of the 1930s. From this perspective, early American Studies literary critics, far from creating a political unconscious that was of use to the State Department, created a critical apparatus that both respected close reading of the literary text and re-connected such readings to politics.[13] Pease's essay was not really a history of Cold War literary criticism, but an almost entirely unfootnoted attack on founding figures in the field of American Studies such as Perry Miller and F. O. Matthiessen. Pease, who has assiduously promoted the post-nationalist view of American Studies at summer seminars, was extravagantly praised in Radway's 1998 presidential address. With such sectarian spokespersons in the ascendancy, the ASA crossroads was in danger of closing down. As the president read out long lists of scholars whose work she deemed exemplary, she effectively banished those writing in other traditions, by refusing even to name them.

Fortunately, there are also more open perspectives in the ASA. George Lipsitz remarked in 2002 that the debates within American Studies often were based on misconceptions on both sides.

> ...these arguments obscured the value of cultural theory in general, but also obscured the rich critical traditions in American studies that had not named themselves as theoretical schools. I felt that I had learned things of value from all of these traditions. I didn't see why we couldn't have it all—

Alan Trachtenberg and Stuart Hall, Leo Marx and Jacques Derrida, Janice Radway and Henry Nash Smith, Celia Cruz and Gilles Deleuze, Jacques Lacan and Chaka Khan.[14]

Lipsitz sought to be generous, in a sensible approach to the rift in the field. Yet even his list failed to cite any Americanists from outside the United States. The only non-Americans he thought to mention were theorists, who seldom write with the US in mind. For him, as for Radway in her 1998 address,[15] the only meaningful divisions in the field of American Studies remained inside the nation. The protests and the scholarship from abroad were still not being acknowledged.

But there is another way to practice American Studies, as outlined in the next chapter.

Notes
1 ASA Newsletter, September 2006, 29:3, 32-34.
2 Alan Wolfe, "Anti-American Studies," *The New Republic* 10 Feb. 2003: 25-32.
3 I thank their teacher, Professor Jeff Meikle for this information.
4 A small example can suggest how strong these divisions are. In 1994 the University of Minnesota held a three-day conference to celebrate its American Studies Program's 50th anniversary. This was a fascinating event for many reasons, in good part because the leadership of the department clearly sided with the newer tendencies in the field, while most of the more than 100 returning PhDs who graduated from the program sided with the older approach. I looked forward to the event partly because I wanted to meet the current graduate students and to hear what they were doing. However, returning graduates from the 1970s met a cold reception from them. Instead, we had a great time meeting the generally rather left-wing PhDs from the 1950s.

5   For at least 15 years the so-called younger generation has been predominant on the national committee and the official journal in the field, *The American Quarterly*. Yet they have less hegemonic control than one might expect. Inside the US one can also publish in *American Studies, The Journal of American Culture* and *Prospects*. In Europe there is the British *Journal of American Studies, American Studies in Scandinavia*, Germany's *Amerikastudien, Revue française d'études américaines*, and so forth. To this should be added dozens of other journals on American literature, history, film, popular culture, and folklore, published both inside the United States and abroad.

6   Leo Marx, "On Recovering the "Ur" Theory of American Studies."

7   John Kouwenhoven, "What's American about American Culture?"

8   This impulse persists to some degree. For example, Miami University, Ohio, including Roland Barthes, *Mythologies* (New York: Hill and Wang, 1972) in its required senior seminar in 2004. http://www.georgetown.edu/crossroads/syllabi/miami_ohio/miami_ohio_capstone.html Likewise, Umberto Eco, *Travels in Hyper-reality* (New York: Harvest Books, 1990) was part of the reading for the introduction to American Studies at the University of Virginia in 1997. See http://xroads.virginia.edu/~CLASS/am483_97/am483syl.html

9   However, one could argue that this deconstruction revealed a pattern. If there was not a single Edison, the possible Edisons were finite, and they formed a discursive pattern. This second book was very up to date for 1983, as it combined the latest literary theory with archival research. However, the literary side of American Studies was distinctly not interested in a socially conservative, white male inventor, even if he was deconstructed. Likewise, the social history side of American Studies that generally embraced neo-Marxism had little use for deconstruction. I had bridged the divide, but neither side was very interested.

10 It provoked me to write a rebuttal that called for American Studies to remain inclusive. After I posted it on the Internet

many like-minded scholars e-mailed their agreement. Up to that time I was on excellent terms with Janice Radway, and I was careful to praise her scholarship in my Internet posting and to avoid any personal attack.

11 The following anecdote I heard on many occasions while a graduate student at Minnesota in the 1970s, including from David W. Noble and Mulford Q. Sibley.

12 For example, I was actively courted by the Society for the History of Technology. The ASA had never selected me to serve on its committees, but the Society for the History of Technology elected me to serve on several, including its Executive Committee.

13 In my experience as a student, the point was always made that the romance had a larger profile in American literature than in Britain, where the novel of manners was more central to its tradition. Yet the romance was not therefore celebrated as being a superior genre, and other literary forms were also examined.

14 http://www.americanpopularculture.com/journal/articles/spring_2002/lipsitz.htm

15 In her published version, Radway added references to some non-American scholars near the end of her lecture, presumably because of the criticism she received for omitting them in its oral form. She did not weave their publications into the structure of her argument, however.

American Studies from the Outside In

American Studies in Stereo

DAVID E. NYE

American scholars know that important research on French, German, or English history is often done in the United States. But when it comes to their own nation, Americanists have had a hard time noticing scholars and perspectives from other countries. Judging scholarly influences by bibliographies and footnotes, it has only been in the last decade that this has begun to change, but a great deal of the apparent change is still rhetoric. On the airplane home from an American Studies Association meeting in Toronto I found myself seated next to a scholar who was then researching a book on the American West. I told her about a sizeable body of work on the subject written by Europeans, including a conference volume edited by Rob Kroes that also included many prominent American scholars of the West and a larger number of Europeans in a fruitful dialogue (1989). When her book appeared several years later, however, I could not detect that any of this work had been consulted. This is a single example, but considered in the light of what Orm Øverland and Rolf Lundén say in this volume, it is by no means an isolated case.

These essays are not, however, a catalogue of such missed opportunities, for the authors have all gained a great deal through international exchanges. It is rather a friendly critique of American Studies as it has developed in the United States, together with a report on how the field has matured in the Scandinavian countries. The essays to some degree speak for other European Americanists as well, but the intention is to provide a Scandinavian view. Scandinavia consists of Denmark, Sweden, and Norway (but not Finland). While these three nations are by no means identical, they do share a common commitment to the welfare state that includes free university education, free medical care, and a full range of social services. All are constitutional monarchies, with a predominantly Lutheran population. They have significant minorities of fourth world peoples (notably in Lapland and Greenland) as well as new immigrant communities (many from Moslem societies). These nations may be "Americanizing" in some ways, but no one who lives within them can miss the justifiable pride Scandinavians feel in their societies. They may see things to admire in the United States, but their goal is not imitation. Why should they? They have low unemployment, a positive trade balance, national budget surpluses, a high standard of living, and the lowest illiteracy levels in the world. They are just as advanced as the US technologically, if measured by ownership of such things as televisions, mobile phones and computers. Despite their cold climate, they use considerably less energy per capita than the US, and their citizens are healthier and live longer. In short, Scandinavia has a distinctive, viable social system. Their economies arguably are equal to or more advanced than those of the United States, and they have minimized inequality more successfully than most other nations.

Since World War II, a community of Americanists has developed in Scandinavia, as part of an increasing general knowledge about the United States. The Scandinavian television stations do not dub American films or television shows, so the average citizen has seen thousands of hours of American programs. Their town libraries and bookstores hold many American books, including thousands in translation. The local butcher speaks English and can sing quite a few American popular songs from memory. But he has traveled to several other European countries, and knows a good deal amount about them, too. In short, Scandinavians have an especially interesting vantage point from which to develop a friendly but critical view of the United States. This little book is meant as part of a larger dialogue, between Americanists on both sides of the Atlantic.

Until, now, however, this has at times been a one-sided learning process, in which American scholars arrive in Scandinavia as academic missionaries to enlighten the poor natives. I recall one well-meaning visitor who spent half an hour explaining to an overly polite faculty that there was an interesting novel they might want to read, called *The Great Gatsby*. He began to describe the setting of the novel and then its plot, as if we had never heard of F. Scott Fitzgerald. I tried in vain to signal to him that everyone in the room had already taught the novel, but to no avail.

This is an extreme case. But the larger problem was not only that this visitor completely misjudged his audience but also that he had no comparative frame of reference, no conception of the literature produced in Scandinavia at the same time.[1] Even for American Studies scholars with a better sense of their audience, to the extent that they know only the United States, they have nothing to compare it to. It is as if they were deeply familiar with red, white and blue, but had never seen burgundy, beige, and aquamarine. Such visiting Americans become unwitting illustrations of Seymour Martin Lipset's observation, "He who knows only one country knows no country."[2] One does not have to agree with Lipset's other views to see the wisdom in that remark.

A Sketch of American Studies in Scandinavia

How and when did American Studies develop in Scandinavia? Any discussion of this subject must begin with reference to Sigmund Skard's two-volume study published half a century ago, under the title *American Studies in Europe* (1958). Skard compared how Europeans viewed America in the nineteenth century to their views in mid-twentieth century. He looked at each country in turn, emphasizing how the reception of American culture, indeed the selection of what was worth studying about the United States, varied considerably. While generalizations were difficult, he did see some broad patterns.[3] In the nineteenth century "America remained the arsenal of European radicalism, the hope of the down-trodden, the Common Man's Utopia." (26) In contrast, to most European governments at that time the United States "was not only repugnant politically and socially, but it was an upstart culturally." (27) The United States was long viewed as a mere provincial extension of British culture, and its books, art, and other cultural productions were not much collected or put into libraries and museums. Even today the scholar interested in American materials from before 1900 often finds Nordic collections deficient, though improved interlibrary loans, Internet book sales, and the digitalized materials on the Web are fast eliminating this problem. Given the early lack of resources, however, few nineteenth-century scholars focused on the new nation. Europe as a whole was not much different, though the resources available were better in Germany and Britain. With a few stunning exceptions, such as Alexis de Tocqueville and Max Weber, most European scholars often ignored America, though there were many interesting travel books written about the United States for the general reader.

World War I increased European interest in the United States, as it was becoming a great power. In France the first chairs in American subjects were created just as America was entering the War. By 1920 the US had the largest economy in the world, and during the interwar years research foundations began to sponsor trans-Atlantic travel by academics for the first time. In the 1930s interest in the US increased, but so did antagonism to it, most obviously in Germany, but also in other nations. America was often viewed as a cultureless land with an enormous industrial plant. Attacked by intellectuals of both right and left, for different reasons to be sure, the US was no longer seen as the land of revolution (that was now Russia) but rather of capitalist democracy.

To narrow the focus, each of the Scandinavian nations had a different early relationship to American Studies. Sweden and Norway displayed somewhat more interest, presumably because both sent larger numbers of immigrants to the United States, and began to send them earlier, than Denmark. Skard notes that in the 1870s the first rector of Goteborg University wrote a book about American literature. Even so, in all the Nordic countries academic interest in the US was sporadic. Well into the twentieth century there were no chairs in American history, geography, or literature. In the public schools American literature made only slow progress. In 1958, Skard correctly saw how the Second World War had dramatically intensified interest in things American, and realized that this was more than a simple response to America's rise as a world power. Just as importantly, after the Nazi occupation of Denmark and Norway, after the concentration camps, German culture had lost the prestige and pre-eminence it had long held in academic life. Scholars no longer looked to Germany, but rather to Britain and the United States. (The reorientation toward the Anglo-American world has lasted a half-century, but in recent years one notes some reviving interest in a re-united Germany, even as the American invasion of Iraq has soured European-US relations.)

The postwar eclipse of Germany did not immediately transfer attention to America, however. During the 1950s departments of English focused on Britain and enshrined Oxbridge pronunciation as the standard, while giving only grudging recognition to American English. In most universities American literature and history were not required, and few theses were written on American subjects. Yet English did become the leading foreign language in both primary and secondary education. It was required of all students, and

American materials increasingly entered the curriculum. Beyond these generalizations about all of the Nordic countries, Norway early took the initiative, not least due to Skard's leadership. Sweden and Denmark created fewer permanent positions for Americanists in the 1950s. Four decades later, however, Sweden had well developed programs in American literature at Uppsala, Denmark had created two Centers for American Studies (Odense, 1992, and Aarhus, 1996), and Norway had significant concentrations of Americanists in both Oslo and Bergen.

Half a century after Skard wrote his magisterial book, it is obvious that the Nordic countries have made great strides toward institutionalizing American Studies. The tiny library holdings he found have grown much larger, and the possibilities of interlibrary loan are far better. E-mail provides immediate contact with fellow specialists anywhere on the globe, while access to the Internet has gone far to eliminate resource differences. The Nordic Association for American Studies (NAAS) held its first conference in 1961, before the ASA met for the first time in the United States, in 1967. Today, NAAS has more than 300 members. Then it had no journal; in 2008 *American Studies in Scandinavia* will celebrate its fortieth year.

Yet if progress is unmistakable, the road has been neither smooth nor straight. In the 1960s anti-war protest fuelled anti-Americanism. Protesters often did not distinguish between anti-war and anti-American sentiments. The majority of US American Studies scholars were against the Vietnam War, so it seems ironic and misguided that in Scandinavia this field of study often suffered cutbacks as a reaction to American foreign policy. The first Center for American Studies in Denmark was almost established as early as 1970 at Århus University, but the prevailing political climate made this impossible, and a quarter century passed before that university had one. Copenhagen University apparently suffered a similar fate. When

I came there to teach in 1987, American literature was not a required course in the English Department, and no courses in American history were offered in the history department. The English faculty retained its strong orientation to Britain, and as late as 1991, Copenhagen University emphatically rejected a proposal to establish a center for American Studies, even though external funding was offered and sufficient staff were already on hand. To some extent, in all the Nordic countries, with the exception of Norway, the Vietnam era delayed the growth of the field. Even in Norway the leading scholars in the field felt it necessary to write a letter during the height of the anti-Vietnam War protests, disavowing their support for the US position, but asserting their continued interest in studying the United States. In contrast, during these very years American Studies inside the United States grew rapidly in part because its scholars offered powerful critiques of violence in America, of racism, and of the mythology of Manifest Destiny.

Some Nordic history departments became anachronistic as a result of isolating themselves from American developments. To my amazement, in the late 1980s some Nordic historians still thought Frederick Jackson Turner's frontier thesis was a viable argument, and some still regarded Richard Hofstadter's *The Age of Reform* as a basic text. In the last two decades, however, student exchanges with the United States, as well as the continual movement of scholars to and from America via the Fulbright Program and other exchanges, has raised the level of knowledge and the intensity of interest. History departments, even if they remain Eurocentric, have hired Americanists; English departments now require all students to take American literature.

As this sketch of American Studies in the Nordic countries suggests, the field differs in many ways from its counterpart in the United States. Visiting scholars need some orientation if they really want to adapt to the new teaching and research environment. A few try to bring all their research materials with them, only to discover many of the books are available. And some try to teach as though they were still in the US, in which case the students do most of the adjusting. One can even argue that this is a good thing for the students, though it does little for the visiting faculty member.

Teaching American Studies inside another culture is a kind of cultural striptease, but not in the sense of removing layers of meaning to get to a naked truth that lies beneath. Rather, American Studies abroad is a process in which whatever seems to be natural turns out to be cultural. No matter how many layers of meaning one examines, there is always another cultural meaning underneath. Things that a visiting American assumes to be universal turn out to be cultural. Take the university as an example. The Nordic university is quite unlike its American counterpart. Nordic students select their major before arriving at the university and take almost no electives in other departments. They are on average older. They seldom seek out faculty for personal advance. They pay no tuition, and they are far more financially independent of their parents than American students. There are no intercollegiate sports teams, no fraternities, no parents' weekends, no homecoming weekend, no alumni newsletter, no fund drives, and often no graduation ceremonies. Almost all faculty are in labor unions and salaries are determined largely on the basis of seniority, with only symbolic merit increases. Given all these differences, the look and feel of a Scandinavian university is not what an American is used to.

The Scandinavian field of American Studies differs in at least five fundamental ways from the same discipline in the US. First, despite the field's progress since World War II, it is rather present-minded. Judging by course enrollments and thesis topics, students generally prefer the recent past, particularly the years since c. 1920.

Second, economic support for American Studies abroad

generally reflects this present-mindedness. It often seems that the US needs to be studied not so much because it is intrinsically interesting, but because it is a superpower. Research and teaching on the three centuries before then is less developed. From the US side, American Studies has been assiduously fostered by the Fulbright exchange and the USIS. This is another way of saying that American Studies exists in the Nordic countries partly by virtue of Washington's continual infusions of funds during the Cold War. The policy motivation was strategic and present-minded, although happily the scholars on the exchanges were free to pursue their own research and teaching agendas. Such exchanges were part of a larger cultural offensive linked to the defense of national security.[4] Now that the Cold War is over, much of this money has been withdrawn. Fulbright budgets shrink year by year, despite the fact that the countries themselves have increased their contributions to the exchange. For example, in Denmark, more than 60 % of the budget now comes from the Danes. With the notable exception of Norway, most universities took a decade or even a generation to move from exchanges to regular appointments in American subjects.

Fortunately, more permanent funding for university appointments has begun to flow from the various ministries of education. (How this is related to the end of the Cold War is too large a topic to take up here.) In terms of permanent appointments, American Studies now has a secure place.[5] But this security is recent, and intellectual marginality remains a fact of professional life. This is the third great difference. American Studies occupies a modest place within the universities. Most students do not major in English, after all, and most do not take any courses on the United States. For most faculty, American Studies exists only on the margin of consciousness. To the shock of some American professors, many people in the Nordic nations really are not particularly interested in the US except as another vacation destination, or as a negative contrast to their welfare economies. And for reasons that I will come to shortly, that is probably a healthy thing for the American visitor to encounter.

The lack of interest is reciprocal. Most Americans have only a shadowy idea of the Nordic countries. They almost never speak any of the languages and usually they do not understand their systems of government beyond the phrase "welfare state." Geographically speaking, Americans often literally do not know where Scandinavians are coming from. They often confuse Denmark with Holland. They think that Copenhagen is the capital of Sweden or that one can enjoy the midnight sun in Oslo, Goteborg, or Helsinki. Like all large nations, the United States is primarily interested in itself. When outsiders write about them, Americans are mildly interested if the comments are appreciative (Alistair Cooke (2004), for example), or they take an interest if the critics are rigorously in line with a current trend (Umberto Eco [1990] or Jean Baudrillard [1989]). Even US graduate students in the field of American Studies are only sporadically aware of research done abroad.

This general American ignorance of the Nordic nations makes it difficult for visitors to negotiate the fourth major difference between US and Nordic American Studies. For as soon as one crosses the Atlantic the field is, and cannot avoid being, comparative. Every topic taken up implicitly has a contrasting equivalent in the Nordic world. Abroad, American Studies scholars inhabit two cultural and linguistic universes, which sometimes intersect, but more often run parallel to or contradict one another. The bi-cultural psychology that develops is founded on a host of collisions, refractions, and reinterpretations that a teacher at first must learn to live with, but eventually can exploit.[6] Such scholars experience stereo cultural vision, and the continual comparisons provide a greater sense of historical depth. One example is the comparison of traditions in painting, notably the invention of landscape painting in the Danish and American traditions during roughly the same period. Such comparisons can make one aware of new research topics. In my case, Denmark provided a dramatic contrast to the propensity, in the United States, to value the sublime in nature, architecture, and technology. The Danish landscape and material culture have been constructed to emphasize the small and the cozy (even the cute); structures are built on a human scale. There are no skyscrapers, for example. This cultural contrast contributed, in ways that are impossible to articulate fully, to the writing of *American Technological Sublime* (1994). The contrasts between Danish and American energy use were also important stimuli to my *Consuming Power: A Cultural History of American Energies* (1997).

Americans living outside the United States experience flashbacks and flash-forwards as sequences from one culture reoccur in the other. For example, same-sex marriage was legalized in Denmark more than a decade before the US. Danes agreed to the change with little debate before and almost none afterwards, in contrast to the United States where the Christian right and much of the Republican Party reject it. Other sequences seem to begin in the US and spread elsewhere. A journalist called me once to discuss whether Danish politicians were adopting American media techniques. I agreed that to some extent they were, but the legislative systems are fundamentally different. The American politician must win at least 50 % of the vote. She needs to appear to the broadest possible range of voters, and tries not to appear controversial on most issues. In contrast, no Scandinavian party ever expects to win as much as half the vote. Furthermore, individual politicians are somewhat less important than in the US. Parties present a slate of candidates and send representatives to the legislature if they collectively win more than a few percentage points in an election. Parties do not try to appeal to such a broad spectrum of voters as American parties do. Rather, each cultivates a profile in a crowded field of parties, seeking to win a well-defined minority. Any party with more than 10 % of the vote can become quite important in the formation of coalition governments. Each uses the media, but the goal is to secure between one twentieth and one third of the vote, and this calls for different tactics than American parties must use to win a majority. As this example suggests, cultural transfer of political advertising is not at all a straightforward process. Generally, there is a great deal of selection, resistance, and modification before an idea, practice, or artifact moves from one country to another. Scandinavian scholarship on Americanization includes Steinar Bryn's short book on Norway (1992) and a collection of essays edited by Rolf Lundén and Erik Åsard on *Networks of Americanization* in Sweden (1992). Two other important early works on this topic are Rob Kroes, et al, *Cultural Transmissions and Receptions: American Mass Culture in Europe* (twenty essays, 1993) and Kroes's own volume, *If You've Seen One, You've Seen The Mall* (1996).

Aside from the complexities of trans-Atlantic cultural transfers, Americanists abroad also witness cultural dissonance when incompatible cultural patterns slam up against one another. For example, when Bill Clinton came in Denmark in July of 1997, during the days immediately before his visit the press discovered a major disagreement had developed between the American embassy and local security people regarding the President's only open-air appearance. The Americans wanted a huge crowd, and photo opportunities for the media as Clinton made his way through the throng. The Danes apparently had imagined a stately wave from the rostrum as the President addressed a carefully screened public. The American approach came from US electoral politics, in contrast to Danish politicians who do not "work" crowds and seldom attract 50,000 people either. The solution to this particular disagreement was to cordon off a square and to ask all who came in to pass through metal detectors, a procedure that took hours.

Another example of the clash of customs emerged when a Danish couple took a vacation in New York City. When they wanted to go into a café, they parked their baby in its carriage next to the door. This is quite common in Denmark, where kidnapping is rare, but it shocked the New York employees. When the Danes refused to bring the child inside, the police came to the scene and arrested them. The Danes thought the café was a safe place. The Americans saw irresponsible parents. The Danish newspapers headlined this story for days, and criticized the New York authorities both for the arrest and for keeping the mother and child apart at the police station. Those with stereo vision can understand both sides during such misunderstandings.

In addition, there are many cases of cultural selection and amplification, in which one aspect of a culture is taken up and exaggerated by the other. For example, a particular song by Louis Armstrong, "Wonderful World" is often replayed on Danish radio and television, and has been appropriated for advertising. The song is less often heard in the US, probably because in it Armstrong seems the stereotype of 'the happy Negro,' and "Wonderful World" says nothing about racial injustice.

But are Danes wrong to hear the song in their own way? Similar recontextualizations occur during the transmission and reception of all aspects of culture. This realization led me and Mick Gidley, a British colleague, to invite thirteen other scholars to contribute to a volume on *American Photographs in Europe* (1994). These essays examined such things as the reception of American art photography at German exhibitions from 1893-1929, the arrival of the Kodak camera in Britain and the response to its democratization of image-making, the role of photography in immigrant writing, the reception of American photography in France after World War II, and the "Family of Man" photographic exhibit in Moscow during the Cold War. In these and many other cases, the representation of America is not a simple matter, but rather one of selection, recontextualization, and (often unanticipated) response. Finally, one sees in the daily news the selective (in)attention of each of the Scandinavian nations to the US, and vice-versa. Sweden, Norway and Denmark seldom bulk large in the American press, and on both sides there is a tendency to cover only sensational events such as riots, shipwrecks, assassinations, and natural disasters. Detailed cultural analysis is rare.

This is only a partial list, but it is sufficient to demonstrate that American Studies scholars living in the Nordic countries develop a creolized consciousness, a complex awareness of similarity and difference that deepens over the years. It is often difficult to convey this tapestry of perceptions to visiting American academics, some of whom can only see the Scandinavian (and the larger European) world with one eye and cannot comprehend it in the original tongue. Full stereo perception can only come with language acquisition and cultural immersion, or in other words only after years abroad.

For Scandinavian students, the problem of perceiving the US is far different. They begin to study English before they reach gymnasium, but the content of that early training is only sporadically American. Their free time is partly filled with American films, television programs, and rock music, which collectively provide a stylized sense of the US. At the gymnasium students (aged 17-20) read some American literature, but entire courses are seldom organized in terms of US cultural themes or historical developments, and texts usually remain subservient to the goal of language acquisition. Those who decide to study English at the university arrive with a spotty and impressionistic knowledge of the US, and once there take a good deal of coursework on British language and culture as well as American subjects. They consciously compare the United States and Britain. In short, they cannot get a great depth of knowledge of US culture before reaching the age of 21, or about when US students are completing their BA. Nordic students who decide to specialize in the United States only become deeply engaged in the subject as adults, and their education is a highly self-conscious process.

In contrast, Americans are immersed in their own society and they can have difficulty imagining or understanding a different culture. When teaching in the United States in 2003, I found few students with an international perspective. Those who majored in American Studies had little knowledge of the rest of the world, and they had little basis upon which to compare the US and anywhere else. Even when students go abroad, American magazines, television programs, and books are everywhere to hand, and the Internet is always there, providing a comfortable cocoon of familiar cultural reference points. Since foreign students tend to stick together, they can easily spend as much as a year abroad without learning a foreign language, without making foreign friends and without ever losing contact with the American slant on the news. It is more difficult now to become immersed in the host culture than it was two decades ago, when I went to Spain as a Fulbright lecturer. In 1977 I could not see a single American TV program, there were few expatriates to talk to, and virtually all conversations took place in Spanish. Since then, however, the spread of multinational companies, the deregulation of European television, the increasing number of exchange students, and the arrival of the Internet and e-mail have changed that, leading many Americans to believe that a new global culture is emerging. Such a belief is misguided but convenient, since it makes it unnecessary to learn the language of the host country or to worry about cultural differences. In effect, a belief in globalization justifies hearing and seeing the world in mono rather than stereo.[7]

For this reason, American Studies students ideally ought to spend a full year abroad in a setting where they are not always with other exchange students. By experiencing this contrast, they could realize how profoundly every aspect of their lives is a cultural product, and how resistant foreign cultures are to Americanization. American Studies graduate students, as well as their teachers, would benefit tremendously from spending time abroad not as tourists but as part of their education, in order to see the United States from the outside. They may better understand (though not always agree with) international observers of the US as a result, notably Alexis de Tocqueville, Max Weber, Henry James, and Umberto Eco. A comparative perspective illuminates an American's own cultural identity.

African-Americans have been especially sensitive to these possibilities. James Baldwin, who lived for several years in Paris during the 1950s, found himself listening to Bessie Smith records and pondering his own identity, which seemed easier to understand through contrast with a foreign culture (1955). Interviews with African-American expatriates are quite revealing on this point. While they may go abroad in order to escape American racism, usually they find themselves more American than they realized. An African-American woman who sold everything she owned and moved to Africa found that she missed American food, and that she did not really "fit. I just cannot fit. *My* conduct is all different from theirs and they can't cope with me because of my background." Indeed, after associating with Ghanians almost exclusively for a long time, she felt "very lonely" and realized that she "had nothing in common with many Ghanaians. You know, like being able to crack a joke and have someone here *really* understand it." Ironically, she found herself turning to white Americans, "because they were the only people here who understood my need. Nobody else could understand what was wrong with me, not physically, mentally. Because of our backgrounds, they understood *exactly* how I felt, but nobody else."[8] Americans who feel deeply alienated from the US may eventually discover cultural linkages to home that are stronger than they suspected. Even those convinced that there is no such thing as an American national character may be surprised that Europeans can identify them as Americans by the way they walk or how they hold a knife and fork.

Overall, there is a fascinating asymmetry between the cultural position of Nordic students who begin the study of the US as adults, seeking to acquire a new culture self-consciously, and an American who begins to understand the United States in a new way when abroad by discovering unconscious assumptions and realizing how deeply and thoroughly every aspect of his or her being is shaped by culture. Such realizations are vital in American Studies.

There is a fifth and final difference. Scandinavian American Studies scholars must remain to a degree generalists, in contrast to their counterparts in the US who are typically in large departments, where each is expected to cover only a small part of American history or literature, often less than 50 years. In contrast, the few Americanists at a typical European university must cover far more ground. It is unusual for a university to have more than three American historians, for example, so it is not unusual for a single scholar to teach graduate courses on both immigration and African American history, or on both urban history and the history of the American landscape. With at best half a dozen Americanists to cover all fields, each scholar must be something of a generalist. Combining these teaching demands with stereo vision encourages scholars to become generalists and comparativists.

This outline of the differences between American Studies on two sides of the Atlantic suggests how European Americanists occupy a distinctive intercultural location. Americans usually just assume that they are experts on their own nation. They are native speakers, thoroughly imbued with their culture, and they need seldom wonder about what everyday things mean. Not so the Nordic student, who knows the US first in books, television, and music, and only later in person. I tell my students when they go to the US that their comparative view will give them insights, but I know they are dubious. Of course, there are areas where they can feel particularly confident: theory, where their mastery of languages gives them an advantage, immigration studies, foreign policy as it touches their home country, and comparative work. All of these are worthy fields, where Nordic scholars have long stood in the first rank. But Nordic scholars need not restrict themselves to these interests. Both the comparative view and the interdisciplinary context of Nordic American Studies make possible work of the highest quality on any American subject. Americans can learn things from their creolized perspective, from stereo vision.

There is no reason to suppose that the acquisition of stereo vision will decline. Nordic interest in the US is growing stronger, as measured in exchanges with American universities and enrolments in American Studies courses. The spread of the Internet is also important, as it eases access to information. Another measure of improvement is the ability of *American Studies in Scandinavia* to attract excellent articles, and the success of Nordic-based scholars in publishing their work in the US.[9] But the transformation of the biannual conferences is perhaps the most striking example of maturation. In 1982 the majority of the papers given at the NAAS conference in Copenhagen were delivered by visiting Americans. The organizers of the following conference in Bergen felt that it was time for Nordic scholars to take a more active role than listeners at their own meetings, and they found no lack of qualified people in their own ranks to supplement the American contribution. This practice continued at the following meetings in Uppsala, Tampere, and Reykjavik, and from the time of the 1992 NAAS conference in Odense an average of more than 75 papers are usually delivered, primarily by NAAS members, and mostly in parallel workshop sessions.

A concurrent sign of health is the funding of more Ph.D. candidates in recent years. All of these things point to the coming-of-age of Scandinavian American Studies.

It is maturing, but to what end? Are Nordic scholars about to embark on grand comparative studies backed by massive funding? Is there a distinctive Nordic school of thought in American Studies? Should one expect the appearance of a Nordic Tocqueville? No doubt the United States could benefit from a thorough-going analysis undertaken from abroad, of the kind that Tocqueville once managed on his own, but which now would require teamwork. Such a thing has been sponsored before, notably in Gunnar Myrdal's seminal *An American Dilemma: The Negro Problem and Modern Democracy* (1944) and it could be done again. Yet such an outcome can hardly be expected, as it would require considerable funding over an extended time, plus the selection and coordination of a team of researchers who would need to stay together over a period of years. Such an expensive and long-term project is unlikely, but by no means impossible. Far more feasible are the publication of good monographs and the emergence of new teaching materials, notably interdisciplinary textbooks on the United States seen from the creolized Scandinavian perspective, and aimed at non-Americans.[10]

If there is no official Scandinavian school of American Studies, there is a distinctive perspective. To paraphrase Emerson, "Our day of dependence, our long apprenticeship…draws to a close."[11] Today's scholars from Scandinavia, especially the new Ph.D. students, do not parrot American thinking. They seek to become *European* American Scholars. For them, Emerson's project needs considerable revision. They will immerse themselves not in transcendental Nature but in comparative culture. They will not automatically defer to American colleagues, but test their ideas against Nordic perspectives. Because they see the United States in stereo, they cannot fail to develop new and valuable work.

Scandinavian American Studies has been fully institutionalized in recent decades. It has achieved cultural independence and thrives in a creolized form, making its own distinctive contribution. The same process is taking place in American Studies within all the European countries, particularly those that have been active in the field for decades, notably the Netherlands, Germany, France, Italy, Spain, and Britain. These multilingual scholars, with their stereo vision and methodological expertise, are especially well equipped to rethink American Studies for the 21st century.

Notes
1. Horwitz (1993) edited a useful collection of essays on exporting American Studies.
2. Cited by William B. Bader speech in Vienna celebrating the fiftieth anniversary of the Fulbright Program, "The Last Three Feet: A Fulbright Experience," Viewed Jan 3, 2007 at http://www.google.dk/search?hl=da&q="The+Last+Three+Feet %3A+A+Fulbright+Experience"&btnG=Google-søgning&meta=
3. The subject of the European view of America is vast, of course, but aside from the major figures such as Alexis de Tocqueville and Lord Bryce, one might begin with the eighteenth-century debate on the New World as chronicled in Commager and Giordanetti, *Was America a Mistake?* (1967).
4. See Pells, (1997), 62-63 and Wagenleitner, (1994).
5. The number of faculty in Slavic studies is still larger at some universities, but student interest in things American has never been greater.
6. For more on bi-cultural perceptions based on living in the Nordic countries, see Thomas (1990).
7. I find that "cultural studies" approaches tend to use a small number of theories to describe all cultures and as a result are often reductionist.
8. Dunbar (1968), 63-64.

9   Most would agree that the first four journals in American Studies are *American Quarterly*, *American Studies*, *Prospects*, and the British *Journal of American Studies*. But what are the next four? It would be difficult to reach consensus, not least because many are published in part or in their entirety in their national languages. *American Studies in Scandinavia* is entirely in English.
10 For my attempt, see Nye, (2006, 6th ed.). See also Duncan and Goddard (2005).
11 This is, of course, a paraphrase of Ralph Waldo Emerson's "The American Scholar."

Re-thinking American Studies for the 21st Century

MARK LUCCARELLI

In a deliciously polemical article published in *The New Republic*, sociologist Alan Wolfe tore into a spate of new books by "New Americanist" scholars debating the direction of American Studies. In the piece, entitled "The Difference between Hatred and Criticism," Wolfe – a Boston University sociologist – accuses leading American Studies scholars of carrying the antifoundationalist assumptions of poststructuralism to the point of absurdity: defining away the object of their scorn, America itself. "Revealing America as non-existent," Wolfe tells us, "is supposed to ease the task of those oppressed groups that are struggling to overcome its hegemony." Citing various articles and talks, Wolfe reveals, and revels in, the spectacle of a coterie of bright, young scholars whose misplaced political agenda has led them to the brink of defining away the topical and even the physical boundaries of the very society they purport to be studying. Although one may well choose to take strong exception to Wolfe's patriotism (Americanist scholars, he demands, should undertake a certain "responsibility" in depicting the USA and show a "willingness to convey both its possibilities and its pitfalls."), he nonetheless succeeds admirably in calling into question the spirit of contemporary American Studies as practiced in the USA, and does us a service by suggesting that it is actually foreign programs of American Studies that are more representative of its true purpose – the study of the United States (2003). Whether we agree with Wolfe's criticisms of the New Americanists or not, his article brings up some important questions – questions which were debated at the 2003 NAAS conference at Trondheim: What is the direction of American-based American Studies today? Is there a gap between American and European American Studies programs, and – if so – why? Finally, what should be the direction of American Studies in Scandinavia and Europe? I will offer some reflections of my own concerning these issues, before presenting some of the positions taken by scholars speaking during a roundtable debate that I chaired, entitled: "Re-thinking American Studies for the 21st century."[1]

Genesis of the American Studies Movement
Never an academic discipline in its own right, American Studies is best characterized as an area studies program, the boundaries of which were (and for the most part still are) defined by the object of study – the United States of America. In Europe, American Studies was established as a consequence of American geopolitical preeminence that followed the Second World War and was supported, first by private American foundations and later by the State Department as a part of a larger effort to hold together the western alliance during the Cold War.[2] Most American Studies programs were attached to foreign language departments. By contrast in the United States, American Studies may be best understood as an intellectual movement, an expression of a critical cultural nationalism. Originating in the 1930s (the seminal program at Harvard was established in 1937), American Studies followed in the footsteps of a tradition of essay writing by men of letters, beginning with the reports of European travelers in the 18th century and maturing with the work of a number of American-born cultural critics and critical public intellectuals – figures such as Van Wyck Brooks (1915), Waldo Frank (1919), Harold Stearns (1922), Paul Rosenfeld (1924), and Lewis Mumford. Indeed two of Mumford's early works – *Sticks and Stones: A*

Study of American Architecture and Civilization (1924) and *The Golden Day: A Study in American Experience and Culture* (1926) – could be said to be the two founding texts of the American Studies movement, both in form and content. These works were synthetic: they characterized "American civilization"[3] as a whole, often by bringing into relation what in the academy were disparate fields of inquiry. The studies also tended to work on a balance between criticism and celebration. The academic inheritors and amplifiers of this tradition of letters shared a commitment to uncover an American cultural inheritance that was democratic, pragmatic, creative. American Exceptionalism, it could be argued, was only a wrapping, an attempt to frame and present some important elements of a new and vital society. It was an idealized America, certainly, an expression of a Euro-American hope; but there was also a frank criticism of another side of American life – one so powerful that it moved Harold Stearns to dismiss what had become in his mind nothing more than "a business civilization." Their stance of seeking a balance between hopeful optimism and biting criticism is nicely illustrated in this short passage from Paul Rosenfeld in an essay on Carl Sandburg: "The man respects and loves sincerely the rocks and rills and woods which Americans have always dimly wished to respect and love and not to exploit; known they needed to, and never quite come to love and be good to."[4] It was indeed a lost America of love that they hoped to recover.

The subtlety of Rosenfeld's position (and that of the first order academic Americanists) simply made no sense to a generation of young men and women coming to age in the 1960s and seeing America through the lens of the anti-racist and anti-war movements. What they saw in American Studies was its presumptive political complicity with American imperialism masquerading as a staid, consensus-oriented approach to American culture. In a recently published article in the *Boston Review*, Leo Marx, one of the best practitioners of the old American Studies, gives us as good a version as any of the received view of the change in the field: there was, as Marx humorously calls it, a "Great Divide" in American Studies. Before the divide (BD) American Studies was "holistic, affirmative, nationalistic." It had been founded on a synthesis of literary and historical studies. Literary scholars were of the "myth and symbol" school; their investigations of mythic themes around the conception of a "virgin land" coincided with the consensus school of national historians: both contributed to the development of the idea of American Exceptionalism. Technique and objective combined to give a view of the USA as a "society and culture so nearly homogenous as to be free of significant sociocultural conflict." But the 1960s changed all that. After the divide (AD) literary scholars shifted their attention to texts seen as representative of the unacknowledged voices of American culture, while AD social historians "turned their attention to concrete particulars – to the precise, close-up, empirical," indeed to carrying out virtually ethnographic studies of particular shared identity groups. (2003).

Marx does not join in this view of the great divide largely because he sees it as a fundamental misrepresentation of the first American Studies paradigm. The founding scholars (Henry Nash Smith, F. O. Matthiessen, Perry Miller and Daniel Boorstin) were themselves left-liberals who had combined their appreciation of American ideals and values with sharp criticism of the actually existing society. They were all critical of American capitalism, but they could still be relatively sympathetic to the United States because of their hopes for New Deal reformism. Even more fundamentally, these scholars lived in a world that, having faced down the real possibility of complete economic collapse, was soon confronted with the specter of fascism; consequently they felt grateful pride in the "egalitarian Enlightenment principles of the American Revolution" which, it seemed to them, had been instrumental in staving off the collapse of civilization. I think that Marx makes an important point here – though he is also missing something essential. What he doesn't fully acknowledge is that many contemporary scholars can never accept first school American Studies, regardless of the political instincts or real political positions of the people involved or indeed despite the actual existing alternatives of that era. The disagreement is more fundamental than that; it cannot be addressed by historicizing the old American Studies because in rejecting history (or at least the "old" history), these scholars have radically reconceived the relation between intellectual work and the social-political world. The old American Studies was neo-humanist. Like the Renaissance humanists, the first American Studies scholars had identified a set of foundational texts (canonical American literature and other high cultural productions) which were seen in relation to, but distinct from, the actually existing political and social institutions. In fact, they provided a useful commentary on those institutions. By contrast, poststructuralism, the reigning influence in today's American Studies, is anti-humanist: foundational texts are understood to construct culture out of a binary logic which once exposed reveals underlying social structures of oppression. Consequently, the supposedly critical canonical texts are actually the sources of social oppression, in this view. I want to return to these matters briefly, but before I do it is important to carry the development of American Studies one step further toward the present.

New Americanists: Supplanting the Second American Studies Paradigm

Like Leo Marx, virtually everyone acknowledges the development of the second American Studies paradigm – or the "the new American Studies." But Janice Radway's essay "What's In a Name?" (2002) suggests that we have entered a third paradigm of American Studies, or, alternately, are approaching the fragmentation and death of the American Studies movement altogether.

For Radway, the dominant poststructuralist discourse of what might be labeled the "New Americanists" (or trans-cultural American Studies) has already undermined the neo-liberal second order American Studies paradigm by questioning what the word "American" could possibly signify in an age of mass human migrations and declining national identities. The question is, why should the diversity of various cultures – originating all over the globe, migrating to North America, adapting to new conditions, creating various syncretistic cultural expressions – be expressed in the terms of a national entity – the United States?

This has led to a reassessment of the American Studies revolution of the 1960s and 1970s. The American Studies that emerged after the "Great Divide" was clearly committed to the study of cultural diversity – though I would say that "diversity" was expressed almost entirely in terms of race and gender as opposed to the diversity of ideas. American Studies (i.e. AD) was sharply influenced by the postcolonial politics of the 1960s Left. At the same time, American Studies scholars remained traditional Americanists in the sense that they saw the object of their study to be the United States, including the national political framework. There were both practical and theoretical underpinnings to this synthesis. Theoretically, American Studies embraced new departures in the study of specific social groups: this was particularly true as there was a rising social-science-influenced branch of American Studies rooted in ethnographic theory and headquartered at the University of Pennsylvania – which for a time hosted the *American Quarterly*. Practically, there was a strong commitment to a (neo)liberal reform program which linked the study of various identities of socially disadvantaged groups to concrete social programs aimed at bettering the conditions of life for these peoples – most particularly and increasingly through affirmative action programs. Specifically, AD American Studies developed a powerful politics of the academy as the field became a kind of umbrella organization for the organization of African-American, Chicano, Puerto Rican and Women's Studies programs. The second order paradigm of American Studies, in summary, was an intellectual expression of liberal multiculturalism, and an attempt to make an ethical/political commitment to minority groups compatible with the study of national institutions and history. From this perspective, the present model of neo-liberal multiculturalism was the outcome of a long national process. Over time, I would argue, neo-liberalism has asserted its influence over the national agenda in two ways: first, it involved a reassertion of the interest-group political model updated through affirmative action programs, effectively contributing its part to the reduction of American politics to backroom lobbying; second, it conducted a kind of rapprochement with "free market" neo-conservatism, whereby the model of identity creation is analogous to the creation of consumer-based identities – "an open marketplace of identities" replacing the traditional liberal "open marketplace of ideas."

According to Radway, the dual-sided character of second order American Studies – its commitment to the study of culturally specific groups within the context of *the national society* – has made it unsustainable in the light of poststructuralist theory. Tying standard categories to the development of the American nation state has lead to both the "essentializing" of group identities and to an unrealistic, or at the very least, to a highly contestable view of American polity as a progressive unfolding of American liberal promise. For radical New Americanists such as Radway, adherence to the multicultural liberal model has resulted in a loss of American Studies' critical edge. Liberal multiculturalism's promotion of the category of "minority group" and its focus on the issue of distribution of entitlements by the national state do not go far enough in freeing people from the oppressive traits attributed to "America."

In promoting radical new ways of thinking about difference, poststructuralism has undermined liberal multiculturalism, opening the way for a broader critical appraisal of the entire idea within the context of American political and cultural life. For the New Americanists the disagreement is fundamental, beginning with liberal multiculturalism's foundation: the idea that subaltern groups should be classified as "minorities" in relation to a majority society. The minority group concept – the key category of second paradigm American Studies – assumes relatively stable social identities. This stability is important because it is necessary to a reformist politics of identity which seeks to be inclusive – that is, to make space for minority groups within the framework of the larger national community, you must know who you are trying to include: social facts must be gathered. It is precisely for this reason that representatives of minority group organizations, such as the NAACP, lobbied vigorously against the move to include a new multiracial category on the US Census form and other official documents that ask people to declare their race and gender. (The objection was that mixed-race people are not counted in the US government's statistical accounting of minorities.) Like the official racial and ethnic categories maintained by the US government, the category "minority" rests on an essentialist definition of identity. Poststructuralist American Studies, by contrast, perceives identities to be inherently unstable, shifting "cross-cutting, insurgent, oftentimes oppositional identifications." (58-59) Identities can no longer be bound by essential characteristics of stable social groups, because culture "is the always shifting terrain on which multiple social groups form, actively solicit the identification of some, hinder that of others, and ignore the counter claims made by still others." (58) Just as social identities lack stable meanings, so do they lack definite geographic boundaries: a culture, in this view, can no more be fixed and mapped than it can be described as a concrete thing. In part this idea reflects awareness of the realities of the early 21st century, a world in which human migrations across the globe have increased markedly, to near historic levels. But it also reflects the poststructuralist claim that all meanings are socially constructed and that geography, rather than being a particular space or "container" existing through time, must be seen as "spatially situated and intricately intertwined networks of social relationships that tie specific locales to particular histories."(55) By far the most appealing framework for expressing this idea of social networks as the defining geographical principle is the notion of the borderland – a convenient metaphor for seeing all peoples through multiple cultural frames, resulting in a complex and rich understanding of various cultures. "Borderland" takes its name from real places, but it describes a cultural position akin to the older idea of "in-betweeness" (social marginality)[5] – except that there are no inherently stable identities to be in-between. There is only a kaleidoscope of "multiple, shifting, imagined communities" (57) in relation to which various identities are constructed. Such identities must of necessity be trans-national and trans-cultural, developing through the nexus of cultural contact, influence and contestation conducted through the forces of globalization, in particular through the global media.

Now, I should point out that though I am earnestly and faithfully rehearsing these ideas – even to the point of proceeding with deterministic-sounding statements about how "identities can no longer be thought of in old ways" – I don't mean to be taken literally. Nor am I endorsing the poststructuralist ideas that stand in back of this discourse. Of course, we are *free* to re-imagine social identities, political formations and historical trajectories in multiple ways; at the same time we are *restrained* by actually existing social and political conditions, if we hope to accurately represent how such social identities take institutional form in the US today. I think the writings of the New Americanists are important, not because I find them the best approach to the study of the United States, but because they have done some necessary work in opening up space for critical reassessments (as of liberal multiculturalism, for instance) and for a second reason as well. The New Americanists represent what I take to be the current state of the discourse in American Studies as expressed by its most vocal and persuasive practitioners today. In implying that this discourse has become hegemonic,[6] Radway has accurately evaluated the direction of American Studies, and perhaps of the humanities as a whole, in the American academy, at least for the foreseeable future. It is important, in my view, to address this discourse – and not by simply reasserting positions that date back to the early 1970s, positions which have already been dismissed. One must contest (or engage) the New Americanists on the global turf, in terms of new spaces opened up by the dramatically changing cultural and political environment of our time. This involves examining assumptions about globalization and looking very carefully at related notions of trans-nationality.

The stakes are fairly obvious. At the most immediate level there is the question of the survival of American Studies itself. There is a neat (if somewhat simplistic) parallel between influence of the borderland concept on American Studies, on the one hand, and the globalization concept's impact on the study of the politics of the nation-state. Globalization theories have challenged the assumptions about the locus of political power – seeing it operating in global networks of various sorts and questioning the ability of nation-states, or any entity based on a territorial conception, to explain or control events. In a similar way, the idea of trans-national cultural networks challenges the importance and truth of national identities, and national territories, to the people they are said to characterize.

American Studies & European Americanists: Responses at Trondheim, 2003

What we have described thus far is the state of American Studies discourse in the United States. But what is the situation for Americanists working outside the United States and how do these developments affect us?

For the most part, European and European-based Americanists have been second-class citizens when it comes to American Studies – as has been commented on by many scholars, including Radway. Despite recent efforts to be more "inclusive," a perusal of the Proceedings of the last ASA conference shows that European and other "International" Americanists are more often than not segregated into their own special programs.[7]

One possible response is to join forces with postmodern thinkers who advocate an unequivocally global focus and perspective. A case for the privileging of the global was made by University of Minnesota historian David Noble in his recent *Death of a Nation* (2002). His point is that Anglo-Saxon Protestant American culture was always predatory and contradictory – ultimately a weak foundational culture, which in turn leads him to argue "that the modern nation [is] not the end of history and that the international marketplace [has become] a more important space." (269) The character of the global market is subject to sharp disagreement, but stating an unproblematized maximalist view of its influence – to the exclusion, or virtual exclusion, of the continuing importance of traditional conceptions of polity – is a key assumption on the part of the globalizers. The consequence for American Studies – its absorption into cultural studies – is made abundantly clear by Madina Tlostanova (Moscow):

> In my view the most promising of all the models of the future American Studies are those based on the principles of trans-cultural, trans-national and

> in some cases trans-imperial elements, and thus on the study of imperial-colonial configurations – obviously not only of the Western Hemisphere, but of the whole Western modernity, as it is not possible to divide the history of the Americas and Europe. This would lead eventually to the blurring of the boundaries of American Studies, while the lacuna of the national will likely be taken by the global.

Tlostanova's position that American Studies should take on the assumptions of postcolonial studies assumes, as she puts it, the existence of a common "European and American 'community of fate' in the sense of the common logic of western modernity."[8]

Even without interrogating her position from a theoretical perspective, one immediately comes up against an ingrained reluctance on the part of European-based Americanists to give up on the idea that the US exists as an entity, that it has a national history and a national experience which, however complicated it may be, is real and alive. As Markku Henriksson (Helsinki) puts it,

> there are a number of common elements in tastes, values, politics, economic behavior, etc., which set the people of the United States apart from people of other countries, states or whatever the political-economical-cultural formation or structure may be. Comparisons between the "USeans" and other peoples are important and fruitful, and this has often been the European approach to American Studies.

Henriksson's central point is empirical – that there are clear similarities of taste in the United States (regardless of how basic the common denominators may be) – and his common-sense-like observation that people who share a space are "a people" is, perhaps, very European in perspective, but still true enough in the experience of everyday life to be worth repeating.

Another important point that favors the continuance of the national approach rests on a bald, and these days an often rather uncomfortable reality of international power: the world is increasingly subject to the exercise of American unilateral decision making, a point Raili Põldsaar (Tartu) makes clearly: "It would… be premature to abandon the study of the USA as a unified entity, the great 'other' for most countries of the world. The contradictory ways in which 'America' is conceptualized internationally, often simultaneously as a source of liberation and domination, and summoned in local public discourses, deserve greater attention from the American Studies community." The point is that "America" as an entity exists still in the popular mind – and it is incumbent upon foreign-based Americanists to study how the societies perceive the United States and how "America" is used in the various discourses.[9] Taking up the conceptions (and misconceptions) of "America" or "American culture" in various countries is something that only foreign-based Americanists are positioned to do. Thus the great advantage of foreign Americanists adheres to place: living somewhere outside the USA means we see American culture/cultures from the outside, but far more importantly, we can study the assumptions of American cultural forms and motifs as they take shape within the boundaries of other societies. This would gain further explanatory power, in my judgment, if such work were put in relation to the on-going cross-cultural work of historians and political scientists – who have been looking comparatively at political and social institutions in relation to the nation-state, and to both long-forgotten and emerging political forms as they compete to capture and reshape social identities and economic structures. This would enable us, for example, to look at different models for constructing a multicultural society, and at least be open to critical perspectives on the liberal model. Moving in this direction might invite some of us to take up the purpose and spirit of the original American Studies movement, in the one limited sense of granting creative expressions (literature, art, popular culture) insight into, rather than determinative power over social and political structures.[10] This hope aside, obviously an international approach is quite different from studying a culture/society as a unique culture, as the original American Studies largely did.

Perhaps the best way to hold onto the idea of national experience and to make it relevant to the situation in American Studies today is to draw it out through a specifically *internationalist* perspective – in the literal sense that international means "among nations," and along the lines of a useful theoretical distinction made by Paul Hirst between the global and the international conceptions of the world economy.[11] If societies are still to be understood in national terms – and through international perspectives – what are we to make of the undeniable growth of transnational cultural scenes and discourses – of everything from rap music to shared Norwegian ancestry? Kristin Solli (Iowa/Oslo) argues that the transnational dimension of culture need not abrogate the national:[12] "I would like to see American Studies as a discipline in which national and transnational perspectives are not considered mutually exclusive. Quite on the contrary, if lived experience can be understood as multi-layered negotiations between national, subnational, and supranational loyalties and obligations, the national – as defined by US geographic borders – is certainly a dimension that should still concern American Studies scholars."

Extending an international perspective on American Studies need not do away with transcultural approaches. However, it is important to see the transcultural in historical and political perspective. "Borderlands," transcultural phenomena, cosmopolitan identities – formulations of cultural identities that extend beyond political borders – are not really new; they are important today, but it remains to be seen exactly how important they will become. In addition, a good case can be made for continuing to see culture in relation to territorial definitions of political entities (meaning bordered entities of some kind), for not only is the modern nation-state still extant, new polities are arising in the form of sub-national politics (cities and micro-regions) and super-national politics (sub-global regions). Many of these new political developments are most pronounced in Europe; the creating of a European region, for example, is a process that helps define European places and contributes to different and still emerging European senses of place that might well prove important points of departure for critical reassessments of the United States.

Migration, the porosity of borders, cosmopolitan identities, and creolization all suggest the value of studying the immigrant experience from a European as well as an American perspective, a subject that Jørn Brøndal explores in the following chapter.

Notes

1   Position statements by all the participants of the roundtable debate followed the text of my essay in *American Studies in Scandinavia,* as an Appendix. I would like to credit Walter Mignolo for conceiving the roundtable. My thanks also to David Mauk for helping to organize it, to the American Embassy in Oslo, Norway, for funding the participation of panelists from the Baltic countries, and to Danny Postel for helping locate sources for this article.

2   Skard (1978), 70, recalling his 1946 decision to press for the development of an independent American Institute, argued that "American civilization was no longer an appendage to Great Britain," and that it was far too important in the world to be ignored. Skard, by the way, had had many doubts about

American "vulgarity" and barbarism, but these, he tells us, were swept away by the (apparent) triumph of the New Deal in the 1930s.

3 At Harvard, the American Studies program was originally called "American Civilization."

4 Rosenfeld, *Port of New York*, 67. It may well be that to be effective in reaching a wider audience and influencing on-going debate, a public intellectual in a democratic society must always seek the kind of tension Rosenfeld achieves in this statement.

5 I'm thinking of Handlin's *The Uprooted* (1951).

6 I realize "poststructuralist hegemony" could be said to be an oxymoron, but is it really?

7 On the other hand, to be fair I must point out that in his 2002 inaugural address the new ASA president, Stephen Sumida, has called for a greater internationalization of ASA.

8 See Roundtable Discussion in *American Studies in Scandinavia* 36:1 (Spring 2004).

9 I was reminded of this point by the way in which "the American system" of higher education was used and misused by both sides in the recent debate over the administration's reform program at the University of Oslo. See also Alm, "America and the Future of Sweden," (2003).

10 In an area studies program there should be room for courses in the study of politics and society, geography, literature, art, popular culture and ideas – and for courses that provide various syntheses of these fields. Two practical difficulties in actuating this approach are pointed out by Pells (2001), namely that most of the cross-cultural work involving North America is done by American historians, as European historians have been reluctant to study North America; at the same time, the overwhelming percentage of European-based Americanists are literary scholars.

11 See Hirst and Thompson, *Globalization in Question* (1999), 1-18.

12 Some "New Americanists" concur with this position. See Spanos, in Pease and Wiegman (1982), 387-415, especially 396.

Research Trajectories

Who Were They? Writing Scandinavian-American History

JØRN BRØNDAL

Of the infinite number of questions that the historian may ask of the past, one has remained particularly pertinent to the study of the Scandinavian-American migrational and ethnic experiences: Who were they?[1] Since the closing decades of the nineteenth century, when the exploration of the field was first undertaken, and up to the present, however, the way in which this simple question was asked changed repeatedly. Whereas the inquiry originally was formulated in a manner to invite confirmation of preconceived ideas about national character, during the years 1930-60 it was rephrased so as to take into account some kind of Americanization that was taken for granted in the interplay between the immigrant's cultural habits and the pressure from the American environment. Later still, in the years 1960-80, "Who were they?" came to address statistically and socially defined groups, at the same time that the main geographical focus shifted from America to the Scandinavian countries. Finally, in recent decades, research has tended to revolve around a double "Who were they?" with some scholars focusing attention on locally or regionally defined ethnic identities, while others concentrate on invented, nationally inclusive ones. At the same time, the traditional chronological and geographical scope of the field widened.

Research prior to 1930: Preconceived ideas about national character

Even though official Scandinavian statistics tell us that migration from the Scandinavian countries to the United States in the years 1820 to 1930 comprised 2,243,630 Scandinavians, i.e., 1,127,304 Swedes, 780,708 Norwegians, and 335,618 Danes, it took a long time before Scandinavian historians truly began to address the migration and adjustment to American conditions of this mass of people.[2] In Sweden, due to growing concern over the supposed negative effects of emigration, a commission chaired by the statistician Gustav Sundbärg was established in 1907 to investigate statistically the repercussions of emigration on Swedish society, particularly agriculture, with a view to making recommendations on future emigration policy.[3] The resultant 21-volume report that was completed in 1913 did not, however, cause much of a stir among Swedish historians. Indeed, according to the Danish historian Kristian Hvidt, the very size of the report may have inhibited further scholarly exploration of Swedish emigration until the 1960s.[4] In 1912, an emigration commission was likewise established in Norway, but it only published short papers, and, again, historical scholars showed little interest in the subject.[5] In Denmark, three economists, V. Falbe-Hansen, William Scharling, and Adolph Jensen, each wrote statistically based studies of emigration, once again with no repercussions among actual historians.[6]

As some scholars have suggested, this passivity may have expressed a certain reluctance among nationally minded historians to grapple with a phenomenon that at least by the early twentieth century had begun to cause apprehension in wide circles in many western European countries, including Sweden and Norway.[7] In Denmark where a debate over the potentially negative consequences of emigration never really developed, the silence of the historians was equally remarkable, but this may have been due to the less dramatic volume of Danish emigration.[8] In short, even though the relationship between history and the social sciences was widely discussed during these years in Germany, France, and the United States, as part of the call to enlarge the study of history beyond the political and biographical spheres, the work on migration by statisticians and economists had no appreciable effect on Scandinavian historians.[9] Instead, the early accounts of the fate of Scandinavian emigrants were written by travel writers, typically journalists and ministers.[10]

Even more remarkable was the relative silence among American historians concerning not only the relatively modest Scandinavian-American exodus but immigration in general. After all, the immigrant was central to the whole American experience, and between 1820 and 1930 immigrant authorities recorded the arrival of some 37.8 million immigrants to the United States.[11] The attempt by such progressive historians as Frederick Jackson Turner and James Harvey Robinson to challenge the monopoly of political history in favor of a history that in principle encompassed all aspects of human existence might have argued in favor of a greater interest in American migration studies.[12] However, Turner's own frontier thesis, presented at the meeting of the American Historical Association in Chicago in 1893, pointed in another direction. Turner's thesis suggested that the American environment was much more important than the European heritage in the genesis of American democracy.[13] Even though he definitely saw immigrants as central to the frontier experience, Turner emphasized the ease with which the immigrant was Americanized and thus disappeared from the historical stage: "In the crucible of the frontier the immigrants were Americanized, liberated and fused into a mixed race, English in neither nationality nor characteristics."[14]

If Turner's assimilation model through its simple metaphorical language and its focus on the strength of the American environment contributed to dampening scholarly interest in immigration studies, so too did increasing public hostility toward mass migration in the late nineteenth and particularly the early twentieth century. The statistician Richmond Mayo-Smith had maintained already in 1890 that the "immigrants" arriving in America after the birth of the United States did not match the "colonists" landing in the 17th and 18th centuries. In 1911 the conclusions of the forty-two-volume report of the federal Immigration Commission similarly made prejudicial distinctions between "old" immigrants from Northern and Western Europe and "new," supposedly racially inferior, immigrants from Southern and Eastern Europe.[15] Edward A. Ross was the most prominent of a number of American sociologists who argued that the "new" immigrants never would be able to assimilate to true American standards.[16] The frenzied patriotism emerging out of the American World War I experience intensified the credence given to such distinctions and contributed to the immigration restriction of the 1920s.[17]

Despite widespread ethnic chauvinism, immigration was never totally ignored by American historians. Thus, in 1921 Arthur M. Schlesinger, Sr., published "The Significance of Immigration in American History," arguing that the immigrant was as important to American history as Turner's frontier, and asserting that restrictionism and irresponsible US isolationism were two sides of the same coin.[18] Even though the immigrants were never entirely forgotten, Henry Steele Commager later suggested that when American historians did deal with immigration during this epoch, the impulse tended to be romantic and moralistic, rooted either in the urban reform program of the Progressive movement or in a fervent, often racially inspired, nationalism based on "Anglo-Saxon" nativism or ethnic filiopietism.[19]

The Scandinavian Americans, like America's other ethnic groups, were usually considered peripheral to the writing of American history. As Odd S. Lovoll pointed out, in the late nineteenth and early twentieth centuries representatives of the elite within some ethnic groups reacted to this situation by establishing their own ethnically based historical societies, in effect challenging the Anglo-American monopoly of US history and highlighting the positive contributions of their own group to American historical development.[20] The 1889 attempt to establish a Swedish-American Historical Society failed, but in 1905 the Swedish Historical Society of America was founded, survived until 1934, and was succeeded in 1948 by an association soon to be named the Swedish Pioneer Historical Society (from 1983 the Swedish-American Historical Society) which in 1950 began publishing the *Swedish Pioneer Historical Quarterly* (from 1982 the *Swedish-American Historical Quarterly*).[21] The Norwegian Americans were somewhat slower in establishing a historical society, but in 1925—during the centennial of the first Norwegian group migration to the United States—the Norwegian-American Historical Association (NAHA) began. From its inception it maintained high academic standards under the leadership of Theodore C. Blegen in its *Studies and Records* (1926-1977; *Norwegian-American Studies*, 1977-).[22] The Danish Americans did not establish a similar institution in the United States, but some prominent Danish Americans contributed financially to the founding in 1932 of the Danes Worldwide Archives in Aalborg, Denmark. Only in 1977, when the Danish Heritage Society was organized, did the Danish Americans get their own historical association, which has published *The Bridge* since 1978.[23]

When the early writers of Scandinavian-American history—most of them amateur historians representing the elite layer of their ethnic group—asked the question, "Who were they?" the answer was almost a given: the idea was to present the ethnic group in its American context, with special attention to how it had contributed positively to the growth of American society, thus providing the group with what Orm Øverland (2000) called a "home-making myth."

Had not the Norwegian Vikings arrived in America before Columbus? Had not Swedish pioneers established the New Sweden colony along the Delaware River as early as 1638? Had not Danish dairymen contributed to the development of American agriculture? Generally, Scandinavian Americans prided themselves with their economic success stories and with being underrepresented in US statistics on crime and insanity.[24]

Even those writers moving beyond pure and simple filiopietism remained entrenched in national stereotypes. George T. Flom of the State University of Iowa, writing about the early Norwegian-American settlements in the Midwest (1909), insisted, for instance, that Norwegian Americans through their greater astuteness and flexibility were more fit for life in the United States than the Danish Americans whose attachments to the homeland were particularly powerful (66-71). Inspired by the strongly racialized—and racist—historical discourse of the early twentieth-century, historian Kendrick C. Babcock, who was not of Scandinavian background, found the Scandinavian immigrants interesting to study because they belonged to the "Baltic race" whose purest breed was to be found in central and northern Germany and in Scandinavia and who, unlike other races, did not stall American historical development but contributed positively to it. Among the Scandinavians, all of whom in Babcock's view were freedom-loving, the Swedes were the most aristocratic, the Norwegians the most democratic, and the Danes the most conservative in a manner reminiscent of Southern (white) culture.[25] When historians like Flom and Babcock asked, "Who were they?," the answer was given by their own prejudice.[26]

1930-1960: An Assimilationist "Who Were They?"
Little migration history was written in Sweden and Denmark between 1930 and 1960, while Norwegian migration history experienced a single breakthrough with the publication in

1941 of the first volume of Ingrid Semmingsen's two-volume emigration epic, *Veien mot Vest* (*The Way West*). In contrast, this epoch witnessed an important expansion in American migration research, including a strong focus on Scandinavian immigrants. When the question, "Who were they?," was now posed, American scholars concentrated on studying the new arrivals as *immigrants*, leading to analyses—strongly influenced by the Turner tradition—of the interplay between the European cultural heritage and the American environment

Characteristically, it was a Turner student, Marcus Lee Hansen, of Danish and Norwegian background, who truly introduced migration research to the American historical field. He never completed his ambitious work on immigration, but after his death in 1939 Arthur M. Schlesinger, Sr., edited his manuscripts that were published as *The Atlantic Migration, 1607-1860* (1940) and *The Immigrant in American History* (1940). The former book earned Hansen the Pulitzer Prize posthumously.[27] Even though time and again Hansen emphasized the powerful role played by the frontier in the shaping of American history, he rejected Turner's idea that it represented some kind of uncomplicated melting pot. Instead, Hansen suggested that the Yankee, energetic and ever on the move, and the European immigrant, conservative and more strongly attached to the soil (and usually only following in the footsteps of the "pioneer"), represented differing conceptions of land usage.[28] As Jon Gjerde has pointed out, Hansen proposed, at least implicitly, that the American land masses represented a resource allowing *different* visions to be realized. One central Yankee vision had to do with land speculation and moving west; one central "European" vision had to do with the conservation of traditional lifestyles that back in Europe were under threat from the interplay between the demographic and industrial revolutions.[29] Thus, Hansen's interpretation of the relationship between the transforming powers of the American environment and the strength of the

European heritage was much more complex than Turner's.

Hansen did not focus particularly on Scandinavian immigrants. Two other American immigration historians, George M. Stephenson, of Swedish background, and Theodore C. Blegen, of Norwegian, centered precisely on their respective ethnic groups. Together with Hansen and German-American Carl Wittke, they made up the elite among America's interwar migration historians.[30] Even though both Stephenson and Blegen, like Turner, saw "Americanization" as the eventual outcome of the meeting between the immigrants and the American landscape, they found the *process* by which this assimilation took place worth studying.

In *The Religious Aspects of Swedish Immigration*(1932), Stephenson, another Turner student, focused on the religious dimension of immigration, and within that field his book remains a major work.[31] When Stephenson asked, "Who were they?," he attempted first of all to identify Swedish-American religious leaders, particularly those representing the powerful Augustana Synod. Like Hansen, Stephenson situated his protagonists in the interplay between the pressure from the American environment and the power of the European heritage. In his view, the American environment triumphed over the attempts to conserve Swedish culture in America: "[T]he fight to preserve a distinctive Swedish culture in this country was, in spite of the influence of the church, a losing one. Transplanted to American soil, the Swede was placed in an inexorable environment." (v) Despite this "defeat," the process of Americanization was not generally characterized by crisis. Below the surface Stephenson viewed the frontier as a liberating force that in fact might contribute to unleashing what he viewed as the best, vital parts of Swedish Lutheranism, thus avoiding the stale dogmatics of the state church in Sweden and ultimately uniting Swedish Lutheranism with American Protestantism: "[I]t...grew stronger in a frontier environment, where it was unhampered by the trammels of a declining ecclesiastical establishment."(176-177) Thus, the Swedish immigrants participated in an emancipatory assimilation process that the egalitarian and democratic atmosphere in the Midwest only encouraged. (426) The stamp of Turner was unmistakable; yet in his analysis of the interplay between environment and culture Stephenson had nevertheless decided to zoom in on the one factor that he found most important in the attempt to *preserve* a Swedish identity in the United States, the immigrant church.[32]

Theodore C. Blegen was the main force behind the founding of the Norwegian-American Historical Association and for several years acted as NAHA's editor. His main intellectual accomplishment, however, consisted in the two-volume *Norwegian Migration to America* (1931 and 1940), an ambitious and well-documented work that covered 1825 to 1915.[33] His starting point was that while the study of the frontier had led most American historians to ignore immigration, a number of fictional works illuminated the interplay between immigration and the American environment. In his landmark *Giants in the Earth* (1927), the Norwegian-American author Ole E. Rölvaag thus provided deep insights into the psychological dimensions of the migration experience.[34] Blegen's ambition was to transfer this type of empathetic understanding to the historical discipline. Writing this type of history would require, first, introducing new types of source material, such as immigrant songs, ballads, and letters, second, taking inspiration from linguists who had analyzed the language of the immigrants and, third, drawing on the writers of fiction "who have probed immigrant souls."[35] Thus, as Odd Lovoll remarked, Blegen became an early exponent of a non-statistical type of social history written "from the bottom up," a term that Blegen in fact employed.[36] Blegen and his fellow Scandinavian immigrant historians thus anticipated the kind of work that would characterize American Studies, when it emerged a generation later. However, there seems to have been little direct contact or inspiration involved, even at the University of Minnesota, which eventually named a building for Blegen and also fostered one of the first, and largest, American Studies programs.

Blegen's understanding of the interplay between nature and culture paralleled Stephenson's, and both saw "Americanization" as the ultimate outcome of the immigrants' saga. Characteristically, the second volume of *Norwegian Migration to America* was subtitled *The American Transition*. Yet again, as with Stephenson, rather than taking assimilation for granted, Blegen found it worth pausing at and studying. Blegen found a key to the "Americanization" of the Norwegian Americans in the development of their language. Whereas Ole Rölvaag had asserted that the Midwest housed two cultures, one hidden and inhabited by the memories, traditions, and language of the immigrants, the other visible and populated by the institutions and habits of the English-speaking world; and whereas the linguist Einar Haugen saw an internal battle within the Norwegian immigrant between an old and new self, Blegen found that the *collective linguistic development* among the Norwegian Americans actually bridged the two worlds. "What happened needs to be interpreted by linguist and historian as well as by novelist and editor; and the totality of the picture that emerges is somewhat different from what has been suggested. ... What he [the immigrant] did was to create, by gradual and normal processes of change, adaptation, and growth, something like an intermediate language—Norwegian-American, which combined both languages, broke the shock of his new-world plunge, and on the whole served his needs effectively."[37] Thus, when Blegen posed the question, "Who were they?," the group that he sought and found was America's Norwegian-American population group that in a gradual, non-traumatic process of adaptation based on the utilization of their own cultural resources *developed* into Americans.

Stephenson and Blegen both saw harmonious assimilation as the eventual outcome of the meeting between the Scandinavian immigrant and the New World, and Marcus Lee Hansen even inferred that some kind of European cultural heritage still subsisted in America. Oscar Handlin, however, overturned the meaning of basic concepts. For this reason, his Pulitzer Prize-winning immigration epic, *The Uprooted* (1951), is worth considering in this context, even if Handlin did not deal specifically with Scandinavian immigrants.

Hansen, Stephenson, and Blegen wrote in the interwar years, during the apotheosis of the "progressive" historians, when the idea of expanding the historical field to embrace a broadly based social history began to be realized, often at the expense of economic history.[38] The works of both Marcus Lee Hansen and Theodore C. Blegen should be viewed in this context, and, symptomatically, they ignored the push-pull model of international migration that the economist Harry Jerome had developed in 1926, with a particular emphasis on the American "pull."[39] Handlin, in contrast, wrote in the aftermath of World War II, an era dominated—in the view of a critically inclined posterity—by the so-called "consensus" school whose representatives emphasized how American democracy, unlike several European versions, had survived the Great Depression of the 1930s, succumbing neither to communist nor to fascist extremism. Arguably, the consensus historians replaced the progressive historians' focus on "substantial," economically and morally based conflict with psychologically inspired ponderings over "American character," reflections that focused on cultural tension rather than class struggle, on irony, ambiguity, and paradox rather than development.[40] Their concentration on conformity should also be viewed in the light of the circumstance that America now for nearly a generation had not experienced large-scale migration, and that the civil rights movement, despite much grassroots activism, had not yet gained nationwide attention.

To the degree that Handlin may be viewed as a consensus historian, however, he must be counted among this school's most culturally pessimistic and critical scholars. Influenced directly by Robert E. Park, the University of Chicago sociologist who had developed his theory of "marginal man" in the 1920s, Handlin suggested in 1951 that the European immigrant in his confrontation with the American environment—now presented more in the shape of the urban ghetto than the West—was placed in a marginalized position of culture shock. Under these circumstances the European cultural heritage, based on collective village traditions, disintegrated under the dual impact of industrialism and individualistic liberalism, and the creation of modern, alienated man took its painful beginning: "[S]een from the perspective of the individual received rather than of the receiving society, the history of immigration is a history of alienation and its consequences." In principle, this agonizing process of adaptation might last for generations, dependent on the intensity of the culture shock. The loss of the European heritage, however, was swift and merciless, the outcome being the uprooted immigrant.[41]

In his analysis of the migration process, Handlin not only expanded the understanding of the American environment to include the urban ghetto. He also rejected the notion of a generally gentle and harmonic assimilation process, and he discarded the notion of the retention of aspects of the European heritage implied by Marcus Lee Hansen. Hansen, Stephenson, and Blegen had let their prototypical immigrant go through a largely positive *development process* that ended in assimilation, but Handlin's archetypical immigrant immediately experienced alienation in a modernizing world. Handlin, like many other post-World War II scholars, abandoned the very notion of "progress".[42] Even so, he did agree with his three senior colleagues that some kind of "Americanization" had taken place.

If US historians intensively worked on aspects of Scandinavian-American history between 1930 and 1960, the only Scandinavian country to exhibit even fledgling interest in the field was Norway.[43] *Normanns-Forbundet* (Norse Federation)—founded in Norway in 1907 with a view to enhancing contact with the emigrants in America—decided to support Norwegian research on the migration experience. In practice, this work was undertaken largely by one historian, Ingrid Semmingsen.[44] Even though Blegen and Semmingsen's work overlapped, particularly in the treatment of early Norwegian-American history, Semmingsen viewed the Norwegian exodus as an *emigration* process, whereas Blegen focused on *immigration* and assimilation. As Birgitta Odén has noted, Semmingsen's methods and manner of posing the question, "Who were they?" pointed toward the extensive post-1960 Scandinavian debate on immigration, a debate in which she participated actively. Therefore, her work will be treated in the following section.[45]

"Who Were They?" The Influence from the Social Sciences, 1960-1980

The Danish historian Inga Floto has suggested that since the end of the Second World War the discipline of history has developed "in two phases with the time around 1960 forming a watershed. … The new form of explanation, the new paradigm, if you will, that crystallized in the individual countries was a *structural functionalism* of some kind, varying from country to country."[46] Certainly for Scandinavian-American migration history and ethnic research in general, the 1960s decade represents a divide.[47] Up through the 1960s and 1970s, inspired by the growth of the civil rights movement, the United States experienced an ethnic revival with ever more groups, as many descendants of European immigrants "rediscovered" their ethnic roots, at least at the symbolic level.[48] Some researchers also found that the United

States—despite immigration quotas since the 1920s and political conformity since the onset of the Cold War—remained more ethnically diverse than one might have expected. In his classic study, *Assimilation in American Life* (1964), sociologist Milton M. Gordon suggested that superficial "acculturation" notwithstanding, many Americans still shaped their daily social lives within the confines of an ethnic group. From the point of view of "structural assimilation," he wrote, the United States remained a pluralist society. (77-81). Similarly, sociologist Peter A. Munch found during his fieldwork in the Midwest in the 1950s that Norwegian Americans in their daily life patterns and church affiliations still acted ethnically selectively and continued to view themselves as Norwegian Americans.[49]

During the 1960s, a fledgling interest in American ethnic history emerged, notably within the field of political history. The writers of the so-called "new political history" or "ethnocultural interpretation"—a field pioneered by Lee Benson and Samuel P. Hays—shifted the focus from the political elite to the grassroots. In studies packed with statistics they suggested that voting behavior in the late nineteenth century tended to be colored more by ethnic and religious factors than by socioeconomic status.[50] A few of these studies concentrated on voting patterns among Scandinavian Americans.[51] Critics feared that the "new political history" would turn political history into a subdiscipline of the equally quantitatively oriented "new social history" with its focus on the grassroots rather than the elite.[52] As a result of the newfound interest in parameters like race, ethnicity, gender, and class this social history in its turn threatened, as it seemed, to tear a comprehensive American historical narrative to bits and pieces. In his 1980 presidential address to the Organization of American Historians, Carl Degler warned that "the present version [of US history] is more chaos than history."[53]

Despite its ethnic orientation, in America the impact of

the new social history on the writing of the history of the Scandinavian Americans was limited, even if Odd Lovoll (1975) did undertake a study of the Norwegian-American *Bygdelag* movement and Dorothy Burton Skårdal attempted to interpret immigrant assimilation from an analysis of Scandinavian-American immigrant literature (1974).[54] In Scandinavia, however, notably in Sweden, the picture was different. There, a parallel growth of interest in social history resulted in a strong focus on Scandinavian migration to America.

Again, the year 1960 is crucial. At the international meeting of historians in Stockholm that year, Frank Thistlethwaite reported on the state and development of migration history. His conclusion was that since the pioneering work of Marcus Lee Hansen in the 1930s, migration history had been kept confined within superficial national boundaries, with US historians dominating the discipline yet being hampered by a "saltwater curtain" descending across the Atlantic. This US dominance had led to investigations of the *consequences* of migration rather than its *causes*; to an understanding of migration as *immigration* and consequently a strong focus on the phenomenon of assimilation; to a US-centrism that left no room for the study of European migration to other overseas areas nor of massive internal movements within Europe; to a stereotypical understanding of the immigrant as a poor European peasant with no appreciation for national, regional or local variation. Furthermore, Thistlethwaite pointed out that much American migration history had focused on movement into rural areas even though most migrants actually moved to the city. He urged historians to seek inspiration from the social sciences—in his view clearly the leader within the field of migration research—and to reorient inquiries toward the European roots of mass migration, notably the industrial and demographic revolutions.[55]

Besides direct inspiration from Thistlethwaite—acknowledged explicitly by several Scandinavian historians in the

1960s and 1970s—Vilhelm Moberg's four-volume folk epic on the Swedish migration experience stimulated Swedish interest in the exodus, with Moberg in fact criticizing historians sharply for ignoring the topic.[56] The Danish historian Niels Peter Stilling has suggested that when many Swedish historians acknowledge their debts to Thistlethwaite rather than to Moberg, this may be due to a reluctance to admit the scholarly value of fictional work.[57] We should note, however, that the founding of the Swedish Emigrant Institute in Växjö in 1965 had much to do with Moberg's enthusiastic promotional work; moreover, the importance of the paradigmatic shift taking place within the field of history in the 1960s should not be underestimated.[58]

The newly roused interest in Swedish emigration found its strongest institutional expression at Uppsala University where in 1962 Sten Carlsson launched the remarkable research project, "Sweden and America after 1860," a project that continued until 1976 and over the years involved no less than forty Swedish scholars. Besides resulting in numerous Ph.D. dissertations, the research project also led to a number of reports, the most important of which was *From Sweden to America* (1976), summarizing the project's main results.[59] Beyond the formal confines of the research project, other scholars, including Lars Ljungmark and Nils Runeby, studied aspects of the Swedish exodus.[60] In Denmark, during those same years, Kristian Hvidt single-handedly began his study of Danish emigration, resulting in 1971 in the publication of his doctoral dissertation, *Flugten til Amerika* (*Flight to America*). How central a role Hvidt's work attained may be seen from the circumstance that whereas the Swedish historian Birgitta Odén in 1963 derisively noted that Erling Olsen's recent work, *Danmarks økonomiske historie siden 1750* (*The Economic History of Denmark Since 1750*, [1962]) did not at all discuss Danish emigration, by 1990 it was Hvidt himself who wrote volume 11 of *Gyldendal og Politikens Danmarkshistorie* (*The Gylden-*

dal and Politiken History of Denmark), a volume that included an extensive discussion of Danish emigration.[61] Following Hvidt's groundbreaking work, several other studies of Danish emigration appeared, including Erik Helmer Pedersen's *Drømmen om Amerika* (*American Dream*), a supplementary volume to *The Politiken History of Denmark*.[62]

Besides these nationally defined projects, Nordic migration research was strengthened during those years by the launching of the project, *Nordic Emigration*, a main item on the agenda of the Nordic historians' meeting in Copenhagen in 1971.[63] By this point, migration research had become marked by considerable openness across national boundaries, an openness based both on the use of parallel historical methods and on strikingly similar ways of asking the question, "Who were they?" In their methodological approach to migration history, the Uppsala group, Kristian Hvidt, and to some extent also Ingrid Semmingsen differed notably from their American predecessors, above all by their extensive use of statistics and their openness to the social sciences. On the other hand, these scholars did not discuss any possible inspiration from, say, Marxism or the *Annales* school. Nevertheless, their works represented an important dimension of the new orientation of history towards the social sciences. True, Hvidt's attempt to map Danish emigration in its statistical totality on the basis of the emigration protocols of the Danish police was unique and won him international recognition; but to a large extent the Uppsala group also based its works upon statistics.[64] Notably, Sune Åkerman's study of the growth phases of emigration and of the relationship between internal and external migration exemplified this trend. Characteristically, when in 1975 Åkerman provided a point-by-point "answer" to Thistlethwaite's ground-breaking 1960 argument, one of the subheadings of his manuscript read, "The Historian as a Social Scientist."[65]

The work of the Norwegian historian Ingrid Semmingsen

was not based on statistics to the same extent as that of her Swedish and Danish colleagues. Even so, she did discuss the correlation between economic trends and emigration, criticizing the economists Harry Jerome and Arne Skaug for focusing too exclusively on short-term change and ignoring long-term cyclical variation.[66] Moreover, in 1972, Semmingsen defended the British migration researcher Brinley Thomas' center-periphery theory (on the inverted relationship between internal and external migration, based on the direction of the flow of capital within the Atlantic economy) in the face of criticism from Sune Åkerman and Kristian Hvidt who were wary of Thomas' use of primary sources.[67]

Frank Thistlethwaite's clarion call to study the migrational experience in the light of the European industrial and demographic revolutions, along with the inspiration from the social sciences, had a major impact on the way in which Scandinavian scholars posed the question, "Who were they?," in the 1960s and 1970s. The question no longer concentrated on how immigrants adapted to American society but, rather, on how and why they broke away from the Scandinavian countries. Additionally, new quantitative methods shifted the focus from the prototypical individual or the idealized national group to statistically defined categories of people. Moreover, previous attempts to empathize psychologically with the migrants were largely discarded, with the partial exception of Ingrid Semmingsen's works.[68]

What the Scandinavian scholars now found when they asked the question, "Who were they?," were first of all *socially defined groups* in Scandinavia that left for America under the impact of considerable demographic growth and dramatic—if erratic—urban-industrial development at home. Likewise, the availability of cheap land and better wages abroad encouraged the mass exodus, a departure gathering additional force as the first settlers began sending letters and prepaid tickets home to kith and kin in Scandinavia.

A comparison of emigration from the Scandinavian countries between the late 1860s and the outbreak of World War I showed that few Danish emigrants were peasants and cotters, but many were landless people from the countryside, including the adult children of many peasants and cotters. Moreover, an exodus from the Danish cities also took place, consisting primarily of unskilled laborers and servants but also including some artisans and apprentices.[69] Among the Swedish emigrants, on the other hand, one in four was a peasant or cotter, though Swedish "peasants" often owned farms so small that they would have passed for "cotters" in Denmark. Among the Swedish emigrants, moreover, the adult children of peasants and cotters constituted a larger share of the total number of emigrants than among the Danish. Finally, it turns out that a relatively larger percentage of Swedish migrants were of rural background, in good part because Denmark was more urbanized than Sweden in the late nineteenth century.[70] Semmingsen did not have access to material that permitted as detailed a picture of the social composition of the Norwegian emigrants; she estimated, however, that 90 percent of Norway's emigrants belonged to the lower—if not the lowest—class of the country's toiling population. Moreover, apparently more peasants than cotters emigrated. The incomplete statistical information suggested that rural artisans and particularly the landless adult children of cotters and rural laborers formed the backbone of the masses of emigrants. From the cities, moreover, large numbers of unskilled laborers emigrated, along with numerous artisans and people affiliated with the maritime trades.[71] On the basis of the Swedish material, Sune Åkerman attempted to outline a theoretical stylized pattern of migration from Europe, where emigration was viewed as a phase-divided innovation process that gradually spread to large sections of the sending society, and where the social composition of the emigrants changed from one phase to another.[72]

It was at this statistical level that the question, "Who were they?," was posed in these years. Among the many questions discussed were: the geographical patterns of the diffusion of emigrants; the "urban influence field" that seemed to dampen overseas migration from the surrounding area of larger cities; the relationship between internal and external migration; return migration to Scandinavia; and a question of particular relevance to our present discussion: who were the emigrants from Scandinavian *cities*. For if the majority of the Scandinavian emigrants came from rural areas—with the rural population still by far outnumbering the urban population despite ongoing urbanization—still, *relatively* more people left the city for the United States than the countryside in Denmark, Sweden, and Norway.[73] Semmingsen interpreted this phenomenon as migration in steps: first the emigrants moved from the countryside to the cities, and then only later from the cities to America. The circumstance that family migration from the cities was larger than from the countryside in the 1880s she viewed as a sign that many rural families only migrated to the United States after having been rootless inhabitants of the cities for a significant period of time. Their migration was thus first of all to be seen from a rural history perspective.[74]

Semmingsen's point of view, however, was challenged by Birgitta Odén and later also by Fred Nilsson. Inspired by Thistlethwaite, Odén in 1963 suggested that ever since Gustav Sundbärg's emigration report in the early twentieth century, scholars had focused on the countryside, yet emigration from the cities simply was too extensive to be viewed merely as part of a step-by-step process originating in the countryside: urban emigration had to be viewed on its own terms.[75] In his analysis of emigration from Stockholm, Fred Nilsson concurred: many rural arrivals in the cities dwelled there so long (i.e., at least five years) before migrating to the United States, that they had to be viewed as fully urbanized and therefore should be studied from an urban rather than a rural point of view. Kristian Hvidt shared this opinion.[76] An interesting dimension of this discussion—never resolved—was that Semmingsen and Nilsson actually agreed that many rural people dwelled in the cities for relatively long periods before emigrating. They postulated *whom* these people were only from their differing views of larger theoretical constructs regarding the urbanization of rural people.[77]

What had happened to the migrants as *cultural beings* in this rather formalistic, quantitatively oriented discussion? This was a question that had begun to trouble a growing number of researchers within the field of social history, including some migration historians. As Sune Åkerman pointed out at the historians' conference in San Francisco in 1975, much work remained to be done within the field of social psychology.[78]

History Since 1980: A Culturally Colored Double "Who Were They?"

According to Inga Floto, despite the breakthrough of social history in the 1960s and the subsequent emergence of explanation models based on structural-functionalist thinking, these explanation models are no longer dominant. "To the contrary, the latest developments may be seen as a showdown with the history of structures, an attempt to return to the human being as the central object of history, as the being that "structures the structures."[79] This, Floto adds, is particularly true of the discipline of micro history and more generally of the "new cultural history." At this point we may remark that just as the Scandinavian-American history of the 1960s and 1970s did not debate possible inspiration from the *Annales* school or from Marxism, more recently only a limited discussion took place on the possible influence from poststructuralist-inspired new cultural histories. Still, we may nevertheless note a certain relationship between broad historiographical trends on the one hand and some tendencies in the writing of Scandinavian-American history on the other. For this same reason, Kathleen Neils Conzen's 1987 warning that one must be wary of constructing "a historiography content to talk only to itself and debate only within its own context" seems somewhat superfluous as far as research into Scandinavian-American history is concerned.[80] Since 1980 much scholarship has focused on a two-fold "Who were they?," each case characterized by close attention to people's cultural habits. At a micro level, several researchers decided to follow Thistlethwaite's advice to view the migration process in its trans-Atlantic totality, a perspective that dominated Scandinavian-American migration research in the 1980s and early 1990s. At a macro level, ideas about broad, largely constructed ethnic identities based on national background have also been debated in recent years.

Among historians in general the departure from the "new social history" and the concomitant introduction of a more culturally inspired history was not characterized by such ruptures that an epistemological development from a quantitatively based belief in the possibility of objective knowledge toward a poststructuralist breakdown of both object and subject and a reading of culture as "text" might have inspired. In practice, many historians, including those dealing with Scandinavian-American history, stuck to a vision of cultural history that granted discourse a major role, yet it did not become "a substitute for social reality but... a guide to it."[81] Within Scandinavian-American history, new, culturally oriented viewpoints complemented rather than simply replaced those inspired by the new social history.[82] One characteristic of this development was that older, nationally based divisions within research traditions appeared even less meaningful than previously. Moreover, at least as far as Swedish-American history is concerned, part of the research initiative now returned to America following the massive efforts by the Swedes in the 1960s and 1970s.[83]

Already Marcus Lee Hansen had made note of the strength of the trans-Atlantic ties connecting the immigrants in the United States with friends and relatives in the home locality.[84] Likewise, Theodore C. Blegen had observed that when Norwegian immigrants crowded together in America, regional or local loyalties usually counted for more than national ties.[85] Yet neither Hansen nor Blegen allowed those insights to color much of their research. Hansen was interested in the immigrant first of all as a prototypical individual, and Blegen, in search of a Norwegian-American psyche, wanted to investigate the fate of a whole nationality group.[86] Oscar Handlin, on the other hand, completely ignored the existence of any such loyalties: "I shall touch upon broken homes, interruptions of a familiar life, separation from known surroundings, the becoming a foreigner and ceasing to belong."[87]

In 1964, Rudolph Vecoli challenged Handlin's point of view in his analysis of turn-of-the-century life among Chicago's south Italian *contadini*, which concluded that to a remarkable extent these people actually succeeded in shaping their lives in the New World in a fashion that preserved important social and cultural patterns from the Old.[88] Three years later, Charles Tilly and C. Harold Brown followed up by decrying the great influence that Robert Park's theory of crisis-ridden "marginal man" had exerted upon migration research. They pointed out that people studying internal migration had found that such migrants often moved within networks of relatives and friends.[89] Several of the special studies of the Uppsala project reached similar conclusions concerning Swedish migration to America, and within econometrics the term "stock effect" was introduced to describe the phenomenon of migrants venturing abroad and establishing colonies, only to see other immigrants from the same region or locality in the Old World join them later.[90]

Only in the 1980s, however, was research into these networks of migration truly launched. Responding to Thistlethwaite's call to view the migration experience in its *trans-Atlantic totality*, a number of historians and cultural geographers performed microstudies of the departure of people from small rural communities of one location in the Old World and their migration to one or a couple of destinations in the New. Due undoubtedly to the remarkable quality of the Scandinavian sources—in the shape not least of Lutheran church books offering detailed demographic information—Scandinavian migrants became the focus of this research.[91] Even though these scholars recognized that the type of rural migration they were investigating did not necessarily represent the most typical form of migration, their micro studies nevertheless inspired a broader understanding of ways in which migration could be organized, and of the interplay between the imported cultural habits of the newcomers and the novel American surroundings.[92]

When these researchers posed the question, "Who were they?," they found neither prototypical individuals nor whole national groups, nor statistical conglomerations of social groups. Instead, they discovered small, closely-knit clusters of people endeavoring—through group migration to the American Middle West in the second half of the nineteenth century—to conserve traditional ways of life in the face of demographic and economic pressures at home. In some cases it could even be shown that people who had been neighbors in the Old World became neighbors again in the New, even if the degree of success in establishing such ethnic enclaves usually depended on the economic dynamics of the specific Midwestern locality. These people were not individualists in a modern sense. They represented village cultures characterized by such strong attachments to the soil that land-ownership patterns typically defined marriage arrangements. These people tended to identify with family, parish, or region and only to a lesser extent with nation.[93] Rather than being *uprooted*, these migrants experienced a *transplantation* of sorts which did not result in the complete replication of the lost community back home, to be sure, but which did inspire a complex interplay between imported, regionally defined cultural habits and a broad spectrum of local New World environments. In this interplay, the immigrant church served as a conserving power—even in those cases when regionally and culturally defined Old World tensions erupted into conflict and led to religious schism—whereas the expanding American economy represented change.[94]

Thus, we would seem to have returned to the relationship between cultural heritage and environment that occupied Marcus Lee Hansen, Theodore C. Blegen, and George M. Stephenson in the interwar years. There is a marked difference, however. The earlier historians concentrated on describing what was essentially an Americanization process, while recent researchers acknowledge the diverse and continuous nature of the interplay between the forces of ethnic resilience and those of economic change, seen from the viewpoint of the ethnic group, with Americanization not necessarily representing "progress." Did a *homogenizing* Americanization in fact ever take place? Developments of more recent decades still leave the whole idea of assimilation open to debate, even if some contemporary ethnic categories tend to be more inclusive than older ones.[95] More recent discussions of American identity revolve around ideas of ethnic pluralism rather than simply assimilation, typically in combination with reflections over the political-constitutional origins of the United States.[96]

In his prize-winning book, *The Minds of the West* (1997), Jon Gjerde combined a number of demographically based micro studies primarily of Norwegian Americans, German Americans, and "Yankees" with readings into contemporaneous travel literature and fictional works. He insisted that the interplay between imported cultural habits and the new environment resulted in myriad variation and diversity, with the late-nineteenth-century and early-twentieth-century Midwest emerging as an ethnic patchwork quilt. True, one of his main points was that even within this ethnic mosaic two basic typologies—already hinted at by Marcus Lee Hansen—could be distinguished, on the one hand the geographically mobile, land-speculating "Yankee" representing an individualist family organization, on the other hand the conservative, patriarchal "European" who remained attached to the soil and epitomized a corporate family organization. Despite the acknowledgment of these two typologies, Gjerde emphasized the Midwest's basic ethnic diversity that he viewed as an essential building block in the construction of an American multicultural national identity.[97]

Gjerde added that when locally and narrowly defined ethnic identities came under pressure in the New World, assimilative, "Americanizing" forces did not dominate the field on their own: broader ethnicities, constructed by ethnic leaders intent on appealing to large numbers of people by emphasizing common national roots also played a role.[98] This leads us to the second manner in which more recent research has grappled with the question, "Who were they?" Whereas the "trans-Atlantic" tradition dealt with delicately defined, grassroots-level ethnic loyalties, a second category of scholarship operated with much coarser, constructed identities based on national attachments rather than local or regional background. In recent years, this orientation has led to a focus on ethnic elites and their endeavors to construct broad ethnic identities based on national background and also to questions of whom the elite endeavored to appeal to.

Within the field of Danish-American history, the study of identity with a national twist has led to examinations of the role of religion for the retention of a specifically "Danish" identity in America, the idea being that leaders of the Grundtvigian, moderately high-church Danish Church were more "nationally" minded than the more pietistic leaders of the Inner-Mission United Danish Church. The former not only focused strongly on their Danishness but also headed endeavors to found religiously based "Danish" colonies in the United States (even if Inner-Mission members at a later point attempted something similar).[99]

Interest in broadly defined ethnicities rooted in Old-World national attachments received a boost, however, first of all in connection with the postmodernist-inspired examination by Benedict Anderson and also by Eric Hobsbawm—despite his Marxist background—of the concepts of nationalism and the nation-state as "cultural artifact" or "invented tradition." In the same spirit, Werner Sollors portrayed the concept of ethnicity as an ever-changing cultural construct.[100] Again, however, we must add that to the degree that ethnic historians accepted the idea of ethnicity as a construct, they insisted on studying the concept as it was rooted in a perceived social reality, "grounded in real life and social experience."[101]

It was from this "pragmatic" angle that ethnic historians dealing with the Scandinavian-American population group undertook to study ethnic identity with a focus on national background. An important work in this tradition was Dag Blanck's investigation of the construction of a Swedish-American identity among the leaders of the Augustana Synod—by far the most important Swedish-American ecclesiastical body—between 1860 and 1917.[102] Whereas the social anthropologist Fredrik Barth had argued in 1969 that the ethnic group should be studied first of all by shifting focus away from its supposed cultural values and examining instead the processes of boundary maintenance going on among different ethnic groups, Blanck, referring to the prominent migration historian Kathleen Neils Conzen, found that Clifford Geertz's view of culture as "socially produced structures of meaning engendered by and expressed in public behaviors, language, images, institutions," permitted a closer analysis of the cultural manifestations of a constructed Swedish-American identity.

By studying the demographic makeup of the student body of Augustana College in Rock Island, Illinois, the changing kinds of teaching material employed there, and the types of publication work that the Augustana Synod engaged in, Blanck gave his investigation a practical slant.[103]

When Blanck posed the question, "Who were they?," his focus was primarily on the elite within the Augustana Synod and on its attempts—particularly after 1890—to construct a Swedish-American identity through its teaching and publishing activities. Secondarily, he concentrated on the target audience, i.e., both the students at Augustana College and more generally the many Swedish Americans who between 1860 and 1917 were members of the Augustana Synod (ca. 20 percent of all Swedish Americans, or at least half of those Swedish Americans affiliating with the Swedish-American institutions)(56).

Due to the generational change taking place around 1890, when the second generation of Swedish Americans came of age, the Augustana leaders found it imperative to educate the new generation to understand their Swedish background and learn to view themselves as Swedish Americans. National background was emphasized in celebrations of representative Swedish icons like the warrior king Gustav II Adolph, and of Swedish Romantic literature, in combination with a strong focus on the contributions of Swedish *Americans* to US history, for instance the founding of New Sweden in the 1630s or the technical exploits of engineer John Ericsson during the Civil War. The aim was not only to strengthen Swedish-American claims to recognition in the United States but in all likelihood also to distance the Swedish Americans from other ethnic groups, not least those of Catholic background. Moreover, the construction of a Swedish-American identity became one building stone in the overall construction of an ethnically pluralist American identity. "Looked at from this perspective, the Swedish immigrants and their children living in turn-of-the-century America were, by becoming Swedish Americans, also becoming Americans." (216-221) Like Jon Gjerde, Dag Blanck thus found the key to an understanding of Swedish-American, as well as American, identity in pluralism rather than in a simple process of assimilation. The question of to what extent the Swedish-American grassroots adopted this culturally elitist Swedish-American construct, or *who* did, Blanck did not really answer. He acknowledged the existence of a continuum of ethnic identities, spanning from the grassroots level to the elitist constructed level, and suggested that the "practical"—and plastic—versions of what it meant to be Swedish-American unfolded in a field of tension between those two extremes (28-29).

Besides Blanck's study, other works within this invention-of-tradition or construction-of-ethnicity category included April Schultz's study of the Norwegian-American centennial celebration in Minneapolis in 1925, Per Nordahl's examination of radicalism among Swedish-American organized laborers in Chicago 1890-1940, Peter Thaler's work on ethnic activism among Norwegian America's intellectuals in the late nineteenth and early twentieth centuries, and Jørn Brøndal's investigation of Scandinavian-American involvement in Wisconsin politics and the Progressive movement, ca. 1890-1914.[104]

Thus, when the question, "Who were they?," was posed in recent decades, two important approaches focused on cultural identity, one—the trans-Atlantic tradition that had its heyday in the 1980s and early 1990s—at the grassroots level, the other—the invention-of-tradition perspective that predominated in more recent years—at the elite level.

In finally looking over the entire field of Scandinavian-American history, two areas of research cry out for increased attention. The first is women's history and gender studies. Strikingly few works have been produced within this field, even if gender relations do play a fairly prominent role in Jon Gjerde's *The Minds of the West* and in various articles.[105] Much more research remains to be done. The other relatively neglected area is the more recent one of "whiteness" studies. In this case, however, prospects look somewhat brighter. Orm Øverland wrote a pioneering article in 2000, and sociologist Karen Hansen of Brandeis University is working on a project investigating the relationship between Scandinavian settlers and Dakota Indians in the years 1900-1930.[106]

These two areas of comparative academic neglect notwithstanding, other dimensions of the history of Scandinavian-American migration underwent scrutiny in recent years, broadening the sweep of the question, "Who were they?," both chronologically and geographically. One scholar to break the traditional time frame—ca. 1815 to 1930—was Odd Lovoll whose *The Promise Fulfilled* studied the fate of the Norwegian Americans right up to the present, with a special focus on their explicit, in several cases *chosen* ethnic identity in an America that David A. Hollinger hopefully looked forward to as "post-ethnic."[107] Another scholar to widen the chronological scope was the Danish historian Torben Grøngaard Jeppesen whose investigation of the fates of more than 800,000 Danish Americans on the basis of the original US census rolls for the whole time period 1850 to 2000 is truly breathtaking. This work, which was inspired by the disciplines of demography, social history, and cultural geography, may be viewed as an important sequel to Kristian Hvidt's studies in the 1960s and 1970s when the latter, adopting a social-science perspective, undertook to map a whole nationality group's emigration patterns statistically. Hvidt provided a picture of emigration from Denmark; Grøngaard Jeppesen created an overview of immigration into—and internal migration within—the United States.[108]

In a sense, Grøngaard Jeppesen also expanded the geographical scope of investigation. Whereas most studies of

Scandinavian Americans focused on the *ethnic communities* of Scandinavian Americans, Grøngaard Jeppesen attempted to look at *all* Danish Americans, whether or not they settled in ethnic enclaves. Especially as far as the Danish-American group is concerned, this approach made a whole lot of sense, since by far the majority of Danish Americans lived outside the "Danish" colonies. Even though the angle is quite different, scattered Scandinavian Americans likewise form the topic of folklorist Jennifer Eastman Atteberry's forthcoming study of Swedish Americans writing home to Sweden from the Rocky Mountain West.[109] Recent years have witnessed yet other ways of changing the geographical focus. Ulf Beijbom pioneered the study of Scandinavian-American immigration to metropolitan cities as far back as 1971 when he wrote a book on Chicago's Swedish Americans; but in more recent years his work was supplemented by several others scholars likewise dealing with the sizeable Scandinavian migration to American metropolitan areas, including also New York City and Minneapolis-St. Paul.[110] Yet other historians expanded the geographical scope simply by concentrating on Scandinavian migration to other overseas destinations.[111] A reversal of the geographical focus also took place. Whereas a few scholars undertook to study return migration to the Scandinavian countries, recently others also began to discuss the impact back home not only of the return migrants but also of those visions of America that began to develop in Scandinavia with the increased trans-Atlantic contacts.[112]

In conclusion, the field of Scandinavian-American history continued to expand also in recent years. Even though some areas, notably that of women's history and gender studies, tended to be neglected, overall the way in which the question, "Who were they?" was posed tended still to reflect the changing meta-discourses within the whole discipline of history. In addition, one can see that immigration history has increasingly become a dialogue between scholars in Scandinavia and the United States. This transnational perspective suggests how fruitful an international dialogue between Americanists can be. Yet it must be admitted that for decades the field of American Studies paid little attention to immigration, other than as the story of assimilation. When and how American Studies began to realize the complexity of immigrant history and literature is Orm Øverland's theme in the following chapter.

Notes
1   The following essay revises, updates and translates an article first printed as "Hvem? Udviklingslinjer i skandinavisk-amerikansk historieskrivning," in Due-Nielsen, ed., (2002), 30-57.
2   These figures are based on data provided in Carlsson, (1976), 117-119; Olsson and Wikén, (1995), 27-140; Ferenczi and Willcox, (1929), 747 and 752; Danmarks Statistik, *Statistisk Tabelværk*, Fifth series, Litra A, 5 (1905), 42-43; and *Statistiske Undersøgelser* 19 (1966), 117.
3   Kälvemark, (1976), 110-112.
4   Hvidt, (1971), 48.
5   Semmingsen, (1950), 11.
6   Pedersen, (1873), 273-295; Scharling, (1883), 409-425; Jensen, "Udvandring," (1904), 65-90.
7   Barton, (1961), 31-32; Svalestuen, (1980), 11; on the criticism of emigration, see Kälvemark 1976, 106-113; Semmingsen, "Nordic Research into Emigration," (1978), 125.
8   On the absence of any significant Danish debate on the possible negative effects of emigration, see Hvidt (1971), 44-45; Helmer Pedersen (1987), 9, notes that Adolph Jensen did in 1904 express some concern over the loss of human capital through emigration. This concern was also aired by the otherwise positive V. Falbe Hansen, cf. Falbe Hansen (1873), 281-284.
9   On the debate on the relationship between history and the social sciences, see Floto, (1996), 59-86.

10 Danish examples within this genre are Cavling, (1897), A. Boberg, (1909); Norwegian, Klaveness, (1904), and Takla, (1913); Swedish, Nyvall, (1876), Skarstedt (1917).
11 Calculated from data in *Statistical Yearbook of the Immigration and Naturalization Service*, 1998, 8 (http://www.ins.usdoj.gov/graphics/aboutins/statistics/imm98.pdf).
12 Burke, (1992), 15; Higham, (1965), 111.
13 Turner (1920), 1-38; see also Hofstadter, (1968) 65-68, 164; Floto (1996), 47-48; Iggers, (1997), 42.
14 Turner (1920), 23.
15 Mayo-Smith quoted from Lovoll, (1986), 225; Brøndal, (2001), 336-337. On the racial dimension to this debate, see Higham, (1988), 264-330; Jacobson, (1998), 39-90.
16 Gleason, (1992), 50-55.
17 Higham (1988), 268.
18 Schlesinger, (1927), 72 and 85.
19 Commager, (1961) 3-5.
20 Lovoll (1986), 226.
21 Three other minor Swedish-American historical associations were organized during this era: the Swedish Colonial Society (1909) which focused on the New Sweden colony on the Delaware River in the seventeenth century; the Augustana Historical Society (1930), and the American-Swedish Historical Foundation which in 1929 opened a museum in Philadelphia, cf. Barton (1978), 14-15.
22 Lovoll (1986), 228-231; Barton (1978), 7-10. In 1981, a Norwegian department of NAHA was established, NAHA-Norway.
23 Bender, (1992), 235. Even though the Danish Americans were slow in founding an historical association, Dana College in Blair, Nebraska (established in 1884 by Danish immigrants of the Inner Mission Lutheran faith), soon became home to an important Danish-American archive; so did Grandview College in Des Moines, Iowa (established in 1896 by Danish immigrants of the Grundtvigian Lutheran faith), cf. Iversen (2001), 73-74. With the establishment in the mid-1980s in Denmark of Dansk Udvandringshistorisk Selskab (the Danish Emigration History Society), the journal *Emigranten* appeared between 1985 and

1988. Since then the Society has cooperated with the Danes Worldwide Archives in putting out publications.
24 Anderson, (1874); Johnson (1911); Sørensen (1908); Nelson (1900). See also Blanck, (1997), 184-209.
25 Babcock (1914), 11, 17-18. On the racialized discourse of the early twentieth century, see Higham (1988), 264-330; and Jacobson (1998), 39-90.
26 Gustav Sundbärg also excelled in such national stereotypes, cf. Hvidt (1971), 47-48.
27 Ander (1961), 294.
28 Hansen (1940), 60-66, 76.
29 Gjerde, (1993), 35 and 40.
30 Commager (1961), 5-6; Ander (1961), 290.
31 Gleason (1992), 250-251.
32 See also Ander (1961), 292.
33 Other Norwegian-American works from this period include Qualey's geographically oriented *Norwegian Settlement in the United States* (1938); Bjork (1947); Bjork, (1958).
34 Blegen, (1931), v; Rölvaag, incidentally, had been co-founder of the NAHA two years earlier.
35 Blegen (1931), vii; Blegen, (1940), vii.
36 Lovoll (1986), 229.
37 Blegen (1940), 71-72.
38 Floto (1996), 120-121.
39 Jerome, (1926), 208; on Hansen's lack of interest in the push-pull model, see "Introduction," in Larsen *et al.* (1993), 14. When Blegen discussed the forces behind mass migration to America, he restricted his analysis largely to quoting an article by Semmingsen, cf. Blegen (1940), 464.
40 Wise (1980), 89-92; Floto (1996), 158-160.
41 Handlin, (1951), 4-6; Park, (1996), 165-166; Tilly and Brown, (1967), 140; Hirschman, (1983), 399-400; Gleason (1992), 54-55.
42 Cf. Floto (1996), 155.
43 In Sweden, it is true, geographer Helge Nelson published *The Swedes and the Swedish Settlements in North America*, vol. I: *Text*; vol. II: *Atlas*, (1943).

44 Semmingsen (1950), 11; Svalestuen (1980), 11.
45 Odén (1963), 262.
46 Floto (1996), 241.
47 In the related discipline of American Studies, Leo Marx referred to a "Great Divide" in the aftermath of the political upheaval of the Vietnam era, (2005), 121.
48 Gans, (1979), 193.
49 Munch, (1954), 140.
50 The pioneers within this field were Benson (1961) and Hays (1959, 1980). Two prominent works within the "new political history" are Kleppner, *The Cross of Culture* (1970) and Jensen, *The Winning of the Midwest* (1971).
51 Weibull, (1965), 209-211; Brye, (1977), 163-193; Soike, (1991).
52 McCormick (1986), 62-63.
53 Degler (1980), 17; see also Higham (1994), 1298-1301.
54 See also Barton, (1975); Mortensen (1967); Nyholm (1963).
55 Thistlethwaite, (1964), 73-80, 88-89. One important work by an American sociologist on the connection between Swedish emigration and economic trends was Thomas' *Social and Economic Aspects of Swedish Population Movements, 1750-1933* (1941).
56 Semmingsen (1978), 107. Moberg's epic: *Invandrarna*, (1952); *Nybyggarna*; and *Sista brevet till Sverige*, (1956-1959).
57 Stilling, (1979), 97-98. For recognition of Moberg's role, see Beijbom (1993), 7; Runblom, (2001), 33.
58 Barton (1978), 16.
59 Runblom and Norman (1976), 369. Other reports were Kälvemark, ed. (1973); Hasselmo (1978).
60 Ljungmark (1971); Runeby (1969).
61 Odén (1963), 261; Hvidt, (1990), 253-267.
62 Stilling (1979); Holt, (1976), 76-120; Pedersen, (1985); Jørgensen *et al.* (1987); Jørgensen, (1991).
63 [Hvidt (ed.)], *Emigrationen fra Norden...* (1971); see also *Nordic Emigration: Research Conference in Uppsala, September 1969*, (1970); Kronborg *et al.*, eds. (1977).
64 Hvidt (1971), 65-79; Daniels, (1991), 176-183.
65 Åkerman (1976); Åkerman (1975), 6 and 17.
66 Semmingsen (1950), 499-500.

67 "Emigration from Scandinavia," (1972), 51; Åkerman (1976), 56-63; Hvidt (1971), 52-53, 145-146. For a defense of econometric migration models, see Odén, (1971). Besides Semmingsen's work, the most important Norwegian contribution during these years was Svalestuen's local-history study (1972).
68 Attempts to empathize psychologically with the migrants were now mainly found in popular introductions such as Hvidt, (1976) and Ljungmark (1965).
69 Hvidt (1971), 212-213, 237; on the considerable methodological problems in employing Hvidt's categories of occupation (problems that Hvidt himself discussed), see also Stilling (1979), 107.
70 Hvidt (1971), 240-245; Hvidt (1990), 315; Carlsson (1976), 140-148.
71 Semmingsen (1950), 50, 192-197, 215.
72 Åkerman (1976), 27-32; see also Carlsson, (1968), 101-122.
73 On urbanization in the Scandinavian countries, see Hvidt (1990), 315; on emigration intensities from rural and urban areas, see Hvidt (1971), 118; Semmingsen (1950), 195; Nilsson (1970), 11.
74 Semmingsen (1950), 232-236 and 498-499; see also Semmingsen (1972), 52-54.
75 Odén (1963), 268.
76 Nilsson (1970), 61-87; Hvidt (1971), 124-127.
77 On the unresolved historiographical debate on step-by-step migration, see Ostergren (1986), 133.
78 Iggers (1997), 102; Appleby, Hunt and Jacob (1994), 220; Åkerman (1975), 46; Runblom (2001), 33.
79 Floto (1996), 261.
80 Conzen, in Lovoll, ed. (1985), 196; also quoted in Runblom (2001), 39.
81 Iggers (1997), 126-127 and 133; see also Appleby *et al.* (1994), 222-223; Burke (1992), 121-122.
82 Characteristically, in his discussion of the impulses that migration networks sent across the Atlantic, Ostergren wrote, "The impact was perhaps first and foremost a matter of values and

culture, but it ranged far beyond that to social and economic relationships, as well." (1988), 24.
83 Ostergren (1986); Barton, (1978), 159-161; Beijbom (1983), 156; Runblom and Tedebrand, (1979), 129-140.
84 Hansen (1940), 70.
85 Blegen (1940), 464.
86 On Hansen's strong focus on the individual, see Higham, (1989), 11-12.
87 Handlin (1951), 4.
88 Vecoli (1964), 408.
89 Tilly and Brown (1967), 42-43, 64; according to Choldin, (1973), 163, fn 2, Litwak pioneered this type of research (1960), 385-394.
90 Ostergren (1986), 131-132; Åkerman, Kronberg and Nilsson (1977), 105-122; Dunlevy and. Gemery, (1976), 143-152; Ljungmark (1987), 104-116.
91 For an acknowledgment of Thistlethwaite as a source of inspiration, see Gjerde (1985), 2; Ostergren (1988), 24; and Mackintosh (1993), 12; on the source material, see Tedebrand,(1976), 76-93; Gjerde (1985), 2-4. Mackintosh (1993), 13, points out that Danish church books provide less detailed information than the Swedish and the Norwegian ones.
92 Gjerde (1985), 5; Ostergren (1988), 149, 210.
93 Gjerde, (1979), 406, 413; Ostergren (1988), 134-135, 184-185.
94 Ostergren (1988), 241-242; Gjerde (1997), 108, 154-156; Gjerde, (1986), 681-697; see also Mackintosh (1993), 13-14. Furthermore, see Bodnar's *The Transplanted: A History of Immigrants in Urban America* (1985). The title represents a direct challenge to Handlin's *The Uprooted*.
95 One of the more inclusive recent ethnic categories would be that of "European Americans," cf. Alba, (1990), 9-14.
96 Gleason, (1980), 31-34; Huntington (1981), 27. See also Gerstle (2001), 3-4. The idea of juxtaposing America's political ideals with ethnic realities dates back to Myrdal (1944).
97 Gjerde (1997), 60, 159-185; see also Ostergren (1988), 20, 241-242.

98 Gjerde (1997), 225-228. A central term in this connection is that of "ethnicization" which refers to the establishment of broader ethnic loyalties out of local or regional Old World ties; such loyalties might arise when members of the ethnic group came under sufficiently strong pressure from the surrounding American environment; see Sarna (1978), 370-378.

99 Simonsen (1990), 8, 86-87; Mackintosh (1993), 127-128. The reflections of Jon Wefald on the role of the national background of the Norwegian Americans in Midwestern politics seem more dubious: on the basis of a very selective reading of a number of Norwegian-American newspapers he romantically postulated a connection between what he on the one hand considered the Midwestern radicalism of his Norwegian Americans, on the other hand—without further documentation—cooperative traditions back in Norway. (1971), 4, 46.

100 Hobsbawm, (1983), 13; Anderson, (1991), 4; Sollors, (1989), x-xiv.

101 Conzen, et. al., (1992), 5; see also Blanck (1997), 20-21.

102 Discussion based on Blanck's Ph.D. dissertation (1977), not the republished version (2006).

103 Barth, (1969), 15; Blanck (1997), 26-27.

104 Schultz, (1994); Nordahl (1994), 11-12; Thaler, (1998); Brøndal, (2004). See also Barton (1994); Lindmark (1998); Gradén (2003); Nordström, Anderson, and Blanck, eds. (2004); Thaler, (2004).

105 Gjerde (1997), 159-185; see also Rice (1978), 136-150; Gjerde and McCants, (1995); Rönnqvist, (1999), 91-120; Brøndal, (2004), 173-188.

106 Øverland, (2004), 132-141. Karen Hansen's project, for which she received a John Simon Guggenheim Memorial Fellowship, bears the title, "In the Wake of the Land Rush: Scandinavian Settlers and Dakota Indians at Spirit Lake, 1900-1930." See also Bergland, (2000), 319-350.

107 Lovoll, (1998), 34, 137, and 214-215; see also Hollinger (1995), 2-3. In Denmark an interview-based study among Danish Americans was undertaken recently, cf. Larsen, (2001), 9.

108 Jeppesen, (2005); see also Jeppesen, (2001), 41-45, and (2000). Over the years the Danes Worldwide Archives in Aalborg have organized conferences and edited various publications about Danish emigration, including Larsen and Bender (1992); Larsen *et al.* (1993); and Stilling and Olsen (1994).
109 Jennifer Eastman Atteberry, *Up in the Rocky Mountains: Writing the Swedish Immigrant Experience*, Minneapolis-St. Paul 2007 (forthcoming).
110 Beijbom, (1971); Lovoll, (1988); Mauk, (1997); Anderson and Blanck, eds. (1991 and 2001). David Mauk currently directs a project on Norwegian Americans in Minneapolis-St. Paul.
111 See for instance Pedersen, (1986); Larsen, ed. (2000).
112 On return migration, see Tedebrand (1972); Djupedal, (1997); Mackintosh, (2001). On the influence of one group of return migrants, Swedish engineers, see Grönberg, (2003). On the visions of America that began to develop, see Lagerkvist (2005). A seminar, "Americanization Processes in the Nordic Countries" at the University of Southern Denmark, Odense, Dec. 2, 2005, indicated that Scandinavian interest in the process of Americanization is on the rise, with Danish contributions from Nils Arne Sørensen and Klaus Petersen and Norwegian contributions from Helge Danielsen and Hallvard Notaker seeming imminent.

Studying Myself in the United States – Studying the United States in Myself

ORM ØVERLAND

As the transnational becomes more central to American studies, we are likely to focus not only on the proverbial immigrant who leaves somewhere called 'home' to make a new home in the United States, but also on the endless process of comings and goings that create familial, cultural, linguistic, and economic ties across national borders. (Shelly Fisher Fishkin, 2004)

We have to write out of who and where and when we are, whether we like it or not, and disguise it how we may." (Margaret Atwood, 1998)

In the end, the future of American Studies in Europe will ... depend on the ability of European scholars ... to establish their American work according to their own methods and standards, learning from each other as much as from the Americans; and it will depend on the spirit of that scholarship. (Sigmund Skard, 1958)[1]

My first NAAS conference, which was also the first conference organized by the Nordic Association for American Studies, was in Sigtuna, Sweden in 1961, when I was still a student.[2] NAAS has been important in my life for half a century, so now, back in Sweden where it all started, seems a good time to come to a conclusion. I am myself a Norwegian, but from the beginning I have thought of NAAS as a Nordic community of scholars. To me it has seemed that being a part of this Nordic community is more important than also coming from Denmark, Finland, Iceland, Norway or Sweden. My sense of feeling at home in all the Nordic countries and having close historical and cultural ties with my colleagues from these countries has become central to my identity. This identity has to a large degree been shaped by my study of the United States and my involvement in organizations such as NAAS and the European Association for American Studies (EAAS).

Much of my adult life has been focused on the study of the United States. I have found myself happy with my preferred object of study for more than four decades – even though not always happy about the political decisions that have been made in the country of my choice. This is neither a simple position nor a facile statement; it has become increasingly difficult to harmonize my fascination with and love of the United States with my abhorrence of aspects of American policy. However, I have come to realize that I may have been led to, rather than chosen the study of the United States as my vocation. Indeed, I may have been genetically predisposed to American Studies: two of my grandchildren are Americans.

A Migrating Family
I say this only partly in jest; for these two young Americans are the latest manifestations of the more than century-long multigenerational trans-Atlantic migrations of my family. Three of my grandparents were returned immigrants from the United States in the late nineteenth century. My mother's parents immigrated as a family in the 1890s and after some years in Idaho decided to return to Norway; but three of their children later settled in the United States. My father's father

spent seven unhappy bachelor years in Montana working for railroads and on ranches before he wrote to his father in 1893, asking for money for his return ticket.[3] All immigrants did not succeed. My paternal grandfather's older brother, Orm (who in Minnesota changed his name to Tom), became editor of a short-lived Knights of Labor newspaper, *The Industrial Age*, in Duluth, and their sister, Martha, went on her own from Duluth to New York where she eventually became a lawyer specializing in corporation law. A thick book she wrote on this subject may be found in American law libraries.[4] It may be that in writing for publication in the United States I have, sub-consciously, been emulating my American granduncle and grandaunt. My fourth grandparent, my father's mother, did not make it to the United States; but three of her siblings did, and settled in LaSalle County in Illinois. I correspond regularly with one of their descendants.

My family's migrations did not end with my grandparents' generation. In May 1939 my parents took me and my younger brother to North America, to Montreal, where I spent more than seven childhood years. My earliest memory is of a subway ride from Manhattan to Brooklyn on the day of arrival in New York. (I did not understand this memory until my next ride on the same subway line in 1963.) I grew up with the same radio shows and the same magazines, comic books, and Big Little Books as my American contemporaries. Then, in 1963, my wife and I and our first son continued the pattern of migration when I went to continue my study of the United States at Yale. Since then our family has migrated regularly to the United States. And the pattern has persisted into the next generation. One of our three sons is born in New Haven and today he and his family are Americans.

I am not quite an outsider, then, as a student of the United States; and yet, one impact that my American peregrinations have had on my identity has been to make clear to me that I am indeed a European – *not* an American. Although I feel at home in the United States, the United States is not my home. But I am not entirely comfortable in my European homeland either, and this may be one of the necessary consequences of immersion in the culture and traditions of another country. How did this immersion come about?

I understood as a child
My study of America began, then, in May 1939 when I disembarked in New York two days after my fourth birthday and went on by train to Montreal where my father was pastor in the Norwegian Seaman's Mission. My first vague awareness of the larger world came with the Nazi invasion of Norway almost a year later. With it I became an exile. As I now see it, my growing but necessarily childish understanding of being an exile was part and parcel of my gradual awareness of the world outside my family. My earliest engagement with American Studies may not have been scholarly, but it was certainly formative, and it has contributed to my sense of being neither quite an outsider nor quite an insider – whether I am in North America or in Europe.[5]

My study of Europe began in 1944 with D-Day. In the pages of the weeklies, *Colliers*, *Saturday Evening Post*, and *Life Magazine* I followed the progress of the allied forces across Europe in the words and pictures of their reporters, artists, and photographers. On a map of Europe above my bed, colored pins marked the positions of allied armies and divisions. My interest in the war was intensely personal: my return to my land depended on the outcome.[6] This experience at nine of a little understood war moving across a map of Europe has contributed to my adult awareness that the fates of Europe and the United States are one, and that the liberty and strength of Norway depend on the liberty and strength of Europe. The map above my bed started the process that has made me a European.

My study of what it meant to be Norwegian was inseparable from my experience of growing up in a multicultural city. Looking back on those childhood years, it is difficult to accept how completely I internalized the attitude of my English-speaking surroundings to my French-speaking neighbors. We lived close to a Catholic and consequently French parochial school but I never met my French Canadian contemporaries. I looked around corners in their neighborhoods, well informed of the dangers that lurked there. We children had a wide selection of derogatory epithets for the French. At home I was Norwegian and at Sunday school I was Scottish Presbyterian. Most of my childhood friends were Jews and on Friday evenings I was a *shabbas goy*, turning on the lights in the storefront temple (*schul* my friends said) across the street from our apartment and getting a coin wrapped in paper from the rabbi for my services. On major holidays I was called on to turn on the gas stove for my friends' mothers. But I was not really conscious of difference; we were all Canadians except, of course, for the French. So many of the children in the Guy Drummond school were Jewish that when they had their holidays, several classes were merged and we did nothing serious such as arithmetic and grammar until their holiday was over and school went back to normal. In May 1945 I realized that I too had a special holiday and on the morning of the seventeenth – inspired, I later understood, by my Jewish friends – I announced that I was not going to school because this was a Norwegian holiday.[7] Wisely, my parents did not object. I think mine was the strangest 17th of May celebration ever: I simply sat on the front stoop of our apartment house (now one of the buildings of Université de Montreal) until school was out so that all could see that I was not at school. Probably no one noticed, but for me it was – although I did not know the concept – my first public ethnic statement.

We – and by then a sister had been added to the family – returned to Norway in 1946 on a freighter, a Liberty Ship named *Lektor Garbo* carrying wheat from Trois Rivière,

Quebec (to me it was then Three Rivers) to Bergen, Norway.[8] It was a powerful emotional experience for an 11-year old to stand on deck one drizzly, dreary early December morning with his father as the mountains of western Norway came into view. Those mountains, of which I had no memory, told me this was where I belonged. But as my Norwegian identity was being confirmed, my literary interest in the United States had its no less emotional beginning. Our view of the mountains may have inspired my father with the sentimental notion that the pre-war Norway he remembered must be kept pure from pernicious American influences. At least he then and there announced to me that my fair-sized collection of comic books, including many early issues of *Superman* and *Batman*, could not enter our promised land. I was told to get them from the cabin I shared with my brother and dump them over the side of the ship. Disobedience was out of the question. With a heavy heart I carried my pile of literary treasures to the railing and let them fall into the sea. I now see my fascination with American literature as a lifelong attempt to regain that lost treasure.[9]

Studying the "Real" America

I began my academic studies at the University of Oslo in the mid 1950s – first history, and then English, which for me to a great extent meant the opportunity to read more American books. When time came to decide on a MA thesis my choice was nourished by the inspiring teaching and guidance of the father of American Studies in Norway, Sigmund Skard, one of those rare professors who have more students attending lectures in the second half of the term than in the first.[10] But my interest in American culture had grown out of my life story. It was in this personal sense and because of my personal experience that American Studies had become my destined field.

Or so it seemed to me for a long time. For I gave little

thought to my older relationship with the United States through my immigrant forebears and American relatives. I had yet to understand the implications of the truism that the United States is a nation of immigrants and that I was closely related to that developing and migrating nation. Looking back, I realize that nor had my teachers, in Oslo or at Yale, demonstrated an understanding of the United States as a nation constantly in the making.

When thirteen English colonies became the United States of America, Americans of English origin were certainly the largest single ethnic group, but their 48 % of the total did not quite make them a majority. About 20 % were of African origin. Others had forebears from Germany, Holland, Spain (Jews), Finland, Sweden, and other countries. Earlier generations of American historians had arrived at a more inflated percentage of Anglo-Americans. In 1921 Samuel Orth set the percentage of Americans of English origin in 1790 at 82.1 %. There are of course no precise figures; both of these percentages were based on computations. But the difference between Orth's percentage of 82 in 1921 and Roger Daniels's more modest one of 48 in 1991 speaks of a change in the way American scholars perceive American history.[11] This development has also been my development.

Orth called his book *Our Foreigners*. In 1921, "foreigners" was still the common word in American English for Americans of other than English descent. American Studies was consequently not much concerned with them. In the United States the scholarly interest in immigration history as a part of United States history had its slow beginning in the decades between the two World Wars, and three pioneers were of Scandinavian origin: the Norwegian American Theodore Blegen, the Danish American Marcus Lee Hansen, and the Swedish American George Stephenson. But in spite of their efforts immigration history for some time remained a fairly isolated field in American historical scholarship.

An American Citizen

Today it is difficult for me to understand how unimportant immigration seemed to me when I was a doctoral student – both as a field of academic study and research and as a personal interest in my family's participation in the making of America. I visited American relatives in the Midwest a few times during my three years at Yale Graduate School, but mostly I avoided contact with descendants of Norwegian immigrants and their ethnic traditions and culture. My interest was in "real" Americans – and the "real" America was founded by English Puritans and inhabited mainly by their descendants. So blind were my eyes and so deaf my ears that it took many years before I appreciated the significance of an experience I had coming out from the Sterling Memorial Library one wet and dark evening in New Haven in the fall of 1964.

I had finished my work for the day and was on my way out when I was delayed by an altercation at the desk of the guard whose duty it was to check all bags and parcels of those leaving the library. A woman was refusing to open her bag. A line of impatient students quickly grew behind my back. Finally she gave in – as she must – and opened her bag for inspection. The guard glanced in it, gestured toward the exit and said, "good night." I followed on her heels and as we came out she turned around, looked up at me, and said with indignation and a marked accent, "Imagine their doing this to me, an American citizen." What she had been exposed to, I have realized, symbolized all that she had been liberated from by making herself an American. For Americans – like America itself – are in the making. America's strength is the faith of its citizens in the meaningfulness of their citizenship regardless of their many accents and their many places of origin. The patriotic vision of the woman outside the Sterling Memorial Library, however, is at odds with the vision of America that inspires the Patriot Act. The tension between these two visions has been central in the history of the United States.

Two important experiences on my way to realizing and acknowledging the multicultural and transnational core of the America I thought I was studying were contemporaneous with but not actually part of my graduate studies. The first in time was my very modest participation in the Great Freedom Summer of 1964, teaching freshmen at the all-black Texas Southern University. This was also the summer of the Bay of Tonkin incident and I could not but identify with the American anti-war movement as it grew through the second half of the 1960s.[12] Before concluding, I will return to the impact of the anti-war movement on my attitude to the European tradition of criticism of the United States.

But these were extracurricular activities. My tidy image of an Anglo America was not really questioned by my years in American Studies at Yale. Nor did I there reflect on my position as a European in the Yale American Studies Program. In my *The Making and Meaning of an American Classic: James Fenimore Cooper's The Prairie* (1973) and in my early articles on nineteenth- and twentieth-century American literature there is nothing, I now see, to suggest that I was a European student of the United States or that my perspective differed significantly from that of my American contemporaries.[13] Indeed, inspired by my great teachers at Yale, in particular by my mentor, the generous Norman Holmes Pearson, my aim was to be indistinguishable from my American colleagues.[14] Since my ideal was objectivity, my identity was irrelevant. I was well into middle age before I felt free to study the American experience of immigrants and before I felt at home in the ethnic niche of Norwegian Americans. If American Studies is my destined field, this is, I now realize, as much because of my long unrecognized family ties with the United States as of my North American childhood.

A Book about American Literature

In the winter of 1982-1983, after some unproductive years as Dean, I wrote my first notes on a project I foolhardily embarked on, knowing next to nothing about it: a history of Norwegian American literature, American literature, that is, in the Norwegian language. I do not think I would have done this without the example and inspiration of Dorothy Skårdal.[15] In my ignorance I thought that so limited a topic could easily be researched and written in a couple of years. It was all of fourteen years, however, before *The Western Home: A Literary Study of Norwegian America* was published in 1996. This book is about how a European immigrant group brought their language to the United States and used it for literary expression over a period of eighty years.

I now see it as a somewhat belated rebellion against my teachers at Yale. There – twenty years earlier – Norwegian had not been accepted as one of the two foreign languages required for entry into the doctoral program. Norwegian, I was informed by the acting chair of the American Studies Program, was not relevant for American Studies.[16] So there was a certain note of protest in the opening sentence of *The Western Home*: "This is a book about American literature." In the introductory chapter I found it natural to introduce my journalist American granduncle as well as my lawyer-scholar American grandaunt. Only recently have I realized that I should have placed my North American childhood self there as well: I was given my first book about Norwegian immigrants in 1943, when it was read to me by my father. It was called *Muskego Boy* and was lavishly illustrated, as were some other Norwegian American publications of my childhood years, the Christmas annual, *Jul i Vesterheimen*.[17] These and other publications of the Augsburg Publishing House in Minneapolis entered my childhood home in Montreal because of the close war-time relations between the Norwegian Seamen's Mission in North America and The Norwegian

Lutheran Church in America.[18] Clearly – I now see – both my family ties with the United States and my own North American childhood were essential ingredients awaiting the catalyzing effect of Dorothy Skårdal's indefatigable proselytizing.

In the story I was eventually able to tell in *The Western Home*, the earliest attempts at American poetry and prose in Norwegian were published in Wisconsin newspapers in the 1840s and 1850s. By the late 1870s American books in Norwegian included fiction, verse, and drama in addition to the many religious books. This literature, however, never became part of the American literary culture that was conducted in English nor did it get any attention in the European homeland. Today, moreover, the many writers and their books are unknown even to those who claim a Norwegian American identity. Immigrant cultures are both marginal and transitional. An American culture that expressed itself in a language other than English was not actually ignored by the majority culture; it was not heard to the extent that it could *be* ignored. Being transitional, moreover, it was doomed to oblivion. You may say that such is the fate of all cultures, but immigrant cultures and their languages have rarely survived into a third generation in the United States.[19] As newcomers moved into the immigrant culture, assimilated Norwegian Americans were moving out of it. As the grandchildren of immigrants remembered only a few scattered phrases of the language of their grandparents, new immigrants were struggling to learn English. An immigrant culture depended on continuing immigration. When mass immigration was interrupted by the First World War and virtually ceased by the late 1920s it was evident to most actors that the end of a dynamic Norwegian American culture was near. Paradoxically, the 1920s is both the decade with the greatest Norwegian American literary achievements and the decade when, to all practical purposes, American books in the Norwegian language ceased to be published. A single novel, Ole Edvart Rølvaag's *Giants in the Earth* (1927), has entered into the American literary canon in English translation.[20]

Had I realized what a long and arduous project this literary history would be, I probably would not have had the guts to take it up. There was no satisfactory bibliography and no single depository for the work of these obscure authors. During more than a decade, whenever I had the opportunity, I visited American archives and libraries, poring over the dusty pages of long forgotten books and journals in a language now unknown to the descendants of those who had written and read them. It was – I felt – my role to be a medium through whom these forgotten American writers might speak again.[21]

The book's programmatic opening sentence – "This is a book about American literature" – may seem bombastic, but I felt I had to make my governing premise clear from the outset: these American writers who wrote in Norwegian for American readers had created an American literature. American librarians, however, have either disregarded the first sentence or not read beyond the title page: they have catalogued and shelved *The Western Home* as a book about Norwegian – not American – literature.[22] Immigrants and ethnic groups other than the English are still foreigners in an American literary history that begins with English colonists and focuses on what was later written in their language. The still dominant view is that the languages of foreigners cannot be American languages, nor can the literature written in such languages be American. At a conference on early American literature in the early 1980s I asked the presenter of a paper on newspapers in colonial Philadelphia whether his statistics included newspapers in German. In his response he was first bewildered, then irritated. There are, however, some signs of an important shift in the understanding of what is central and what is peripheral and of what is significant and what is insignificant in American Studies.²³ In her Presidential Address to the (United States) American Studies Association in 2004, one of Shelly Fisher Fishkin's several proclamations was, "As the transnational becomes increasingly central to American Studies, we may well seek to recover chapters of the past that have eluded any archive despite their importance."²⁴ One of the recovery projects she mentioned is the large mass of American texts in languages other than English. In such a project languages such as Spanish, German, and French will necessarily loom larger than the languages of numerically smaller groups such as Finns and Norwegians.

European American Studies
I became a member of the board of the EAAS for the first time in 1976 and my active involvement in this organization has played an important role in my changing perspective on American Studies and on my growing awareness of how and why a European perspective must and should be different from an American one.²⁵ One defining experience was the editing of a volume of articles in English translation by scholars from Eastern and Central Europe, the second volume in an EAAS translation project. It was initially planned as a volume presenting the work of scholars in what was then known as East Europe, a political rather than a geographical concept. But during the editing process the political division of Europe underwent radical change. One consequence of this change was that some of the articles were not merely translated but were rewritten in the course of the long editing process because the authors felt increasingly free from the political restrictions that had determined the ideological rhetoric and the once obligatory slanting of their scholarly work. The book was eventually published in 1990 as *In the European Grain: American Studies from Central and Eastern Europe*.²⁶ For the editor the entire process was an education in the potential of a changing Europe, a Europe that was as Russian as it was

French and as Polish as it was British. The realization that the United States did not look the same from the many different countries that were Europe was central to a realization of what a European perspective meant: there are at least as many European perspectives on the United States as there are American perspectives on the United States. One thing that all the many European perspectives have in common is that they include the study of *American* American Studies: when Russian or Norwegian Americanists attend the annual meetings of the US American Studies Association they are studying and observing the meeting as well as participating in it. The ASA culture is also an American culture and you may have to have an outside view in order to include it in your American Studies. The many studies of the United States from European perspectives will, however, remain largely irrelevant to our colleagues in the United States as long as their view of the field is limited to work found in journals and books published in the United States.[27] The first necessary step to make American Studies international may be that American scholars seriously consider the possibility of the relevance of American Studies scholarship from abroad. The references in United States publications and the reading lists of United States graduate courses suggest that we still may have a long way to go.

Homemaking in the United States
It may have been the exclusion of *The Western Home* from the library shelves reserved for *real* American Studies that drew my attention to how immigrants and their descendants in the not so distant past had found it necessary to argue that they were American. During my work on *The Western Home* I had reacted negatively when my research showed up so many instances of what seemed a Norwegian American tendency to boast of being such excellent Americans, indeed the very best Americans.[28] Immigrants from Norway had unpleasantly

high ideas about themselves, I thought. But as my study of immigration history broadened I became aware that all immigrant groups (not only those from Europe)[29] at the turn of the nineteenth century boasted of being more American than others. When I was invited to give the opening lecture at the NAAS conference in Oslo in 1995 I had just completed my as yet unpublished *The Western Home* and knew that I wanted to make use of this opportunity to talk about something new, not about what I had already done (—well, I am older now). That lecture became the beginning of a book published five years later: *Immigrant Minds, American Identities: Making the United States Home, 1870-1930*. (2000)[30]

At the time I gave this lecture I was convinced that such a project would have to be a collaborative effort: no single scholar could master the number of immigrant languages necessary for an account that could make valid analyses of a perceived general feature of European immigrant cultures. When the lecture was published as a "working paper" in David Nye's *Odense American Studies International Series*, it included an "invitation to scholars with knowledge of other ethnic groups and their languages who may wish to contribute to a collective project that would aim at identifying, describing and interpreting American home-making myths with a view to comparative and synthesizing studies on the nature of acculturation and Americanization as well as on distinguishing traits of American ethnicities."[31] There were, perhaps naturally, no responses to this invitation. But on a visit to Minnesota in the fall of 1996 I discovered the rich resources of Rudolph Vecoli's Immigration History Research Center at the University of Minnesota. It was a microfilm copy of a 1930s WPA project that offered me one of the keys that permitted access to what emigrant leaders were saying to the members of their immigrant groups: *The Chicago Foreign Language Press Survey*. Here translated items from the large number of newspapers in languages other than English are organized thematically and chronologically by language, thus providing access to several decades of immigrant expression and activities. Published in Chicago, these newspapers often had a wide geographical distribution. The following year a scholarship from Marc Shell and Werner Sollor's Longfellow Institute at Harvard University gave me access to the rich library holdings of that university. By then I realized that I indeed had the source material I needed for my book.

My point of departure was my understanding that one project shared by members of all immigrant groups has been to make home of a country that insists you are foreign. Let me read to you my opening sentences:

> In common American usage the noun *foreigner* has had one meaning not registered in major dictionaries of American English: *an American or a resident in the United States who is not of British origin.*[32] To be characterized as foreign has been central to the experience of so many Americans of first and second generation who came from a European country other than the United Kingdom that one can only wonder why lexicographers of a nation of immigrants have not noted this meaning of the word.

In this book I demonstrated that European immigrants responded to exclusion by arguing that the United States was their special home. Central to their argument were narratives where characters of their nationality played important roles in the history of the United States, thus proving that the imagined descendants of these characters (such as Kosciusko or Columbus) had a special right to be Americans. I called such arguments homemaking arguments. The stories immigrants told to support these arguments I called homemaking myths. The function of homemaking myths was to make America the rightful home of an immigrant group. There are three genres of such myths:

Myths of foundation — where the main theme is, "We were here first or at least as early as you."
Myths of sacrifice — where the main theme is, "We gave our blood for our country."
Myths of a close ideological relationship — where the main theme is, "We were American before we came to America."

Stories that made such arguments were told by the cultural and intellectual elite of all European immigrant groups. They told these stories to convince their fellow immigrants that they had a special right to be at home in the United States and not be regarded as foreigners in their own land.

These myths may appear self-glorifying. Considered in their historical context, however, they were responses to a politics of exclusion where immigrants and their children were defined as foreigners. These myths supplemented the dominant American historical narrative – equally mythic – where all roles were played by Americans of British descent. The history immigrant children were taught at school had a nation-building function and was intended to make Anglo-American children proud of their heritage. However, these history books did not address the children of immigrants from, say, Finland, Poland or Germany and their need of pride in *their* heritage. In school texts immigrants were not only outsiders but threats to American culture. The alleged mission of the public school was to make Americans of the children of foreigners; the message was often that they had no right to a home in the United States, as David Muzzey's widely used *An American History* (1911) made clear. There the children of immigrants, who were in the majority in many classrooms, were confronted with the question: "Can we assimilate and mold into citizenship the millions who are coming to our shores, or will they remain an ever-increasing body of aliens, an undigested and indigestible element in our body politic, and a constant menace to our free institutions?"[33]

Not Bunk!
This is now history. By the time of the Second World War few seriously questioned that the descendants of European immigrants were Americans. But it is important that today's descendants of European immigrants be aware of this history so that they do not repeat it. The exclusion of Americans from their land did not end with their grandparents and great grandparents. Japanese Americans were regarded not only as foreigners but as enemies when the United States entered the Second World War; the post-war decades saw a culmination of the bitter struggle to keep African Americans out of their American home; and today immigrants and the children of immigrants from Islamic countries again have the experience of being regarded with suspicion as aliens in their own land – and as a menace to its free institutions. History is more than Henry Ford claimed it to be.

In my work I continue to be fascinated by the making of America. My recent publications are on ethnicity, migration and exile, on aspects of entering the United States and making it home.[34] My major project has for some years been a seven-volume edition of immigrant letters of which the first four have been published and a fifth should be out by the end of 2007. This edition is based on a large collection of immigrant letters in the Norwegian National Archives (*Riksarkivet*), a collection initiated in the late 1920s by the American historian Theodore Blegen and the Norwegian-American Historical Association at a time when there was little interest among Norwegian and European scholars in the lives and experiences of the peasants and laborers who had left their countries for what they hoped would be a better life in the United States.[35]

Immigrant and Native Americans

I have had much to learn from these often semi-literate writers. One lesson that has recently given me cause for reflection is of alternative ways to make America home. Immigrant homemaking has not been without its ethical ambiguities. The vast areas of land settled by European immigrants were not empty before they arrived – even though immigration historians have largely avoided understanding immigration as the displacement of a native population. Indeed, barriers and hindrances have been common tropes for Native Americans in the rhetoric of historians of immigration. Letters from three immigrants may illustrate two contrasting approaches to homemaking in the United States. One, that of exclusion, has been the more common, the other, that of inclusion, may suggest an attitude to homemaking that could have led to an America different from the one most immigrants took part in creating.

The first of these three immigrants, Jacob Hilton, came to Socorro, New Mexico in the spring of 1881 and wrote to his father on the farm Hilton in Ullensaker, a little north of Oslo, that this is "a new world where white people have just begun to come. Now I am among Indians, Mexicans and Spaniards.[36] All three are alike in appearance and one is as dangerous as the other." But with the arrival of the railroad, he wrote, "white people are beginning to swarm in the mountains and valleys that used to be populated by these lazy and useless people who live like wild animals. I have never felt better since I left home than after I came to this place." Jacob Hilton acquired a sense of belonging by seeing himself as one of the white people who, he writes in the same letter, have built the United States "from sea to sea. There are still millions of acres of land that have not yet been trod on by white people but as the emigration increases it will all in time be settled by whites. But this place has become my home. Let others go further." In a letter he wrote some months later he again identified himself as one of the "white people [who] have only come this past year" and expressed his sense of being at home in "the wonderful America." Then, in November he wrote about a bloody encounter with Apache Indians, "the *'poor Indians'* that people in the eastern states have so much sympathy for. My judgment on such people is that they should be in hell with broken backbones—both the Indians and those who feel such concern for them." Jacob Hilton created his American identity and his sense of being at home in his new land by defining himself as a white male westerner and excluding the "lazy and useless people" from a place in this home.

In a recent article on the correspondence of Jacob Hilton in *Journal of American Ethnic History*, I observe that he responded not only to his own experience in New Mexico, "but to the heady rhetoric of the local newspapers. For surely Jacob Hilton's characterizations of the 'others,' whether of the 'lazy and useless people who live like wild animals' or of the Indian-loving 'people in the eastern states,' were not original creations of his own mind but part of the language he had been exposed to on his western journey and that he made his own so soon after arriving in Socorro."[37] You may find him an extremist, but one way of trying to understand Jacob Hilton and his sense of belonging in a new home is to see him responding to the dominant culture of Socorro in a manner not all that different from the way the child conformed to his neighborhood's views of the ethnic divisions in Montreal of the 1940s or the graduate student responded to the dominant culture of the American Studies Program at Yale Graduate School in the 1960s and identified himself as a student of the real America.

My second immigrant correspondent, Iver Andersen Lee, came to the present North Dakota in 1882. After he had married in 1891 he wrote to his family in Hedalen in Valdres

March 2 and told them that his new wife was twenty-five years old, short, and rather fat.[38] Among the many other things he thought would interest people in Hedalen he wrote about a five-day journey he had made to visit some friends and buy fish from Native Americans in their vicinity. I would like to share this part of his long letter with you. After telling how he had done a profitable business on his return home with the fish he had bought from the Indians, using some of it to make *rakfisk*, he writes,

> The Indians are rather nice people to visit.… In most of their houses they had a stove but in some there were fireplaces. I must say that it was really nice to see a fireplace again, because I haven't seen one since I left you. And the fire burned so brightly in their fireplace that I really felt at home…. There has been quite a lot of trouble with the Indians last fall and winter and they have rebelled in many places. And the government has made regular war against them. There have been several battles and several hundreds have fallen on both sides, but mainly Indians. At the place where I visited there had not been any uprising, but they are said to have done their so-called war dances some time after I was there and that created quite a scare…. Moreover, quite a few exaggerated and some completely false rumors were in circulation and this made the situation look much worse. Many left their cattle and homes behind and fled from the area. But the scare subsided when the exaggerations and falsehoods were revealed. The government is itself responsible for the unrest among the Indians. The situation is that they are in a way the wards of the government. They do not farm the land but have fed themselves by fishing and

hunting. So as the land has gradually been taken from them, their sources of livelihood have diminished and as compensation the government has agreed to supply them with food and clothes. This is done through government agents but they have been under so little control that they have made themselves wealthy at the Indians' expense. Thus the Indians have often suffered from hunger and this is what has led them on the warpath. It seems quite reasonable that they would rather fight for survival than die of starvation.[39]

The difference between the attitudes of Jacob Hilton and Iver Lee is neither of place nor of time. My third immigrant, Gulbrand Rundhaug, also wrote from North Dakota and at about the same time as Iver Lee. His letter to the farm Elsrud in Ringerike about the unrest among Native Americans is dated 10 February 1891, a few weeks after the massacre at Wounded Knee. He wrote, "We now live in constant fear of the Indians since they have begun to kill the whites. They have already killed and scalped many white people. They burn them alive in the most horrible manner. The soldiers are out to stop them and they slaughter many, and all here in Dakota who do not have rifles are given rifles by the government. They are really awful people. They are red as blood and worse than wild animals."[40] The soldiers are acting on behalf of humanity; there can be no mercy for beings "worse than wild animals." We may imagine later versions of Gulbrand Rundhaug celebrating executions outside penitentiaries.

While two of these writers explicitly denied the humanity of the Native Americans and thus eliminated their occupation of their land as an ethical issue, Iver Lee looked for and found not only a shared humanity but a shared sense of a fireplace as the center of a home. Entering the homes of Indians Iver Lee was reminded of entering a home in his old-home valley of Hedalen. It is important to understand that his letter makes clear that this was a deliberate choice. In his letter he also noted the lack of furniture and the use of the floor for both sitting and sleeping. But rather than focus on what may have felt foreign he chose to focus on what made him feel at home. The situation, the land of origin and the new social and cultural contexts of these three immigrants were much the same; different choices made for their contrasting identity formations and homemaking processes. The historian who writes about Norwegian contributions to the making of the United States must confront the excluding homemaking of Jacob Hilton and Gulbrand Rundhaug. The homemaking of Iver Lee, however, suggests that late nineteenth-century racism was not a historical necessity and that the United States could have developed differently. But the majority of immigrants did not contribute much to such a different development.[41]

The American and the European Projects
The United States is still in the making, is still a project. The inclusive America of Iver Lee is an idea still to be realized. The land of freedom imagined by the woman outside the Sterling Memorial Library is still a vision. I will not live to see the completion of the American project but my identity is as involved in the study of this project as it is rooted in my sense of being Norwegian and European. I hope that my grandchildren on both continents will be able to grow up with faith in the American project.

Europe as a political entity is of course no less a project. For many Norwegians *union* remains a word with negative connotations[42] and my country has placed itself on the sidelines and chosen not to be a full partner in the European Union in the making. As I continue to study the United States in myself I recognize that my positive response to *union* may have been one effect of my American Studies on my Norwegian identity. More important, though, is my experience of the United States as a multi-ethnic nation. Norway so often seems a closed tribal society in comparison: our concept of "immigrant" is entirely based on difference in skin color, clothing traditions, and religion. I am glad that my study of the United States has made me impatient with the xenophobia so characteristic of my culture.

Indeed, my study of the United States has made me impatient with European intellectuals who seem unable to understand the essential difference between the American tradition of criticizing the United States and the European one of criticizing — well, the United States. In the Gospel of Luke (18:9-14) we find the story of two men in the temple who both were highly critical of the behavior of one of them. Without any sense of the irony involved, a Norwegian scholar made the following comment about a book on European views of the United States: "When the authors also observe that the foremost critics of the United States are themselves Americans they could have added that many of them actually say the same as their European counterparts."[43] There is no understanding here of the radical difference between saying "I am a sinner" and "You are a sinner." Of the two who were critical of the same person one day in the temple in Jerusalem we are told that "all who exalt themselves will be humbled, but all who humble themselves will be exalted." Self-criticism is not an exercise much practiced by Europeans.

The Scholar and the Person
When I returned to Norway in 1966 after three years at Yale I could finally take part in something that I felt I could not be involved in while I was a guest of the United States: protests against the Vietnam War. However, I found myself increasingly uncomfortable with the address of these protests: the American Embassy in Oslo. The demonstrations should rather have been organized and aimed at Norwegian institu-

tions such as the *Storting* and addressed to the Norwegian government's support of the war. Americans were criticizing their government; we should criticize our own. I had after all studied Thoreau, who directed his criticism of slavery in the South against the complicity of his own free state of Massachusetts: "What should concern Massachusetts is not the Nebraska Bill, nor the Fugitive Slave Bill, but her own slaveholding and servility. Let the State [i.e. Massachusetts] dissolve her union with the slaveholder."[44] Again it has been my experience that the personal and the scholarly are intertwined and interdependent. Views of the United States from abroad must include that which is abroad, must indeed include the viewer – and the beam that may be in the eye of the viewer.

There are ambiguities involved, however, in American Studies perspectives from abroad. While European scholars may not get the attention they deserve from their American colleagues, there has been a history of considerable and benevolent attention from the United States that speaks through the State Department. The relationship between European American Studies scholars and the official rather than the academic United States has not been without political and ethical complications. Indeed, in the decades after the Second World War American Studies in Europe was heavily sponsored by the State Department, mainly but not solely through the US Information Agency or Service, as it is known abroad. Without this financial support, which of course must be understood in the context of the Cold War, the early work of the EAAS and the growing number of national and regional American Studies associations may not have been possible. The war in Vietnam made this reliance on the American government problematic to many and, beginning with what may be characterized as a blow-out during a US-funded bicentennial conference at Schloss Leopoldskron in Salzburg in the spring of 1975, such funding was a frequent but informal issue of dispute among participants at EAAS conferences. It must be made clear, however, that there were, in my experience, never any strings attached to the often generous US funding of European American Studies.

Two related incidents in the winter of 1972-73 may illustrate both the strained relationship with the official United States in these troubled years and the attitude of many American diplomats to critical scholars. At the initiative of historian Torbjørn Sirevåg, American Studies Scholars at Norwegian universities signed a public declaration published by several major newspapers concluding that the war had made the United States "a travesty of the nation once looked up to by the peoples of the world." There was no public comment from any US diplomat in Norway but our statement was evidently a theme in discussions at the embassy and communications with Washington: some weeks into the next year we received individual letters from the USIS in Oslo offering the payment of travel costs for participation in the coming conference of the British Association for American Studies. There was no mention of our critical public statement. The implied message that our political views were not the concern of the State Department was not lost on those who received these letters. We now live in what appear to be less enlightened times and I somehow doubt that the present administration in Washington encourages this kind of response to the criticism of American foreign policy.[45] While I cannot but be grateful for the generosity that so much of my involvement with NAAS as well as EAAS has depended on, I am also glad that our work is no longer dependent on such generosity.

Writing this essay has been an impetus to reflect on how the scholar and the person cannot and should not be separated. The identity and personality of the scholar are his or her most important tools. We are inevitably in our work as our work is in us. There are no objective interpretations of history, literature, or society; nor should we pretend that our choice of what we study is unrelated to our experience, our beliefs, and our values. Thus the United States has had a significant impact on my experience, my views, and my identity just as the way in which I understand and interpret the United States is necessarily affected by my experience, my views, and my identity. Perhaps the closest a scholar can come to objectivity is to be aware of its impossibility and, indeed, of its undesirability.

Notes

1. Fishkin, (2005), 24. Atwood, (1998), 1504. Skard, (1958), 653-654. – This article is a revised version of a talk at the opening of the conference of the Nordic Association for American Studies at Växjö, Sweden, May 26, 2005 and also published, in a slightly different version, in *American Studies in Scandinavia* 37:2 (Autumn 2005), 1-24.
2. The proceedings of the first conference were edited by the organizer, Lars Åhnebrink, Professor of American literature at Uppsala University, as *Amerika och Norden*. Publications of the Nordic Association for American Studies No. 1 (Stockholm: Almqvist & Wiksell, 1964). This volume includes the program of the conference and a list of participants. The opening was a rather grand affair with speeches by the Prime Minister of Sweden, Tage Erlander, and the U. S. ambassador to Sweden. The second NAAS conference, in Oslo in 1964, had a similar opening, this time with the Norwegian Minister of Foreign Affairs, Halvard Lange and the US ambassador to Norway. The conference proceedings were edited by Sigmund Skard as the second volume in the Publications series, entitled *USA in Focus*. The opening ceremonies of later conferences have been lower keyed.
3. A selection of letters by Hans A. M. Øverland to his father are in Øverland, (2005). In English translation they may be read in Zempel, (1991).

4   Martha Ubo Overland (1866-1914), (1906, and later revisions). Martha first joined her brother in Duluth and Superior, working as a dressmaker and then bookkeeper and stenographer before she went to New York where she got her law degree in 1899 and later had offices in William and Wall Streets in Manhattan. Tom (1850-1899) also worked for several Norwegian American newspapers, in Minneapolis and Duluth. He died destitute at the age of 49 of pneumonia in the spring of 1899 after working all winter in a lumber camp near Duluth. His career in journalism was by then over.

5   In 1989 I paid my scholarly homage to the country of my childhood: *Johan Schrøder's Travels in Canada, 1863*. Edited, Translated, and with an Introduction by Orm Øverland (1989).

6   The war was close. Even a child could sense the seriousness of war with seamen visiting church and home between convoy duty, many never returning, and father had a uniform, also serving as chaplain in the Norwegian Air Force at their training camp, Little Norway, in Toronto.

7   Norway celebrates its 1814 constitution on May 17.

8   The ship was named for Ingvald Garbo, a senior high school teacher in Bergen, who in 1941 was executed by the Nazis for placing his typewritten essays in German military vehicles to make the soldiers reflect on what they were participating in. See Garbo, (2000).

9   When I, towards the end of his life, asked my father about his reason for being so unreasonable he claimed to have no memory of this – for me – so shattering an event. My father was in no way alone in fearing the pernicious effects of comic books on the young nor in seeing them as a potential American cultural infection in the years after WW2. See Ulf Jonas Björk, "American Infection: The Swedish Campaign Against Comic Books, 1952-1957," an unpublished paper presented at the conference of the Nordic Association for American Studies in 2003. For an account of the United States side of this issue, Björk refers to Lent, ed., (1999). An entertaining fictional account of the anti-comic book campaign (and much, much else)

is Michael Chabon, *The Amazing Adventures of Kavalier and Clay* (2000).

10 This MA thesis, carefully edited by Sigmund Skard, was published as "The Impressionism of Stephen Crane: A Study in Style and Technique," *Americana Norvegica* 1 (1966): 239-285.

11 Orth, *Our Foreigners* (1921), 31. Daniels, (1991), 68. The figures in both cases are computations. I assume that one source of error in Orth's percentage is that he did not include slaves in the total. Orth was a professor of history at Cornell University.

12 In 1964, graduate students at some universities in the Northeast organized a "Southern Teaching Program" that offered the services of students for summer courses at what were then known as "predominantly Negro" colleges and universities. I was watching television with my graduate student colleagues at Texas Southern University when the news of the incident in the Bay of Tonkin broke. None of us could possibly believe the official version of the phony incident that triggered a full-scale war. The most shocking event of that summer – the murder of the three voter-registration volunteers James Chaney, Andrew Goodman and Michael Schwerner – has still not been resolved. June 14, 2005 – more than forty years later – *The New York Times* reports on the jury selection for the murder trial of one of the accused.

13 In spite of its title, my anthology, *America Perceived: A View from Abroad in the 20th Century* (West Haven, Connecticut: Pendulum Press, 1974), did not represent a more European or Norwegian orientation in my study of the United States.

14 Once, in a seminar session, Norman addressed me as an outsider, suggesting that I as a European could not fully appreciate the rural New England characters of Robert Frost's poetry. I realized that in my reading these characters were closely related to rural Norwegians as I knew them but did not take this realization to a further reflection on a special perspective.

15 Skårdal, (1974). This was the first book devoted to a study of a broad selection of American literature in languages other than English. It was based on a Harvard dissertation supervised by

Oscar Handlin. For some years I served as external examiner of MA theses on Norwegian American authors by students of Dorothy Skårdal at the University of Oslo.

16 The two standard languages for this requirement were French and German. Strangely, Spanish was then not considered important for American Studies.

17 Edna and Howard Hong, *Muskego Boy* (1943). The Christmas annual *Jul i Vesterheimen* (Christmas in the Western Home) was published by Augsburg from 1911 to 1957.

18 My father, Berge J. Øverland, was on a three week lecture tour in Minnesota in February 1942, resulting in further support for his work in Montreal as well as increased interest on his part in Norwegian American institutions and relations.

19 Although immigrant cultures usually die with the second generation, they often have a distinctly different afterlife as American ethnic cultures. One important difference is that the language of ethnic cultures is English.

20 Ole E. Rølvaag, *I de dage…* and *Riket grundlægges* were published in Oslo in 1924 and 1925. In collaboration with Lincoln Colcord, Rølvaag translated the two volumes as one novel: *Giants in the Earth* (1927). It was long widely used in high school and college English courses but has for some decades been replaced by more recent novels about immigrant experiences.

21 This notion of being a medium has been further realized in translations. Ole A. Buslett's "The Road to Golden Gate" and Dorthea Dahl's "The Copper Kettle" are in Shell and Sollors, eds. (2000), 416-459, 552-575. I have been involved in the republication of two Norwegian American novels: *A Saloonkeeper's Daughter* (2002), and *The Rise of Jonas Olsen: A Norwegian Immigrant's Saga*. A Trilogy by Johannes B. Wist. (2006). Hopefully, more will follow.

22 Colleagues in Europe recognized it as a book about American literature: it was awarded the American Studies Network Prize for the Best Book in American Studies by a European 1996-1997.

23 See Øverland, ed. (2001). The Longfellow Institute at Harvard University has, thanks to the efforts of Marc Shell and Werner Sollors, played an important role in this shift.
24 Fishkin, "Crossroads of Cultures," 25.
25 My participation in an Erasmus thematic network for American Studies with colleagues from universities in Dijon, Ghent, Mainz, Trieste, Vienna, and Winchester was also significant for my awareness that I was a *European* American Studies scholar.
26 Øverland, ed., (1990). A Romanian scholar, whose proposed contribution had to be rejected, excused himself: "This may be of interest as an example of how we have to write here."
27 Two fine series of publications in Germany alone are *Amerikastudien/American Studies* and *REAL: Yearbook of Research in English and American Literature*. Journals devoted to American Studies abound in European countries; some of them have articles in languages other than English.
28 See for instance Schultz (1994).
29 In a reader for Japanese language schools a text on "Good Citizens" admonishes children of Japanese immigrants to "always remember the virtues of the Japanese people…. There is no better way than this for you to serve your nation, America…." Kumei, in Øverland, *Not English Only*, 106.
30 The publisher advised against my original title: "This Land Is My Land."
31 Øverland, (1996), 19.
32 The three American dictionaries consulted were *Webster's Third New International Dictionary of the English Language Unabridged* (Springfield, Massachusetts, 1966), *A Dictionary of American English on Historical Principles* (Chicago, 1940), and *A Dictionary of Americanisms* (Chicago, 1951. *The Oxford English Dictionary*, Second Edition (Oxford, 1989), however, notes a parallel usage of "foreign" in British English: "the word is in British use not applied to parts of the United Kingdom, nor, ordinarily, to (former) colonies chiefly inhabited by English-speaking people" (VI: 51).

33 Quoted by Fitzgerald, (1980), 78. She observes that this and other text books "portrayed the immigrants as nothing more than a problem."
34 See the following articles: Øverland (2000, 2004, 2005, 2006).
35 The first three volumes were in cooperation with Steinar Kjærheim (1992, 1993, 2002) *Fra Amerika til Norge IV: Norske utvandrerbrev i utvalg, 1875-84* (2002). A fifth volume will appear shortly and the last two volumes should be ready by 2008. An American two-volume edition of a selection of letters from the seven Norwegian volumes will eventually be published by the Norwegian-American Historical Association.
36 The earliest Mexican/Spanish settlement in the present New Mexico, led by the controversial conquistador Don Juan de Oñate, was in 1598.
37 Øverland, (2004), 133-141. The correspondence from Jacob Hilton referred to here is in *Fra Amerika til Norge IV*. The encounter with the Apache Indians involves Gus Hilton, the father of the Conrad Hilton of hotel fame.
38 The original letter reads: "Hun er 25 Aar gammel, er liden af Vekst—kort men ganske tyk." The family in Norway spelled their name *Lie*, but for obvious reasons Iver and two brothers changed this to Lee, thus retaining the pronunciation.
39 *Fra Amerika til Norge V,* letter No. 219; my translation. *Rakfisk* is freshwater fish, usually trout, that has been cured by a process of fermentation.
40 *Fra Amerika til Norge V*, letter No. 215; my translation. His phrase for "slaughter" is even more brutal in the original: "Slagter ned meget." The Norwegian word is almost exclusively used for the killing of animals.
41 I have written at greater length about this issue as reflected in immigrant letters in "Norwegian Americans Meet Native Americans," Armstrong and Hestetun, eds., 109-122.
42 Norway did not become fully independent until 1905, when the king of Sweden ceased to be king of Norway.
43 Thomas Hylland-Eriksen in a review of Stian Bromark and Dag Herbjørnsrud, *Frykten for Amerika: En europeisk historie* (Oslo: Tiden, 2003). *Aftenposten* 5 November 2003. It would

have been more accurate to observe that it is many Europeans who actually say the same as their American counterparts.

44 Thoreau, "Slavery in Massachusetts," (1950), 674-675. My own quixotic protest took the form of declaring myself no longer a member of the Norwegian armed forces, where I had the rank of sergeant. American Studies made me a C.O. and took me to court.

45 About his experience as a key organizer of a series of Bicentennial conferences around the world in 1975 and 1976, Robin Winks, scholar and diplomat, has written, "Perhaps the diplomatic community had learned again that healthy criticism was valuable. Perhaps the scholarly community had learned that diplomats could be even-handed, that the government did not interfere with scholarship, that the United States was in fact the free country it boasted itself to be." Winks, ed., (1978), 11-12.

Absent Native Son

DAVID E. NYE

Rolf Lundén, Orm Øverland, Jørn Brøndal, Mark Lucarelli and I each came to American Studies by a different path. Rolf grew up in Sweden and discovered an interest in the United States; Orm and his family moved back and forth many times between Norway and North America. Jørn grew up in Denmark where he had native speakers of English in his family, and gradually his interest in history focused on the United States. Mark, like myself, received an education in American Studies in the United States and came to Scandinavia as an adult. We were not born into the outsider's or the comparative view, but acquired it through the force of circumstance.

In my case, this was hardly foreseeable. I seemed destined to be deeply embedded within American culture. My first American ancestor, Benjamin Nye, migrated from Sussex, England, to Cape Cod in 1636. He built a mill, now gone, but his solid house still stands in East Sandwich, Massachusetts. My personal sense of the United States begins with that two-story house with its many fireplaces, now maintained by a family association and open to tourists. Benjamin Nye had seven children, planting a vast family tree that includes thousands of descendants. Nyes fought in the American Revolution. Most were farmers, but some shipped out on whaling ships, like young Herman Melville, and some were on merchant ships, a few in the China trade. There is a southern branch of the family, too, some of whom owned slaves. Nyes fought on both sides in the Civil War. The Nyes did not become particularly wealthy or powerful, though a few became famous, notably

Edgar Wilson Nye (1850-1896), who is still remembered for a few quips, such as "Wagner's music is better than it sounds." A friend of Mark Twain's, and like him a platform speaker with a deadpan humor, he wrote a comic bestseller, *Bill Nye's History of the United States* (1894). The first line declares: "Facts in a nude state are not liable criminally, any more than bright and beautiful children commit a felony by being born thus..."[1] He went on to suggest that it was his duty as a (comic) historian to dress up the facts and make them more entertaining. Twain also knew James Warren Nye (1815-1876), whom Abraham Lincoln sent out from New York State to be the first territorial governor of Nevada, and to make sure it continued to side with the North during the Civil War. As recounted in *Roughing It*, Twain's brother worked as the secretary to Governor Nye, who ended his career as a Senator in Washington.

I mention these ancestors to suggest how easy it was for me as a child to identify with the development of the United States, intertwining my family past with the nation's history. Such a background provides advantages to the would-be Americanist, but it is also a handicap. I had to learn to see my ancestors and American history critically, first in the classroom, then during the protests of the Vietnam era, and finally by teaching abroad. Living for the last quarter century in Denmark, I have been simultaneously detached from and yet professionally engaged with the American scene, and have learned to see these ancestors more clearly.

Education
Born in Boston, Massachusetts in 1946, I spent my childhood in Pennsylvania, during the Eisenhower years. In 1959 my family moved north again, to Hartford, Connecticut. I entered college the year after John F. Kennedy was assassinated. World War Two pervaded American culture during my childhood, in comic books and toys, in the old newsreels on television, in the conversations of those who had served, and in the

political rhetoric. The Cold War likewise was a tension always already there, defining the political structure of the world. As the previous chapters have made clear, these tensions also shaped American Studies, as the emerging field sought to define the culture of the United States. Little wonder that during these Cold War years the field's research agenda focused on "the national character," "liberal consensus," immigrant assimilation, and the (supposedly weak) class system, while hopefully examining the prospects for "Negro progress" and integration. These themes likewise permeated the *New York Times*, which I was required to read each day as part of my education at the Lenox preparatory school.

Lenox was a boarding institution with no endowment. It was therefore absolutely without luxuries, an economic condition that was raised to a moral advantage in the theology of its headmaster, Reverend Curry. He hammered into us the values of spartan, muscular Christianity. We were to excel in sports, study hard, and embrace a life of service to others. This asceticism was further expressed in rigid rules against smoking and drinking (that we pretty much observed), and against swearing or having a radio (that we routinely ignored). Students wore coats and ties, and had a fixed routine of classes, sports, daily chapel, mandatory study halls, and meals. We each had a daily job to do, such as cleaning a latrine or a classroom. All beds had to be made before breakfast at 7 AM, and everyone had to be in bed with lights out at 10 PM. We could not leave the school grounds without permission, and when granted, it was for only one hour in the tiny town of Lenox, whose worldly temptations consisted of a single grocery store, a library, a newsstand, a small hardware store, and no coffee shop that I can recall.

The school motto – "Not to be served, but to serve." – was repeated in many of Curry's daily sermons. He embraced the Civil Rights movement, and, unlike many prep schools at the time, Lenox was integrated. Between my enrollment in

1959 and graduation in 1964 I heard many visiting African and African-American speakers, as well as some wonderful choirs from Black colleges in the South. The speaker at our graduation was an African bishop, who held forth for an hour on Christian ecumenicism and the social gospel.

Beneath this idealism and ideology of self-renunciation seethed the music of Bob Dylan and the early Beatles and a fascination with the forbidden joys of sex, booze, and cigarettes. Like other teenage boys, we competed for dominance and prestige. Prowess in sports counted for at least as much as brains. (Too small for football, too short for basketball, and unable to hit a good curve ball, I found my niche in fencing, where I eventually became captain.) We aspired to be "cool," which to us meant an emotionally detached and cynical attitude toward authority, coupled with the morbid, glamorous certainty that we would soon be incinerated in a nuclear war. Armed with adolescent nihilism, we planned to enjoy a few sinful pleasures, when not practicing the social gospel. We felt we understood Holden Caulfield and Huck Finn, and dreamed of escape. Before graduation we attained a bookish worldliness by reading *The Brothers Karamozov*, *The Trial*, and *A Farewell to Arms*. We longed for a jazz club in New York, the fabled wild parties of college, and travel abroad.

When I entered Amherst College in the fall of 1964, I was uncertain about whether to major in European history, anthropology, or perhaps English literature. I had never heard of American Studies, and I thought American history was far less interesting than European. But I found the European history survey a bore and English literature a bit stuffy. The following year the two-term survey of American Studies proved fascinating, as much for its method as for its content. I did not realize how gifted the faculty were. I assumed that across America other students also were being taught to approach history as a series of intractable problems of interpretation, to be understood from multiple points of view.

This approach took on a powerful immediacy in the second semester, which focused on the theme of war in American culture, taken in historical perspective, but leading up to the Vietnam War, which was escalating that spring (1966).[2] I was fortunate enough to have John William Ward as seminar leader for this course. A former US Marine and author of an influential study of Andrew Jackson, Ward eventually became President of Amherst and later still the head of the American Council of Learned Societies. In class, he was a persuasive Socratic questioner. The shadow of Vietnam dominated the last weeks of the course even more than the faculty might have expected, because the Amherst Trustees decided to give an honorary degree to the Secretary of Defense, Robert S. McNamara. In protest, many seniors came to graduation that year wearing black armbands and a few refused to accept their degrees. McNamara agreed to meet with students and faculty, and for an hour in a packed Johnson Chapel he answered questions, but seemed unmoved by arguments made against the war. I had the chance to ask one question myself, and, based on I. F. Stone's journalism, I challenged McNamara to prove that any evidence could document the so-called "domino theory". Stone had torn apart a Pentagon "white paper" which purported to document this theory. The argument I tried to sketch out in a few moments seemed to make no impression on McNamara, who had the serene self-confidence of the numbers-cruncher and professional manager. Thirty years later his memoirs revealed that he had doubts about the war too, but these did not shadow his public persona that day.[3]

It was a decorous meeting. We were all well dressed and polite in our disagreements. Almost no one had long hair yet, and the idea of the counter-culture did not exist in my mind in 1966. Nevertheless, the confrontation with McNamara was an intellectual earthquake. I was certain that this apparently well-meaning man was monstrously wrong, following a failed logic that led inexorably to wasted resources, loss of national prestige, the devastation of Vietnam, and the deaths of hundreds of thousands of men, women and children. But he got his honorary degree.

Deepening engagement with the conflicted politics of the time prepared me for the most important intellectual encounter of my Amherst years, Leo Marx's survey of American literature. He lectured on the Puritans, natural depravity, the attempts to define "what is an American" from Crévecoeur onwards, the pastoral dream of America, the madness of Ahab in *Moby Dick*, Thoreau's theory of civil disobedience, and Whitman's barbaric yawp heard over the rooftops of the world. For those of us taking the course, this literature often seemed to be a meta-commentary on the politics and society of our times. The generals in the Pentagon were our Ahabs, the leaders of the Civil Rights and anti-war movements our Thoreaus, and our best hope, it seemed, was to survive the coming apocalypse as the Ishmaels of our generation. This was not the thrust of Professor Marx's course, I hasten to add, which was quite simply the most inspiring and coherent set of lectures I had ever encountered, delivered with passion and ironic good humor in a wonderfully engaging voice.

My yearlong seminar with Henry Steele Commager was also extremely important, partly because of his truly encyclopedic knowledge. When Amherst was recruiting him from Columbia, he demanded and got an immense office, which also served as a seminar room for 20 students. Its walls were lined from floor to ceiling with hardbound books. We soon realized that he had not only read them, but recalled whole passages word for word. There was a density and complexity to his teaching, which often consisted of monologues inspired by the assigned reading in intellectual history. His musings might take us anywhere from the history of science to poetry about the Civil War to Constitutional questions or the opinions of European travelers about American slavery.

Wherever his thoughts happened to go, they traveled not in sentences but marched in full paragraphs with footnotes and cross-references. This kind of detailed knowledge is too little valued by our increasingly theory-driven education. If Ward and Marx had given me a passion for American studies, Commager charted an immense range of topics to master.

The Vietnam War not only dominated my college years but my graduate education at Minnesota as well, darkening and shaping my perceptions in a myriad ways. Some classmates were drafted. Some died. Immediately after college graduation I failed an army physical because I had recently been in a traffic accident, but I easily passed the second physical, three years later, and was found "eligible" for the draft. I then declared myself to be a conscientious objector, a choice that seemed the only logical alternative at the time. I had long been active in the anti-war movement, both in local marches and demonstrations, and in national protests against the war in Washington, DC. The students and graduate teaching assistants at Minnesota, I among them, went on strike several times, stopping all classes. I did not occupy any buildings, but I witnessed many confrontations with authorities. I saw a crowd of policemen severely beat a press photographer with nightsticks in broad daylight on campus. (On another occasion, I saw a group of bikers turn on one of their own and beat him senseless, on what had been, until then, a placid Sunday afternoon.) I attended rallies and heard anti-war speakers as varied as the improvisational Jerry Rubin and the buttoned-down Noam Chomsky.

The two professors whom I learned the most from were David W. Noble and Mulford Q. Sibley. Noble rivaled Marx in his oratorical skills and was a powerful interdisciplinary synthesizer. (It still pains me that they had a falling out after Marx wrote a critical review of one of Noble's books.[4]) Sibley, who became my dissertation advisor, had an incredibly open mind and was as widely read as Commager. He knew political philosophy literally from the Egyptians to the present, but ranged into many other areas, including psychology, utopian literature, and the history of religion.[5] With Sibley, I took a seminar on Plato, followed by tutorials in western political thought that lasted a year, including Hegel and Marx. He was the best Socratic questioner I have ever encountered, a quiet yet charismatic speaker, a prolific author, and a gentle but unswerving anti-war activist. John Ward, who had also studied with him, was hardly a man given to religious analogies, but he once told me straight out, "Sibley is the closest thing to a living saint."

With such mentors I passed through the Vietnam years, which began with the heady but ultimately absurd promise of a new kind of revolution from within the middle class, and ended in counter-revolution and Watergate. It also began as an age of abundance and ended in economic stagnation. The academic job market collapsed, and of the ten Minnesota people who finished their doctorates in American Studies in my year, only three immediately found academic appointments, myself among them. On both the personal and national level, these five years from 1969 until 1974 began with extravagant hope and ended in something close to despair. Allen Ginsberg's famous first line in *Howl* seemed no exaggeration: "I saw the best minds of my generation destroyed..." They were less likely to be destroyed by the drugs, easily available in the seedy West Bank neighborhood where I lived in Minneapolis, than by the tensions and distortions of the draft, the War, the peace movement, and the paranoia caused by undercover agents. Agents posing as students spied on both Noble and Sibley, a fact eventually reported in the newspapers.

Through it all I read avidly, immersing myself in the new social history, African-American culture, and American literature, as well as seminars in music history, structural anthropology, epistemology, and intellectual history. I embraced all of these subjects, but none of them directly suggested a thesis topic. Finally, I decided to write a dissertation on the male, Protestant culture of the 1920s, using three figures as touchstones: F. Scott Fitzgerald, Calvin Coolidge, and Henry Ford. At the outset I had an elaborate methodology and a complex argument that linked these three figures into larger patterns. But once I began reading, I soon found myself fascinated and repulsed by Ford. In retrospect, the choice seems foreordained, because only Ford offered me a way to fuse social and intellectual history with what I had come to regard as the central place of technology in American culture.

This interest in the social meanings of technology had many sources. My father was a mechanical engineer who took an interest in the history of industrialization. He was a member of the Society for the History of Technology, and I used to thumb through its journal on visits home. Leo Marx's central theme of the opposition between the machine and the garden was a second obvious and important source. In addition, I had written a long undergraduate paper comparing French and British industry in the eighteenth century. My directed readings with Sibley were also important. But the most obvious factor to me at the time was the highly technological way Americans were fighting the Vietnam War. In retrospect, I can also see that I was early fascinated by the material culture of industry and transportation, even if this interest was never addressed directly by a teacher. But these "origins" only seem obvious in retrospect.

Why Ford? A life is made of accidents as well as influences. In the summer of 1970, I drove from Minneapolis to the East coast in a decrepit Ford Falcon, along with Dieter, a German exchange student who was studying engineering and lived in the same apartment building. He had purchased the Falcon as a near wreck and restored it. We took a meandering route that went through Iowa, Wisconsin, Chicago, and Montreal. When we reached Detroit. I was all for pushing on into Canada, but Dieter stubbornly insisted we stop at a museum

I had never heard of. I gave in, and we went to see Henry Ford's Dearborn Village. In 1970 Ford was hardly a cultural icon for graduate students, especially students in American Studies. I was interested in the New Left not the Old Right, in workers not capitalists, in the anti-war movement not the assembly line. But at Ford's curious supermarket of history, I became deeply absorbed. I did not then and there decide to write my thesis about him, but the seed was planted. When I told friends about the trip, I recalled what a good time we had in Montreal and how US Immigration tore the Ford Falcon apart at the Vermont border looking for non-existent drugs. I had more hair then.

I had no formal training in the history of technology, a field that was only emerging as an academic discipline in the early 1970s. Consequently, my dissertation combined the tradition of myth and symbol scholarship with intellectual history, while drawing on such works as I could find on technology and culture. My idea of a successful career was to teach in a small college. I took no interest in publication when in graduate school beyond writing a few book reviews for the student newspaper, and I saw myself primarily as a teacher. Since then I have turned into a researcher, and to do so I had to continue educating myself, building on what I learned, particularly from Marx, Ward, Commager, Noble, and Sibley.

Early Research
If I gradually evolved into a specialist on technology in American culture, this was never my intention during graduate school. Instead, one of the main problems I wrestled with was the relationship between the individual life and history, and my first two books were about inventors who also were popular, public figures. A conventional historian would simply have written biographies. But the early American Studies movement had explicitly rejected biography during the 1950s.

The materials that conventionally had been used to write biographies instead served other purposes. Popular figures began to be studied as symbols, whose lives were ultimately less important than the values and ideas that the public believed their lives expressed. This approach still seemed attractive when I entered graduate school, but not by the time I was ready to write my dissertation. My first two books, each in its own way, expressed the radical discontinuity between what was mainstream American Studies in the 1960s and the post-structuralism of the 1970s.

My Amherst education had emphasized individuals far less than the concept of culture, as developed by cultural anthropology. Ward's *Andrew Jackson: Symbol for an Age* (1955) was one of the most successful early works in American Studies, and it remained in print for forty years after its appearance in 1955.[6] My dissertation on Ford and my anti-biography of Thomas Edison were a two-step response to this book. Ward had abandoned the biographical genre. He ignored General (and later President) Jackson as a private person, instead focusing on his public image. First, he showed that there was a remarkable consistency in the way that Americans regarded him, so that it was quite legitimate to see him as a representative figure. Ward was able to connect Jackson's public image to the writings of major orators, artists, and authors of the period, and to show how the same themes also emerged in politics, literature, painting, and landscaping practices. Second, he showed that much of this public representation of Andrew Jackson was historically debatable, somewhat inaccurate, or even incorrect. Third, Ward demonstrated that the public image of Jackson held together three mutually inconsistent ideas (about Nature, Providence, and Will), to form an unstable ideology. Looking back from the 1970s, Cecil Tate argued that Ward had invented an American form of structuralism.[7] As in the work of Claude Levi-Strauss, people thought in terms of symbols rather than facts, and heroic figures, such as Jackson, mediated between and contained contradictory elements. Their public biographies were best evaluated not in terms of historical accuracy, but rather as cultural myths.

In the late 1960s Ward, Marx, Henry Nash Smith, and R. W. B. Lewis were identified as the central figures in the "myth and symbol" school. It was not a term that any of them favored or endorsed as a self-description. Indeed, there was never a conference or a manifesto that self-consciously proclaimed this to be a school of thought. Rather, the label was invented largely as part of the repudiation of their approach, which was (mistakenly, I believe) attacked for being "elitist" and "unscientific." Most of the critiques of Smith, Ward and Marx missed the complexity of their approaches to history and literature.[8]

My selection of Ford as dissertation topic immediately suggested revisions I would need to make to Ward's method. He had treated Jackson's career from the vantage point of his death, and his book assumed a cultural unity that varied little over Jackson's lifetime. This cultural unity was arguably expressed by early nineteenth century media, which were still primarily local and not yet linked together into a national system of wire services and newspaper chains, in an age before professional public relations. In contrast, Ford's public images emerged in a different media environment, and the unities of culture, of time, and of reception that Ward could assume for 1840, did not exist in 1920. The first half of my *Henry Ford: Ignorant Idealist* would show how American society saw him as a quite different figure in 1912 than in 1922 or 1932. There was no unity or coherence. The second half of the book then examined how Ford looked at the world, and showed how the private man was vastly different from any of the public personas.

By the time I had completed my dissertation, however, I was questioning its fundamental opposition between the public and the private. After reading Hayden White, Roland Barthes, Michel Foucault, and Jacques Derrida, I had begun to question the ability of words or images to represent anything accurately.[9] I had begun to wonder if the individual was in fact a useful unit of analysis. The death of the author was widely declared. Could one also declare the death of the public figure? The individual increasingly seemed less important than the circulation of signs and texts through society. Could an inventor's laboratory perhaps be seen as a place where different codes intersected and collided?

Bearing these questions in mind, when I began to work on Thomas Edison, I looked with suspicion at all forms of documentation. I became highly aware of how each archive was organized to encourage particular kinds of interpretation. As before, I was intrigued by public images, but the Edison image seemed to be even more deeply fractured and contradictory than Ford's. I found no less than eight different Edisons prominent in the press of the 1870s and 1880s. I did not know quite what to do with these many figures, until I had dinner with Fredric Jameson, who had graciously read the draft of one chapter.[10] He suggested that I develop the manuscript using the semiotics of A. J. Greimas's,[11] which offered a way to explain the patterns of opposition that I had already discovered empirically.[12] Ward had found his own version of structuralism, and now, it seemed, I had (re)discovered the semiotic square and could use it to deconstruct Edison into binary patterns.[13]

Indeed, I found many intriguing uses for this form of analysis. For example, as the inventor of the phonograph, Edison was often asked to demonstrate it. The early machine could not only record, but play back, and one could even record on top of an earlier recording, creating a verbal collage. On one occasion, Edison first read a poem in a low voice into the phonograph and then recorded comments on the poem in a high voice. The resulting text ran like this:

> A soldier of the legion lay dying in Algiers. **(Oh, shut up!)**
> There was a lack of woman's nursing, there was a dearth of women's tears. **(Oh, give us a rest!)**
> But a comrade stood beside him while his lifeblood ebbed away, **(Oh, what are you giving us!)**
> And bent with pitying glances to hear what he might say. **(Oh, you can't recite poetry!)**
> The dying soldier faltered and he took the comrade's hand **(Police! Police!)**
> And he said: "I never more shall see my own, my native land." **(Oh, put him out!)**[14]

The contrast between the poem and the commentary, emphasized by the bass and falsetto voices, suggests the tension between the working-class culture of Edison's laboratory and the middle-class values of his home. The invention literally mediates between these two realms, giving Edison a way to express both cultures, and at the same time the chance to stand to one side and laugh at the clash of cultural codes. One could even say that the inventor of the phonograph anticipated sampling and developed a Victorian form of rap.

Edison cannot be associated exclusively with one voice (however attractive for psychologists) or with working class protest against gentility (however attractive for a labor historians). Instead, Edison adopted a series of contradictory masks or disguises. One of the early biographies observed that, "He takes great delight in imitating the lingo of the New York street gamin. A dignified person named James may be greeted with. "Hully Gee! Chimy, when did youse blow in?" He likes to mimic and imitate types, generally that are distasteful to him. The sanctimonious hypocrite, the sleek speculator, and others...."[15] Edison authorized the biography where this anecdote appeared, and clearly wanted his playfulness and irreverence to be remembered. He knew that he was a man of contradictions.[16]

My anti-biography of Edison was itself a cultural artifact of post-modernism. By the time it appeared Greimas, Barthes, Foucault, and Derrida all had begun to decline in importance in Europe, even if inside the United States they would remain fashionable for at least another decade. Moreover, there was to be no radical shift in the writing of either history or biography during the 1980s. Disciplinary boundaries proved too strong for deconstruction, and historians kept on writing much as they had before, as though the realist novel of c. 1880 remained the last word in literary experimentation. Furthermore, in 1985 students in the newly emerging fields of gender, ethnicity, and race were looking for their own heroic figures and role models, not for ways to deconstruct them.

And as for me, armed with a sense of the limits of representation and the many ways that one might write history, I turned away from anything like biography, to write a series of books on the social history of American technology. It turned out that my iconoclastic attack on the biographical genre had by no means been a waste of time. Writing *The Invented Self* had been like mastering a complex set of gymnastic exercises, and afterwards I found it easier to conceive, outline, and execute other books that were a little less unconventional.

Union College
The work on Ford and Edison preoccupied me during my first job at Union College, in Schenectady, New York. When I arrived in late summer, 1974, I considered myself extremely fortunate to have a position at all, let alone at a small college in the East, and imagined staying there for my entire career. But it was not to be. The new faculty hired in 1974 were shaped by Vietnam protest, rock music, and the counter culture. We looked different than the older faculty, sporting longer hair and looser clothing. We did not wear neckties

or horn rim glasses. And these outward signs suggested attitudes that many older faculty found anathema. There was an enormous generation gap between those who had finished their Ph.D.'s before c. 1970 (and who had therefore been undergraduates in the fifties and early sixties), and those who completed their doctorates just a few years later.

The combination of this generation gap with the demographics of university life in the middle 1970s was fatal. The baby boomers (as students) had come and gone, and small colleges faced years of stagnant or falling enrollments. Administrations not only hired fewer new people, but they made it harder to get tenure. The majority of the American Studies Ph.D.s in my generation taught for only a few years before being squeezed out of education in one way or another. Those who survived were not necessarily the best. We were the most stubborn. Union College ruled that no more than a certain percentage (I believe it was 60 or 65 %) of any department could hold tenure. In order not to lose bright young faculty who exceeded this limit, Union invented the new job classification of "tenurable," which meant that faculty they wanted to retain after six years received not tenure but four-year renewable contracts.[17] On arrival, I was the only assistant professor in history. Ahead of me were three people who already had these "tenurable" four-year contracts. I calculated that to get tenure I would have to wait at least 15 years. The insecurity of such a system, aggravated by the generation gap, boded ill. In my first term, the English Department decided that two faculty were not eligible even for a four-year contract. Two years later it fired both of their replacements. With American Studies faculty coming and going through such a revolving door, Union was less about ideas than about insecurity and survival.

It dawned on me that focusing on building up an American Studies program and on teaching, rather than doing research, was the sure road to unemployment. Most of the work that I did for "the good of the college," such as administer American Studies, read applications for the Admissions Office, or sing in a madrigal group, had no value on the job market. Beyond the college gates, only publications counted. In the second year I therefore put myself on a rigorous program of twenty hours of research and writing every week, much of it on weekends. By the time I left Union in 1981, I had published my dissertation (1979), a short history of the Youth Conservation Corps (1981), and a catalog of the General Electric Photographic Archives (1981). I had also written the Edison anti-biography, though I did not have a publisher. This work completed my alienation from Union's tenured faculty. They were not in sympathy with these winds of intellectual change. Several university presses also thought my anti-biography rather strange and turned it down, accompanied by requests for a conventional biography instead. This I refused to do, turning instead to a quite different book, on photography at General Electric. This project finally released me from Union, as I received a National Endowment for the Humanities research grant that allowed me in 1981-1982 to go as a visiting scholar to both Harvard and MIT. I never had to undergo a tenure review just to become "tenurable."

In Cambridge I found a lively cohort of other scholars on research grants to talk to. For the first time, and as it has turned out, also for the last time, I was surrounded for a year by scholars working on technology and culture. Leo Marx had left Amherst and helped to found MIT's Science, Technology, and Society program, and his presence made both the transition and personal introductions easier. The famous Thomas Kuhn was there, when not jetting off to give another lecture on his influential studies of scientific revolutions. And Kenneth Keniston, the sociologist of youth cultures, chatted amiably about an enormous range of topics, while down the hall Merritt Roe Smith seemed to know everything about nineteenth-century machines and their social implications.

The young faculty were just as impressive, including David F. Noble, Sherry Terkel, and Chuck Sabel, who won a McArthur Award at the end of that year. In addition, there was a parade of lecturers at Harvard's History of Science Department. Each, it seemed, had completed an important book just last week. After the heavy course load of teaching at Union, where I did all my writing late at night, on weekends, or during vacations, the year in Cambridge was academic paradise.

In May, with my grant running out, I accepted a foreign lecturer position at Odense University in Denmark. I had briefly visited Denmark twice, and I had recollections of lively cities and bucolic, summer landscapes. But I knew almost nothing about what lay ahead. I sold or stored my furniture, shipped a few boxes of books, and bought a one-way airline ticket. I expected to be away for two years. That was twenty-five years ago.

Expatriation
Expatriation opens up a space between the individual and a new cultural world. That space can be the source of creative growth or it can be a realm of dissociation. The expatriate must live in the diffuse region between two cultures and is never in more danger than when he or she imagines himself or herself integrated into the adopted nation. This can be particularly true in a country such as Denmark, where cultural differences are not as obvious as they would be for a white American in Asia or Africa. Yet even in Denmark all surfaces reflect back subtle differences – in the interior layout of a bus, in the organization of time, in the way that strangers meet.

At the beginning, I lived in a state of intense surface awareness, and in this state tried to answer the inevitable, ever-repeated question, "How do you like Denmark?" There can be no satisfying answer, but a polite one is necessary, and I would say something complimentary or ironic, depending on the occasion. Gradually, the country assumed a complexity, fullness, and an immediacy that could only be expressed in hundreds of peculiarities, so that the question became absurd. Denmark had become a complete world of islands and peninsulas, provincial towns and cities, regional dialects and social classes, a realm where an expatriate discriminates between many things, and so the question becomes the unanswerable equivalent of, "What do you think of your life?" Yet, Danes kept asking the question for years, as though I had only just arrived, and by asking it they declared that I was still an outsider. But for me, the real question became, "If I go back, what will I think of the United States?"

Since, as often as not, the questioner merely wants to make conversation, the expatriate develops pat answers. I said that I was in Denmark because I had a chance to work here, because the job I was offered was better than any position I could get in the United States in 1982, because I thought it was interesting to live in Europe, or because family lore maintains that ancestral Nyes migrated from Denmark to England in the fourteenth century, before Benjamin Nye came to Massachusetts in 1636. All these replies were true, but none was the truth. Worse, as I repeated these answers, they took on the ritual quality of some dead liturgy. The real question was not whether I would stay. What are the terms under which it is possible to live in another cultural world where, no matter how well one learns the language or studies the society, one will always bear the mark of the stranger? In Denmark, where there is far less geographical mobility than in the United States, this foreignness is pronounced because Danes have friends for life, starting in their earliest years. Their families are less scattered than American families, and the resulting dense texture of social life makes it exceedingly hard to get inside. Professional associates of decades may never invite colleagues home, for example, as they maintain a firm distinction between work and private life. The image of Danish social life, for the outsider, can easily be that of the empty weekend streets where no cars move, no people appear, and a profound silence reigns from Saturday afternoon until Monday morning. The newcomer has little access to the private, weekend world, but he or she must try to be self-sufficient until the next week begins. And every evening is a smaller version of the weekend.

The expatriate must therefore have some inner resource, some work, hobby, or passion that fills these hours, that makes them not a period of boredom, but an opportunity to read, to write, to work. Eventually, the social circle widens, but far more slowly than in the United States. Danes almost never introduce one friend to another, even when a group of people meet accidentally in the street. They seldom seek to bring like-minded people together, nor do they fill large rooms with strangers for freewheeling cocktail parties. Each connection had to be carefully made and developed on one's own.

Immersion in a foreign social system changes the relationship of a scholar to his work, particularly if writing about the United States. After decades in Denmark, I cannot think in quite the same way about American history as I did before I came. I can still see it from inside, but I can also view it from the outside, from an older context, and from a country with an extensive system of social welfare. Each of these changes makes a difference. Viewing the United States from beyond its borders throws the borders themselves into question. The naturalness of boundaries is an artifice of every culture, reinforced by seeing the weather map on the nightly news. From Europe, the shape of the United States begins to look accidental, even temporary, rather than fixed or given. This sense of possible flux appears all the stronger in the light of Danish history, since the area controlled by the Danes has fluctuated tremendously over the past one thousand years. Once it was one of the great powers of Europe, possessing at various times half of England, most of Sweden and Norway, parts of northern Germany and parcels of real estate in the Baltic States. Today Denmark is but a remnant of its former imperial self, having lost all this as well as Iceland during World War II, though it still controls Greenland and the Færoe Islands. No one can long study the decline of such an empire without wondering what the United States might look like in two hundred years.

When I arrived, Denmark stood on what was then called "the front line" of NATO, which made me constantly aware of the larger set of boundaries then drawn between East and West. With East Germany only a hop across the water, the Cold War could never be far from one's mind. And since Denmark was a rather uneasy NATO partner, refusing, for example, to allow nuclear weapons on its soil or in its ports, the East-West border itself looked less solid than it had when living far away in the United States. This instability of borders became even more obvious with the break-up of the Soviet Union. My point is not that any of these events directly transformed my research, but they did shape my teaching, as they subtlety reframed my thinking. For example, I reflected on how during the colonial period only some North American colonies chose to join the Revolution. What if Jamaica or Nova Scotia had made common cause with Virginia and Massachusetts? And rather than think only of why the Americans won, I began to ponder how and why the British lost.

The age of European societies, likewise, forces any historian to rethink the American experience. While the too-often repeated Danish remark that the United States has no history exaggerates the point (and ignores Native-Americans), certainly there is a vast difference between a society primarily created by immigrants during the last 500 years, which has written records for every time period, and a European society whose roots go back thousands of years, before Christianity, before the invention of writing, before the idea of history itself. These differences do not register in obvious ways, but they exert a quiet pressure on experience. In Denmark the existence of a monarchy, of people with noble rank, of an established church, or of any number of other institutions strange to an American, all remain unquestioned, accepted parts of life. It is impossible to rouse a discussion on the topic of abolishing noble ranks, or tax support for the church. There are virtually no republicans calling for an end to the monarchy.

Danish social life is far more settled than in the United States, a fact made obvious in such things as the fixed seating plans and length of dinner parties, the imposition of closing hours on shops, and the ritual quality of vacation times that are fixed in July for almost everyone. And yet, Danish society in other ways is radically advanced in comparison to most. It has a more extensive system of welfare services than virtually anywhere else, and the United Nations gives it a higher rating than the US on its quality of life index. No one is denied medical care or ambulance service because they cannot afford it. The state sends people to clean the homes, wash the hair, and deliver meals to the elderly. All education is not only free, but all university students qualify for state scholarships, which, though barely enough to meet expenses, certainly make it possible for anyone to attend. There are social classes, but they are harder to see than in America. There is some poverty, but its discovery is a public scandal. There are only sixty murders committed each year in a population of 5 million, and the police solve virtually all these crimes. There are ten times as many murders in Pittsburgh or Detroit during a year, and a great many of them are never solved. In Denmark handguns are completely illegal. Living in a more egalitarian and largely secure world, I cannot see the United States as I used to. Its corporations look far more powerful and dangerous to individual liberty, its skewed division of wealth appears more unjustifiable, its over-reliance on automobiles seems an individualistic cul-de-sac – one could go on for many pages with such a list.

These cultural contrasts register in my work, both as a teacher and as a scholar. In teaching I address Danes about my own country, which forces me constantly to rethink the nation's history and institutions in comparative terms. In my writing, the comparisons are not as explicit. The subjects may be the same as those I would have tackled had I never become an expatriate, but I see them differently. I do not write as a Dane would about the United States, but neither do I write as an American would at home.

Foreign residence makes some features of the United States stand out, but other features look less dramatic in comparative perspective. Too often, American historians write as if US injustices and problems were larger and more difficult than elsewhere. The McCarthy witch hunts, for example, which I condemn as much as anyone, look rather tame when set beside the frequent, systematic denials of human liberties that have occurred in Europe. Or, to take another example, the achievements of the American women's movement seem less radical when seen from a Scandinavian perspective, where women have already been prime ministers in Norway and Iceland, and could easily become so in Denmark and Sweden. Living in Scandinavia challenges the common American tendency to assume that the United States is at the cutting edge, leading everyone else. From Scandinavia, the US can look rather backward and inefficient in such areas as public safety, medical care, transportation, energy use, and urban design.

Stimulated by a foreign environment and buoyed by a modicum of job security, I began my most fruitful period of scholarly work. This began with the publication of my anti-biography of Edison by Odense University Press, which sold rather well. Then, between 1985 and 1998 I completed five works: *Image Worlds: Corporate Identities at General Electric* (1985), a study of photography as ideology; *Electrifying America* (1990), a social and cultural history of the adoption of electrification; *American Technological Sublime* (1994), an analysis of an almost ineffable, yet recurrent public emotion; *Consuming Power* (1997) a history of American energy (over)consumption; and a collection of essays, *Narratives and Spaces: Technology and the Construction of American Culture* (1998). In none of these works are individuals the organizing principle; personal stories do not carry the burden of these narratives. Indeed, I do not even offer a thumbnail sketch of particular individuals. A focus on biography would have made it harder to conceive of books such as *Image Worlds, Electrifying America*, or *American Technological Sublime*. Thus my scholarship between c. 1983 and 1998 resolutely avoided a biographical approach to history and culture, as I quietly kept faith with *The Invented Self*.

Living in Denmark was important to my writing, partly because cultural aesthetics vary. In *American Technological Sublime* I found myself drawn to features of the American landscape that were missing in Denmark, notably spectacular electric lighting, national parks, rocket launches, and sublime landscapes such as the Grand Canyon and Niagara Falls. Likewise, the lack of public transport and the over-reliance on the automobile are familiar themes to any American historian, but they take on added resonance and meaning when seen from a country whose public transport genuinely makes it unnecessary to have a car. Furthermore, American individualism extends at times to absurd lengths, notably in the wasteful practice of putting furnaces in each American home. Danes mostly rely on centralized heat and hot water systems, which are more energy efficient, cheaper, and less polluting. Such contrasts led to me write *Consuming Power* in an effort to understand why Americans are the world's largest per capita consumers of coal, oil, and natural gas. In writing each book, I found that living outside the United States was a creative stimulus to framing the project and to asking new questions. But in each case I also found it essential to do some of the research while in the United States.

If living abroad can fructify intellectual work, however, the expatriate remains caught in a space between two worlds. One may be tempted to seek an impossible submergence in a foreign culture or to retreat to the sanctuary of the old familiar world of the United States. But this choice does not remain static over time. The longer one is away, the harder it becomes to return home to an ever-changing America, where friends constantly move to new jobs, new homes, and new horizons, where family members grow old and begin to pass away, and nieces and nephews are born and grow up whom one scarcely knows. One remains in a precarious middle, vacillating between two languages and sensibilities. This ambiguous position can become the basis for an international point of view. I resist the classifications and mental organizations of both the United States and Denmark, and instead try to understand each culture as a complex whole. What I think of either nation cannot be easily summarized as a result. Ultimately, one feels like an anthropologist in each place; neither inside nor outside, neither alienated from nor fully integrated into either society, which both ceaselessly become more complex and engaging. Thus I learned to understand the United States – and American Studies – as that most privileged of outsiders, the absent native son.

James Baldwin got it right in *Nobody Knows My Name* (1961) when he declared that Americans abroad discover a deeper kinship than they are able to see when immersed in the United States. "The fact that I was the son of a slave and they were the sons of free men meant less, by the time we confronted each other on European soil, than the fact that we were both searching for our separate identities." (18) This is true. But Baldwin did not stay long enough in France; he did not immerse himself deeply in its culture. Perhaps he never met many European Americanists, who were rather scarce in 1959. In any case, he mistakenly concluded that Americans abroad "knew more about each other than any European ever could." (18)

It has been the burden of this book to declare just the reverse, to say that the United States cannot hope to understand itself solely through internal debate and self-referential discussion, whether at home or among expatriates abroad. Only through comparative study, only through seeing the US simultaneously from outside and inside, only from developing the stereo vision this effort requires – and evinced in the essays printed here – will it be possible to move American Studies beyond the acrimonious and futile debates of the last decade toward a more open, international, and comparative field.

Notes
1 Full text at – http://djm.cc/library/Bill_Nyes_History_of_the_US_edited.pdf
2 On the Amherst curriculum during these years, see Guttmann, (1970).
3 McNamara, (1996).
4 Marx's review of *The American Adam in the New World Garden* (1969), 1724-1725
5 Sibley (1970).
6 Ward also used his method to analyze Charles Lindberg in an often-reprinted essay about the public reception of his famous flight from New York to Paris in 1927. See Ward, (1969).
7 Tate, (1973).
8 One of the first critics of the "school" was Kuklick (1972), pp. 435-450. See also Marx, "Afterword," *The Machine in the Garden* (2000).
9 Particularly, the following works affected my thinking in the early 1970s, as they appeared around the time I completed my dissertation. White, *Metahistory* (1973), Barthes, *Mythologies* (1969), S/Z, (1972) and *Image, Music Text*, (1977), Derrida, *Of Grammatology* (1977), and Foucault, *The Archaeology of Knowledge* (1976).
10 Fredric Jameson was also kind enough to correspond with me about the project. At this time he was primarily known

for *Marxism and Form* (1971) and *The Prison House of Language* (1972). His own use of Greimas can be seen in *The Political Unconscious: Narrative as Socially Symbolic Act* (1981).

11 For an introduction, see A. J. Greimas, *Du Sens: Essais Sémiotiques*, (1970).

12 Building on the work of Vladimir Propp and Ferdinand de Saussure, Greimas had argued that any pair of contrary terms (x and y) can become the basis for a sign system. Each of the contrary terms could be negated (-x and -y), yielding a semiotic square.

13 For example, it permitted me to understand Edison's public images within two organized patterns. Each located the inventor within a system of possibilities. The first set of oppositions showed how an inventor, who manipulated materials to produce fundamentally new things, was often regarded as either extremely intelligent (scientist) or lucky (a tinkerer). Such an inventor operated within an ordinary, natural framework. Alternatively, however, an inventor could be regarded as having some sort of supernatural powers. In the Victorian age many people were fascinated with ghosts, spirit rappings, and the possibility that human beings might evolve new senses or acquire new powers. Such concerns suggested two additional Edison figures, one who seemed an alchemist, who tinkered with supernatural forces, the other a masterful wizard whose imagination penetrated directly to the secrets of nature. Indeed, Edison was commonly referred to as "the wizard of Menlo Park." All four of these public "Edisons" could be found in the newspapers and magazines of c. 1880. See Nye, *The Invented Self* (1983).

14 Jehl, (1939), 157.

15 Dyer, *et al.* Vol. II (1929), 774.

16 Edison was married twice, to two quite different kinds of women. The first was shy and lower middle class. After she died, the second was socially adept, well educated, and upper class. (And yet, even these generalizations make me uneasy, for these women were surely as complex as Edison.) He had six children, three by each wife. One of them, his namesake,

committed suicide. Another, by the second wife, became Governor of New Jersey. So was he a bad father or a good father? Biographers invariably find the unity they set out to discover, but I found that it was just as easy to find irresolvable contradictions.

17 The American Association of University Professors (AAUP) criticized this practice, which was at variance with virtually all other universities in the United States.

Bibliography

This bibliography includes all texts cited in this volume. It is organized according to the English alphabet. As a result, words beginning with the Scandinavian vowels, "æ" and "å" are found under the letter "a," while "ø", may be found under "o."

Åhnebrink, Lars. *Amerika och Norden*. Publications of the Nordic Association for American Studies No. 1 (Stockholm: Almqvist & Wiksell, 1964).

Åkerman, Sune. "From Stockholm to San Francisco. The Development of the Historical Studies of External Migration," in *Annales Academiæ Regiæ Scientiarum Upsaliensis* 19, Stockholm 1975, 5-46.

Åkerman, Sune, "Theories and Methods of Migration Research," in Harold Runblom and Hans Norman, eds. *From Sweden to America: A History of Migration.* (Uppsala: Acta Universitatis Upsaliensis, 1976) 19-75.

Åkerman, Sune, Bo Kronberg and Thomas Nilsson. "Emigration, Family, and Kinship," *American Studies in Scandinavia* 9 (1977), 105-122.

Alba, Richard. *Ethnic Identity: The Transformation of White America*. (New Haven: Yale University Press, 1990).

Alm, Martin. "America and the Future of Sweden: Americanization as Controlled Modernization," *American Studies in Scandinavia* 35:2 (Autumn 2003), 64-72.

Ander, O. Fritiof. "Immigrationshistorians utveckling i Amerika," *Historisk Tidskrift* (Stockholm), 81 (1961), 289-304.

Anderson, Benedict. *Imagined Communities: Reflections on the Origin and Spread of Nationalism*. (London: Verso, 1991, second edition).

Anderson, Philip J. and Dag Blanck, eds. *Swedes in the Twin Cities: Immigrant Life and Minnesota's Urban Frontier.* (Uppsala: Uppsala University Library, 2001).

Anderson, Philip J. and Dag Blanck, eds. *Swedish-American Life in Chicago: Cultural and Urban Aspects of an Immigrant People, 1850-1930.* (Uppsala: Acta Universitatis Upsaliensis, 1991).

Anderson, Rasmus B. *America Not Discovered by Columbus. A Historical Sketch of the Discovery of America by the Norsemen in the Tenth century.* (Chicago: S.C. Griggs and Company, 1874).

Appleby, Joyce, Lynn Hunt and Margaret Jacob. *Telling the Truth About History.* (New York: Norton, 1994).

ASA Newsletter, 29:3 (September 2006), pp. 32-34.

Atteberry, Jennifer Eastman, *Up in the Rocky Mountains: Writing the Swedish Immigrant Experience.* (Minneapolis: University of Minnesota Press, 2007).

Atwood, Margaret. "In Search of *Alias Grace*: On Writing Canadian Historical Fiction," *American Historical Review* 103:5 (December 1998), 1504.

Babcock, Kendrick C. *The Scandinavian Element in the United States.* (Urbana: University of Illinois, 1914).

Baldwin, James. *Nobody Knows My Name.* (New York: Dell, 1961).

Baldwin, James. *Notes of a Native Son.* (New York: Bantam, 1955).

Barth, Fredrik. "Introduction," in Barth, ed. *Ethnic Groups and Boundaries: The Social Organization of Culture Difference.* (Bergen: Oslo Universitetsforlaget, 1969).

Barthes, Roland. *Image, Music Text.* (New York: Hill and Wang, 1977).

Barthes, Roland. *Mythologies.* (New York: Hill and Wang, 1969).

Barthes, Roland. S/Z. (New York: Hill and Wang, 1972).

Barton, H. Arnold. "Clio and Swedish America," in Nils Hasselmo, ed. *Perspectives on Swedish Immigration. Proceedings of the International Conference on the Swedish Heritage in the Upper Midwest, April 1-3, 1976.* (Duluth, Minnesota: University of Minnesota Press, 1978), 3-24.

Barton, H. Arnold. "The Editor's Corner: Where Do We Now Stand?" *Swedish Pioneer Historical Quarterly* 29 (1978), 159-161.

Barton, H. Arnold. *A Folk Divided: Homeland Swedes and Swedish Americans, 1840-1940*. (Carbondale: Southern Illinois University Press, 1994).

Barton, H. Arnold. *A Folk Divided: Homeland Swedes and Swedish Americans 1840-1940*. (Uppsala: Studia Multiethnica, 1994.)

Barton, H. Arnold. *Letters from the Promised Land: Swedes in America. 1840-1914*. (Minneapolis: University of Minnesota Press, 1975).

Baudrillard, Jean. *America*. (London: Verso, 1989).

Beijbom, Ulf. "Swedish-American Research: Its Standing Today and Perspectives for Tomorrow," *Swedish-American Historical Quarterly* 34: 2 (1983), 153-170.

Beijbom, Ulf. *Swedes in America: Intercultural and Interethnic perspectives on contemporary research – A report of the Symposium Swedes in America: New Perspectives*. (Växjö: The Swedish Emigrant Institute, 1993).

Beijbom, Ulf. *Swedes in Chicago. A Demographic and Social Study of the 1846-1880 Immigration*. (Växjö: Läromedelsförlagen, 1971).

Bender, Henning, "The Danes Worldwide Archives 1932-1992," in Birgit Flemming Larsen and Henning Bender, eds. *Danish Emigration to the U.S.A.* (Aalborg: Danes Worldwide Archives, 1992).

Benson, Lee. *The Concept of Jacksonian Democracy: New York As a Test Case*. (Princeton: Princeton University Press, New Jersey, 1961).

Bergland, Betty A. "Norwegian Immigrants and "Indianerne" in the Landtaking, 1838-1862," *Norwegian-American Studies* 35 (2000), 319-350.

Bjork, Kenneth O. *Saga in Steel and Concrete: Norwegian Engineers in America*. (Northfield, Minnesota: Norwegian-American Historical Association, 1947).

Bjork, Kenneth O. *West of the Great Divide: Norwegian Migration to the Pacific Coast, 1847-1893*. (Northfield, Minnesota: Norwegian-American Historical Association, 1958).

Blanck, Dag. "Five Decades of Research of Swedish Immigration to North America." In P. Sture Ureland and Iain Clarkson, eds.

Language Contact across the North Atlantic. (Tübingen: Max Niemeyer Verlag, 1996.)

Blanck, Dag. *Becoming Swedish-American: The Construction of an Ethnic Identity in the Augustana Synod, 1860-1917.* (Uppsala: Uppsala University, 1997).

Blanck, Dag. Review of Jon Gjerde, *The Minds of the West,* in *American Studies in Scandinavia* 32:1 (Winter, 2000), 117-118.

Blanck, Dag. *The Creation of an Ethnic Identity: Being Swedish American in the Augustana Synod, 1860-1917.* (Carbondale, Southern Illinois University Press, 2006).

Blegen, Theodore. *Norwegian Migration to America 1825-1860.* (Northfield, Minnesota: Norwegian-American Historical Association, 1931).

Blegen, Theodore. *Norwegian Migration: The American Transition.* (Northfield, Minnesota, 1940).

Bobjerg, A. *En dansk Nybygd i Wisconsin. 40 Aar i Storskoven (1869-1909).* (Copenhagen: G. E. C. Gad, 1909).

Bodnar, John. *The Transplanted: A History of Immigrants in Urban America.* (Bloomington, Indiana: Indiana University Press, 1985).

Bredmose Simonsen, Henrik. *Kampen om danskheden: Tro og nationalitet i de danske kirkesamfund i Amerika.* (Århus: Århus Universitetsforlag, 1990).

Brøndal, Jørn. "Immigration and Immigration Law," in George T. Kurian *et al.* eds. *Encyclopedia of American Studies*, vol. 2. (New York: Grolier Educational, 2001), 334-339.

Brøndal, Jørn. "Woman's Place in a New World: Scandinavian Visions, c. 1850-1900," in Russell Duncan and Clara Juncker, eds. *Transnational America: Contours of US Culture.* (Copenhagen: Museum Tusculanum, 2004), 173-188.

Brøndal, Jørn. *Ethnic Leadership and Midwestern Politics: Scandinavian Americans and the Progressive Movement in Wisconsin, 1890-1914.* (Northfield, Minnesota: Norwegian-American Historical Association, 2004).

Brooks, Van Wyck. "America's Coming of Age," in *Three Essays on America.* (New York: E.P. Dutton, 1934; first published, 1915).

Brye, David L. "Wisconsin Scandinavians and Progressivism, 1900-1950," *Norwegian-American Studies* 27 (1977), 163-193.
Bryn, Steinar. *Norsk Amerikabilete: Om amerikanisering av norsk kultur.* (Oslo: Det Norske Samlaget, 1992).
Buell, Lawrence. "Circling the Spheres: A Dialogue." *American Literature* 70:3 (1998, 465-90.
Bungert, Hans, "Importing the United States, Exporting Internationalism: The First Forty Years of the EAAS, 1954-1994," in: Kristiaan Versluys, ed., *The Insular Dream: Obsession and Resistance* (Amsterdam: VU University Press, 1995).
Burke, Peter. *History and Social Theory.* (Cambridge: Polity Press, 1992).
Buslett, Ole A. "The Road to Golden Gate" in Marc Shell and Werner Sollors, eds. *The Multilingual Anthology of American Literature: A Reader of Original Texts with English Translations.* (New York: New York University Press, 2000), 416-459.
Carlsson, Sten. "Chronology and Composition of Swedish Emigration to America," in Harald Runblom and Hans Norman, eds. *From Sweden to America. A History of the Migration.* (Uppsala: Acta Universitatis Upsaliensis, 1976), 114-129.
Carlsson, Sten. "Från familjeutvandring till ensamutvandring. En utvecklingslinje i den svenska emigrationens historia," in Magnus von Platen, ed. *Emigrationer. En bok till Vilhelm Moberg 20.8.1968.* (Stockholm: A. Bonnier, 1968), 101-122.
Carter, Dale. Review of John Carlos Rowe, ed. *Post-Nationalist American Studies. The NAAS Newsletter* (Spring-Summer 2002), 10-12.
Cavling, Henrik. *Fra Amerika*. 2 volumes. (Copenhagen: Gyldendal, 1897).
Chabon, Michael. *The Amazing Adventures of Kavalier and Clay.* (New York: Random House, 2000).
Cheyfitz, Eric. "What Work Is There for Us to Do? American Literary Studies or Americas Cultural Studies?" *American Literature* 67:4 (Fall,1995), 843-53.
Choldin, Harvey M. "Kinship Networks in the Migration Process," *International Migration Review* 7: 22 (Summer 1973).

Commager, Henry Steele, and Elmo Giordanetti. *Was America a Mistake?* (New York: Harper and Row, 1967).
Commager, Henry Steele, ed. *Immigration and American History: Essays in Honor of Theodore C. Blegen.* (Minneapolis: University of Minnesota Press, 1961).
Conzen, Kathleen Neils, David A. Gerber, Ewa Morawska, George E. Pozzetta, and Rudolph J. Vecoli. "The Invention of Ethnicity: A Perspective from the U.S.A," *Journal of American Ethnic History*, 12 (1992), 3-41.
Conzen, Kathleen Neils. "Commentary," in Odd Lovoll, ed. *Scandinavians and Other Immigrants in Urban America: The Proceedings of a Research Conference October 26-27, 1984.* (Northfield, Minnesota: Norwegian-American Historical Association, 1985), 189-196.
Cooke, Alistair. *Letter from America, 1946-2004. (New York: Knopf, 2004).*
Dahl, Dorthea. "The Copper Kettle", in Marc Shell and Werner Sollors, eds. *The Multilingual Anthology of American Literature: A Reader of Original Texts with English Translations.* (New York: New York University Press, 2000), 552-575.
Daniel Lindmark. ed. *Swedishness Reconsidered: Three Centuries of Swedish-American Identities.* (Umeå: s.n., 1998).
Daniels, Roger. *Coming to America: A History of Immigration and Ethnicity in American Life.* (New York: HarperCollins, 1991).
Danmarks Statistik. *Statistiske Undersøgelser* 19 (1966).
Danmarks Statistik. *Statistisk Tabelværk*, Fifth series, Litra A, 5 (1905).
Davidson, Cathy N. "Loose Change." Presidential Address to the ASA, Nov. 1993. *American Quarterly* 46:2 (Summer, 1994, 123-38.
Degler, Carl N. "Remaking American History," *Journal of American History* 67:1 (June 1980), 7-25.
Derrida, Jacques. *Of Grammatology.* (Baltimore: Johns Hopkins University Press, 1977).
Desmond, Jane C. and Virginia R. Dominguez. "Resituating American Studies in a Critical Internationalism." *American Quarterly* 48:3 (Fall, 1996), 475-90.

Djupedal, Knut. "Some Thoughts on the Influence of Returned Migrants in Norway," in Per Clemensson *et al.* Ed. *Göteborgs-Emigranten 6. Rapport från symposiet "Amerika tur och retur" i Göteborg 18-19. September 1996.* (Göteborg: Göteborgs-emigranten, 1997), 204-210.

Due-Nielsen, Carsten, ed. *Historie og historiografi: Festskrift til Inga Floto på 65-års dagen 26. oktober 2002.* (Copenhagen 2002), 30-57.

Dunbar, Ernest. *The Black Expatriates: A Study of American Negroes in Exile.* (New York: Dutton, 1968).

Duncan, Russell, and Joseph Goddard. *Contemporary America.* (London: Palgrave MacMillan, 2nd ed., 2005).

Dunlevy, James A. and Henry A. Gemery. "Some Additional Evidence on Settlement Patterns of Scandinavian Migrants to the United States: Dynamics and the Role of Family and Friends," *Scandinavian Economic History Review* 24:2 (1976), 143-152.

Dyer, Frank. Thomas Martin, and William Meadowcroft. *Edison: His Life and Inventions,* Vol. II. (New York: Harper & Brothers, 1929).

Eco, Umberto. *Travels in Hyper-reality.* (New York: Harvest Books, 1990).

Elmer Jørgensen, Steffen. "'Emigration Fever' – The Formation of an Early Rural Emigration Tradition on Lolland-Falster and Møn, Three Danish Islands, c. 1830-1871." Unpublished Ph.D. dissertation, Florence 1991.

Falbe-Hansen, V. "Udvandring i vor Tid," *Nationaløkonomisk Tidsskrift* 1 (1873), 273-295.

Ferenczi, Imre and Walter Willcox. *International Migrations*, vol. 1, *Statistics.* (New York: National Bureau of Economic Research, 1929).

Fisher Fishkin, Shelley. "Crossroads of Cultures: The Transnational Turn in American Studies," *American Quarterly* 57:1 (March, 2005).

Fishwick, Marshall W. ed. *American Studies in Transition.* (Philadelphia: University of Pennsylvania Press, 1964).

Fitzgerald, Frances. *America Revised: History Schoolbooks in the Twentieth Century.* (New York: Atlantic/Little, Brown, 1980).

Flom, George T. *A History of Norwegian Immigration to the United States: From the Earliest Beginning down to the Year 1848.* (Iowa City: private print, 1909, 66-71).

Floto, Inga, *Historie: En videnskabshistorisk undersøgelse.* (Copenhagen: Museum Tusculanum, 1996).

Foucault, Michel. *The Archaeology of Knowledge.* (New York: Harper and Roe, 1976).

Frank, Waldo. *Our America.* (New York: Boni & Liveright, 1919).

Friedensohn, Doris. "Towards a Post-Imperial, Transnational American Studies: Notes of a Frequent Flyer." *American Studies* 38:2 (Spring 1997), 69-85.

Gans, Herbert J. "Symbolic Ethnicity: The Future of Ethnic Groups and Cultures in America," in Gans *et al.*, eds. *On the Making of Americans: Essays in Honor of David Riesman.* (Philadelphia: University of Pennsylvania Press, 1979), 193-220.

Garbo, Gunnar. *Nu går jeg fra dere. Fortellingen om en fars liv og død i det 20. århundres Bergen.* (Bergen: Eide forlag, 2000).

Gerstle, Gary. *American Crucible: Race and Nation in the Twentieth Century.* (Princeton, New Jersey: Princeton University Press, 2001).

Giles, Paul. "Virtual Americas: The Internationalization of American Studies and the Ideology of Exchange." *American Quarterly* 50:3 (September 1998), 523-47.

Gjerde, Jon, and Anne McCants. "Fertility, Marriage, and Culture: Demographic Processes Among Norwegian Immigrants to the Rural Middle West," in *The Journal of Economic History*, 55: 4 (December 1995), 860-888.

Gjerde, Jon. "Conflict and Community: A Case-Study of the Immigrant Church in America," *Journal of Social History* 19 (1986), 681-697.

Gjerde, Jon. "The "Would-Be Patriarch" and the "Self-Made Man." Marcus Lee Hansen on Native and Immigrant Farmers in the American Middle West," in Birgit Flemming Larsen *et al.*, eds. *On Distant Shores: Proceedings of the Marcus Lee Hansen Immigration Conference Aalborg, Denmark, June 29 – July 1, 1992.* (Aalborg: Danes Worldwide Archives, 1993), 35-55.

Gjerde, Jon. "The Effect of Community on Migration: Three Minnesota Townships 1885-1905," *Journal of Historical Geography*, 5: 4 (1979), 403-422.

Gjerde, Jon. *From Peasants to Farmers: The Migration from Balestrand, Norway, to the Upper Middle West*. (Cambridge: Cambridge University Press, 1985).

Gjerde, Jon. *The Minds of the West: Ethnocultural Evolution in the Rural Middle West 1830-1917*. (Chapel Hill: University of North Carolina Press, 1997).

Gjerde, Jon. *The Minds of the West: Ethnocultural Evolution in the Rural Middle West 1830-1917*. (Chapel Hill: University of North Carolina Press, 1997).

Gleason, Philip. "American Identity and Americanization," in Stephan Thernstrom, ed. *Harvard Encyclopedia of American Ethnic Groups*. (Cambridge: Belknap Press, 1980), 31-58.

Gleason, Philip. *Speaking of Diversity: Language and Ethnicity in Twentieth-Century America*. (Baltimore: Johns Hopkins University Press, 1992).

Gordon, Milton M. *Assimilation in American Life: The Role of Race, Religion, and National Origins*. (New York: Oxford University Press, 1964).

Goudsblom, Johan. "Dutch and American Sociology in the Fifties: A View from behind the One-Way Mirror," in: Rob Kroes, Maarten van Rossem, eds. *Anti-Americanism in Europe* (Amsterdam: Free University Press, 1986) pp. 112-21.

Gradén, Lizette. *On Parade: Making Heritage in Lindsborg, Kansas*. (Uppsala: Uppsala University Library, 2003).

Greimas, A. J. *Du Sens: Essais Sémiotiques*. (Paris: Editions du Seuil, 1970).

Grönberg, Per-Olof. *Learning and Returning: Return Migration of Swedish Engineers from the United States, 1880-1940*. (Umeå: Umeå Universitet, 2003).

Grøngaard Jeppesen, Torben, ed. *Danskere og danskheden i USA: Rapporter fra Seminar den 18. September 2000 på Hollufgård*. (Odense: Skrifter fra Odense Bys Muséer 8, 2001).

Grøngaard Jeppesen, Torben. "Dannebrog på den amerikanske prærie" – et mikrostudium – samt planer for et makrostudium af danske i USA," in Grøngaard Jeppesen 2001, 41-46.

Grøngaard Jeppesen, Torben. *Dannebrog på den amerikanske prærie: Et dansk koloniprojekt i 1870'erne – landkøb, bygrundlæggelse og integration*. (Odense: Odense Bys Museer, 2000).

Grøngaard Jeppesen, Torben. *Danske i USA 1850-2000 – en demografisk, social og kulturgeografisk undersøgelse af de danske immigranter og deres efterkommere*. (Odense: Odense Bys Museeer, 2005).

Guttmann, Allen. "American Studies at Amherst," *American Quarterly*, 22:2, (Summer, 1970).

Handlin, Oscar. *The Uprooted: The Epic Story of the Great Migrations that Made the American People*. (Boston: Little, Brown and Company, 1951).

Hansen, Marcus Lee. *The Atlantic Migration, 1607-1860*. (Cambridge, Massachussetts: Harvard University Press, 1940).

Hansen, Marcus Lee. *The Immigrant in American History*. (New York: Harper & Row, 1940).

Hays, Samuel P. "History as Human Behavior" *Iowa Journal of History* 58 (July, 1960), 193-206.

Helmer Pedersen, Erik. *Drømmen om Amerika*. (Copenhagen: Politikens Forlag, 1985).

Helmer Pedersen, Erik. *Pionererne*. (Copenhagen: Politikens Forlag, 1986).

Higham, John. "From Process to Structure: Formulations of American Immigrations History," in Dag Blanck and Peter Kivisto, eds. *American Immigrants and Their Generations*. (Urbana: University of Illinois Press, 1989), 11-41.

Higham, John. "The Future of American History," *Journal of American History* 80:4 (March 1994), 1289-1309.

Higham, John. *History: The Development of Historical Studies in the United States*. (Englewoods Cliffs, New Jersey: Prentice-Hall, 1965).

Higham, John. *Strangers in the Land: Patterns of American Nativism, 1860-1925*. (New Brunswick and London: Rutgers University Press, 1988).

Hirschman, Charles. "America's Melting Pot Reconsidered," *Annual Revue of Sociology* 9 (1983), 397-423.

Hirst, Paul, and Grahame Thompson. *Globalization in Question* (Oxford: Polity Press, 1999), 1-18.

Hobsbawn, Eric, and Terence Ranger, eds. *The Invention of Tradition.* (Cambridge: Cambridge University Press, 1983).

Hofstadter, Richard. *The Progressive Historians: Turner, Beard, Parrington.* (Chicago: University of Chicago Press, 1968).

Hollander, Arie N.J. den, ed. *Contagious Conflict: The Impact of American Dissent on European Life* (Leiden: E.J. Brill, 1973).

Hollander, Arie N.J. den, ed. *Diverging Parallels: America As Compared With European Thought and Action* (Leiden: E.J. Brill, 1971).

Hollinger, David A. *Postethnic America: Beyond Multiculturalism.* (New York: BasicBooks, 1995).

Holt, Ane Dorthe. "Udvandringen til Amerika fra Humble sogn," in Hans Chr. Johansen, ed. *Studier i dansk befolkningshistorie 1750-1890.* (Odense, Odense University Press, 1976), 76-120.

Hong, Edna and Howard. *Muskego Boy*; illustrated by Lee Mero. (Minneapolis: Augsburg Publishing House, 1943).

Horwitz, Richard P. *Exporting America: Essays on American Studies Abroad.* (New York: Garland, 1993).

Huntington, Samuel P. *American Politics: The Promise of Disharmony.* (Cambridge: Harvard University Press, 1981).

Hvidt, Kristian, *Danske veje vestpå – en bog om udvandringen til Amerika.* (Copenhagen: Politiken, 1976).

Hvidt, Kristian, *Det folkelige gennembrud og dets mænd (1850-1900).* (Copenhagen: Gyldendal, 1990).

Hvidt, Kristian, ed. *Emigrationen fra Norden indtil 1. verdenskrig: Rapporter til det nordiske historikermøde i København 1971, 9-12 august.* (Copenhagen: Den Danske Historiske Forening, 1971).

Hvidt, Kristian. *Flugten til Amerika eller Drivkræfter i masseudvandringen fra Danmark 1868-1914.* (Århus: Universitetsforlaget, 1971).

Iggers, Georg G. *Historiography in the Twentieth Century: From Scientific Objectivity to the Postmodern Challenge.* (Hanover and London: Wesleyan University Press, 1997).

Iversen, James D. "Danish American Organizations: Then and Now," in Grøngaard Jeppesen, ed. *Danskere og danskhed i USA*, 69-79.
Jacobson, Matthew Frye. *Whiteness of a Different Color: Immigrants and the Alchemy of Race*. (Cambridge: Harvard University Press, 1998).
Jacoby, Russell. *The Last Intellectual: American Culture in the Age of Academe*. (New York: Basic Books, 1987).
Jameson, Fredric. *Marxism and Form*. (Princeton: Princeton University Press, 1971).
Jameson, Fredric. *The Political Unconscious: Narrative as Socially Symbolic Act*. (Ithaca: Cornell University Press, 1981).
Jameson, Fredric. *The Prison House of Language*. (Princeton: Princeton University Press, 1972).
Janson, Drude Krog. *A Saloonkeeper's Daughter*. Translated by Gerald Thorson. Edited, with an Introduction and Notes by Orm Øverland (Baltimore: Johns Hopkins University Press, 2002).
Jehl, Frances. *Reminiscences of Menlo Park*. (Dearborn: Edison Institute, 1939).
Jensen, Adolph. "Udvandring," *Nationaløkonomisk Tidsskrift* 42 (1904), 65-90.
Jensen, Richard, *The Winning of the Midwest: Social and Political Conflict, 1888-1896*. (Chicago: University of Chicago Press, 1971).
Jerome, Harry. *Migration and Business Cycles*. (New York: National Bureau of Economic Research, 1926).
Johnson, Amandus. *The Swedish Settlements on the Delaware: Their History and Relation to the Indians, Dutch and English, 1638-1664*. (New York: D. Appleton & Co, 1911).
Kälvemark, Ann-Sofie, ed. *Utvandring: Den svenska emigrationen till Amerika i historiskt perspektiv*. (Stockholm: Wahlström & Widstrand, 1973; Hasselmo, 1978).
Kälvemark, Ann-Sofie. "Swedish Emigration Policy in an International Perspective, 1840-1925," in Runblom and Norman, eds. *From Sweden to America*, 94-113.
Kaplan, Amy. "'Left Alone With America': The Absence of Empire in the Study of American Culture." In Amy Kaplan and Donald

E. Pease, eds. *Cultures of United States Imperialism*. (Durham: Duke University Press, 1993), 3-21.

Kaplan, Amy. "A Call for a Truce." *American Literary History* 17:1 (Winter, 2005), 141-47.

Kennedy, J. Gerald. "'A Mania for Composition': Poe's Annus Mirabilis and the Violence of Nation-building." *American Literary History* 17:1 (Winter, 2005), 1-33.

Klaveness, Toralv. *Det norske Amerika*. (Oslo: A. Cammermeyers Forlag, 1904).

Kleppner, Paul. *The Cross of Culture: A Social Analysis of Midwestern Politics, 1850-1900*. (New York: Free Press, 1970).

Koht, Halvdan. *The American Spirit in Europe: A Survey of Transatlantic Influences*. (Philadelphia: University of Pennsylvania Press, 1949).

Kouwenhoven, John. "What's American about American Culture?" *The Beer Can By the Highway*. (New York: Doubleday, 1961).

Kroes, Rob, "America and the European Sense of History," *The Journal of American History*, 86, 3 (December 1999), 1135-56.

Kroes, Rob. "European Anti-Americanism: What's New?" *The Journal of American History*, 93, 2 (September 2006), 417-32.

Kroes, Rob. *If You've Seen One, You've Seen the Mall*. (Urbana. University of Illinois Press, 1996).

Kroes, Rob. *Predecessors: Intellectual Lineages in American Studies* (Amsterdam: VU University Press, 1999).

Kroes, Rob, ed. *Cultural Transmissions and Receptions: American Mass Culture in Europe*. (Amsterdam: Free University Press, 1993).

Kroes, Rob, ed. *Straddling Borders: The American Resonance in Transnational Identities* (Amsterdam, VU University Press, 2004).

Kroes, Rob, ed. *The American West as Seen by Europeans and Americans*. (Amsterdam: Free University Press, 1989).

Kroes, Rob, ed. *Within the US Orbit: Small National Cultures vis-à-vis the United States* (Amsterdam: VU University Press, 1991).

Kronborg, Bo *et al.* eds. *Nordic Population Mobility. Comparative Studies of Selected Parishes in the Nordic Countries, 1850-1900. A Collective Work of the Nordic Emigration Research Project*. (Oslo: Universitetsforlaget, 1977).

Kuisel, Richard. *Seducing the French: The Dilemma of Americanization.* (Berkeley: University of California Press, 1993).

Kuklick, Bruce. "Myth and Symbol in American Studies," *American Quarterly* 24:4 (1972), 435-450.

Kumei, Teruko I. "Making 'A Bridge over the Pacific': Japanese Language Schools in the United States, 1900-1941" in Øverland, *Not English Only.*

Lagerkvist, Amanda. *Amerikafantasier: Kön, medier och visualitet i svenska resaskildringar från USA 1945-1963.* (Stockholm, Institutionen för Journalistik, Medier, och Kommunikation, 2005).

Larsen, Birgit Flemming, ed. *In Denmark Born – To Canada Sworn.* (Aalborg: Danish Emigration Archives, 2000).

Larsen, Birgit Flemming. "Impressionistisk billede af danskheden i Chicago og Racine: Udvalgte resultater fra en spørgeskemaundersøgelse," in Grøngaard Jeppesen, 2001, 9-18.

Lauter, Paul. "Reconfiguring Academic Disciplines: The Emergence of American Studies." *American Studies* 40:2 (Summer 1999), 23-38.

Lent, John A. ed. *Pulp Demons: International Dimensions of the Post-War Anti-Comics Campaign* (Cranbury, NJ: Associated University Presses, 1999).

Lindmark, Daniel, ed. *Swedishness Reconsidered: Three Centuries of Swedish-American Identities.* (Umeå: Kulturens Frontlinjer, Skrifter från forsningsprogrammet kulturgräns Norr 18, 1999).

Lipsitz, George. "Our America." *American Literary History* 17:1 (2005), 135-40.

Litwak, Eugene. "Geographical Mobility and Extended Family Cohesion," *American Sociological Review* 25 (June 1960), 385-394.

Ljungmark, Lars. "The Organized Stock Effect," in Steffen Elmer Jørgensen *et al. From Scandinavia to America: Proceedings from a Conference Held at Gl. Holtegaard.* (Odense: Odense University Press, 1987), 104-116.

Ljungmark, Lars. *Den stora utvandringen: Svensk emigration till USA 1840-1925.* (Stockholm: Sv. Radio, 1965).

Ljungmark, Lars. *For Sale-Minnesota: Organized Promotion of Scandinavian Immigration 1866-1873.* (Göteborg: Akademiförlaget, 1971).

Lovoll, Odd S. "Norwegian-American Historical Scholarship: A Survey of Its History and a Look to the Future," in Dorothy Burton Skårdal and Ingeborg R. Kongslien, eds. *Essays on Norwegian-American Literature and History.* (Oslo: NAHA-Norway, 1986).

Lovoll, Odd S. *A Century of Urban Life: The Norwegians in Chicago Before 1930.* (Northfield, Minnesota: Norwegian-American Historical Association, 1988).

Lovoll, Odd S. *A Folk Epic: The Bygdelag in America.* (Boston: Norwegian-American Historical Association, 1975).

Lovoll, Odd S. *The Promise Fulfilled: A Portrait of Norwegian Americans Today.* (Minneapolis: University of Minnesota Press, 1998).

Lundén, Rolf and Erik Åsard, eds. *Networks of Americanization: Aspects of the American Influence in Sweden.* (Uppsala: Studia Anglistica, 1992).

Lundén, Rolf, and Erik Åsard. *Networks of Americanization: Aspects of American Influence in Sweden.* (Uppsala: Acta Universitatis Upsaliensis No. 79, 1992).

Mackintosh, Jette. *Danskere i Midtvesten: Elk Horn-Kimballton bosættelsen 1870-1925.* (Copenhagen: Akademisk Forlag, 1993).

Mackintosh, Jette. *Øst, vest – hjemme bedst? Danske emigranters oplevelser ved gensynet med Danmark.* (Copenhagen: Borgen. 2001).

Maddox, Lucy, ed. *Locating American Studies: The Evolution of a Discipline.* (Baltimore: Johns Hopkins University Press, 1999).

Marx, Leo. "Afterword," *The Machine in the Garden.* (New York: Oxford University Press, 2000, revision of 1965).

Marx, Leo. "Believing in America: An Intellectual Project and a National Ideal," *Boston Review* at http://bostonreview.net/BR28.6/marx.html. Accessed 15 December 2003.

Marx, Leo. "On Recovering the 'Ur' Theory of American Studies." *American Literary History* 17:1 (2005), 118-34.

Marx, Leo. "Reflections on American Studies, Minnesota, and the 1950s." *American Studies* 40:2 (Summer 1999).

Marx, Leo. review of David W. Noble, *The American Adam in the New World Garden, American Historical Review*, Vol. 74, No. 5. (June, 1969), 1724-1725.

Marx, Leo. *The Machine in the Garden*. (New York: Oxford University Press, 1965).

Matthiessen, F. O. *American Renaissance*. (Oxford: Oxford University Press, 1968).

Mauk, David. *The Colony That Rose From the Sea: Norwegian Maritime Migration and Community in Brooklyn, 1850-1910*. (Northfield, Minnesota: Norwegian-American Historical Association, 1997).

May, Elaine Tyler. "The Radical Roots of American Studies." Presidential Address to the ASA, Nov 1995. *American Quarterly* 48:2 (Summer, 1996), 179-200.

McCormick, Richard L. *The Party Period and Public Policy: American Politics from the Age of Jackson to the Progressive Era*. (New York: Oxford University Press, 1986).

McDowell, Tremaine. *American Studies*. (Minneapolis: University of Minnesota Press, 1948).

McNamara, Robert. *In Retrospect*. (New York: Random House, 1996).

Mortensen, Enok. *The Danish Lutheran Church in America: The History and Heritage of the American Evangelical Lutheran Church*. (Philadelphia: Board of Publication, Lutheran Church in America, 1967).

Mumford, Lewis. *Sticks and Stones: A Study of American Architecture and Civilization*. (New York: Norton, 1924).

Mumford, Lewis. *The Golden Day: A Study in American Experience and Culture*. (New York: Boni & Liveright, 1926).

Munch, Peter A. "Segregation and Assimilation of Norwegian settlements in Wisconsin," *Norwegian-American Studies and Records* 18 (1954), 102-140.

Murphey, Murray G. "American Civilization as a Discipline?" *American Studies* 40:2 (Summer 1999), 5-21.

Myrdal, Gunnar. *An American Dilemma: The Negro Problem and Modern Democracy*. (New York: Transaction, 1996, reprint of New York: Harper and Brothers, 1944).

Nelson, Helge. *The Swedes and the Swedish Settlements in North America*, vol. I: *Text*; vol. II: *Atlas*. (Lund: C. W. K. Gleerup, 1943).

Nelson, O. N. "The Nationality of Criminal and Insane Persons in the United States," in O.N. Nelson, ed. *History of the Scandinavians and Successful Scandinavians in the United States*, vol. 2. (Minneapolis: O. N. Nelson & Company, 1900).

Nilsson, Fred. *Emigrationen från Stockholm till Nordamerika 1880-1893. En studie i urban utvandring.* (Stockholm: Läromedelsförlaget, 1970).

Noble, David W. *Death of a Nation: American Culture and the End of Exceptionalism* (Minneapolis: University of Minnesota Press, 2002).

Noble, David W. *Historians Against History: The Frontier Thesis and the National Covenant in American Historical Thought.* (Minneapolis: University of Minnesota Press, 1965).

Nordahl, Per. *Weaving the Ethnic Fabric: Social Networks Among Swedish-American Radicals in Chicago, 1890-1940.* (Umeå: Almqvist & Wiksell, 1994).

Nordström, Byron, Philip Anderson, and Dag Blanck, eds. *Scandinavians in Old and New Lands: Essays in Honor of H. Arnold Barton.* (Chicago: Swedish-American Historical Society, 2004).

Norman, Hans and Harald Runblom. *Transatlantic Connections: Nordic Migration to the New World after 1800.* (Oslo: Norwegian University Press, 1987).

Nye, David E. *A Catalogue of the General Electric Photographic Archives, 1890-1940.* (New York: General Electric Company, 1981, 175 pp. + 200 illustrations. 2nd edition, 1998).

Nye, David E. *A History of the Youth Conservation Corps.* (Washington: U. S. Government Printing Office, 1981).

Nye, David E. *America As Second Creation.* (Cambridge: MIT Press, 2003).

Nye, David E. *American Technological Sublime.* (Cambridge: MIT Press, 1994).

Nye, David E. and Mick Gidley. *American Photographs in Europe.* (Amsterdam: Amsterdam Free University Press, 1994).

Nye, David E. *Consuming Power: A Social History of American Energies.* (Cambridge: MIT Press, 1998).

Nye, David E. *Contemporary American Society*, sixth edition. (Copenhagen: Academic Press 6th edition 2006).

Nye, David E. *Electrifying America: Social Meanings of a New Technology.* (Cambridge: MIT Press, 1990).
Nye, David E. Henry Ford and Time, dissertation, University of Minnesota, 1974.
Nye, David E. *Henry Ford: "Ignorant Idealist"* (Port Washington, New York: Kennikat Press, 1979).
Nye, David E. *Image Worlds: Corporate Identities at General Electric.* (Cambridge: MIT Press, 1985).
Nye, David E. *The Invented Self: An Anti-biography, from documents of Thomas A. Edison.* (Odense: Odense University Press, 1983).
Nye, Edgar Wilson. *Bill Nye's History of the United States.* (Philadelphia: Lippincott, 1894).
Nyholm, Paul C. *The Americanization of the Danish Lutheran Churches in America.* (Minneapolis: Institute for Danish Church History, 1963).
Nyvall, C.J. *Reseminnen från Amerika af C.J.N.* (Kristinehamn: H. Halls Boktryckeri-aktiebolag, 1876).
Odén, Birgitta, "Emigrationen från Norden till Nordamerika under 1800-talet. Aktuella forskningsuppgifter," *Historisk Tidskrift* (Stockholm), 1963. 261-277.
Odén, Birgitta. "Ekonomiska emigrationsmodeller och historisk forskning. Ett diskussionsinlägg," *Scandia* 37: 1 (1971), 1-70.
Olsson, Nils William, and Erik Wikén. *US Passenger Arrival Statistics for Swedes Landing in the US 1840-1850.* (Stockholm: Kungl. Biblioteket, 1995).
Orth, Samuel P. *Our Foreigners: A Chronicle of Americans in the Making.* The Chronicles of America Series (New Haven: Yale University Press, 1921).
Ostergren, Robert C. *A Community Transplanted: The Trans-Atlantic Experience of a Swedish Immigrant Settlement in the Upper Middle West, 1835-1915.* (Uppsala: Studia Multiethnica, 1988), 125-147.
Ostergren, Robert. "Swedish Migration to North America in Transatlantic Perspective," in Ira Glazier and Luigi de Rosa, eds. *Migration across Time and Nations: Population Mobility in Historical Contexts.* (New York: Holmes & Meier, 1986).

Ostergren, Robert. *A Community Transplanted: The Trans-Atlantic Experience of a Swedish Immigrant Settlement in the Upper Middle West, 1835-1915*. (Madison: University of Wisconsin Press, 1988).

Overland, Martha Ubo. *A Manual of Statutory Corporation Law*. (New York: The Ronald Press, 1906).

Øverland, Orm, and Steinar Kjærheim. *Fra Amerika til Norge I: Norske utvandrerbrev 1838-1857* (Oslo: Solum Forlag, 1992).

Øverland, Orm, and Steinar Kjærheim. *Fra Amerika til Norge II: Norske utvandrerbrev 1858-1868* (Oslo: Solum Forlag, 1992).

Øverland, Orm, and Steinar Kjærheim. *Fra Amerika til Norge III: Norske utvandrerbrev 1869-1874* (Oslo: Solum Forlag, 1993).

Øverland, Orm, ed. *In the European Grain: American Studies from Central and Eastern Europe.* (Amsterdam: VU University Press, 1990).

Øverland, Orm, ed. *Not English Only: Redefining "American" in American Studies*. A Longfellow Institute Book. European Contributions to American Studies 48 (Amsterdam: VU University Press, 2001).

Øverland, Orm, ed. *The Rise of Jonas Olsen: A Norwegian Immigrant's Saga*. A Trilogy by Johannes B. Wist. Edited, translated and with an introduction and notes by Orm Øverland. (Minneapolis: University of Minnesota Press, 2006).

Øverland, Orm. "Becoming White in 1881: An Immigrant Acquires an American Identity," *Journal of American Ethnic History* 23:4 (Summer 2004), 133-141.

Øverland, Orm. "Norwegian Americans Meet Native Americans: Exclusion and Inclusion in Immigrant Homemaking in America," Charles I. Armstrong and Øyunn Hestetun, eds., *Postcolonial Dislocations: Travel, History, and the Ironies of Narrative* (Oslo: Novus Press), 109-122.

Øverland, Orm. "Recovering an Unrecognized Novel—Discovering American Literature," Alfred Hornung, ed. *Multicultural America* (Heidelberg: Universitätsverlag C. Winter, 2006).

Øverland, Orm. "The First World War Americanization Movement and Immigrant Resistance to the Melting Pot," William Boelhower and Alfred Hornung, eds. *Multiculturalism and the*

American Self (Heidelberg: Universitätsverlag C. Winter, 2000), 139–156.

Øverland, Orm. "The Impressionism of Stephen Crane: A Study in Style and Technique," *Americana Norvegica* 1 (1966), 239-285.

Øverland, Orm. "*The Jungle*: From Lithuanian Peasant to American Socialist," *American Literary Realism* 37:1 (Fall 2004), 1-23.

Øverland, Orm. "Visions of Home: Exiles and Immigrants," Peter I. Rose, ed. *The Dispossessed: An Anatomy of Exile* (Amherst: University of Massachusetts Press, 2005), 7-26.

Øverland, Orm. *America Perceived: A View from Abroad in the 20th Century.* (West Haven, Connecticut: Pendulum Press, 1974).

Øverland, Orm. *Fra Amerika til Norge IV: Norske utvandrerbrev i utvalg, 1875-84.* (Oslo: Solum Forlag, 2002).

Øverland, Orm. *Home-Making Myths: Immigrants' Claims to a Special Status in Their New Land*. Odense American Studies International Series No. 20 (Odense, 1996).

Øverland, Orm. *Immigrant Minds, American Identities: Making the United States Home, 1870-1930.* (Urbana and Chicago: University of Illinois Press, 2000).

Øverland, Orm. *Johan Schrøder's Travels in Canada, 1863.* Edited, Translated, and with an Introduction by Orm Øverland. (Montreal and Kingston: McGill-Queen's University Press, 1989).

Øverland, Orm. *The Making and Meaning of an American Classic: James Fenimore Cooper's The Prairie.* (Oslo: Universitetsforlaget, 1973).

Øverland, Orm. *The Western Home: A Literary History of Norwegian America.* (Northfield, Minnesota: The Norwegian-American Historical Association; distributed by University of Illinois Press, 1996).

Park, Robert E. "Human Migration and the Marginal Man" (1928), in Werner Sollors, ed. *Theories of Ethnicity: A Classical Reader.* (New York: New York University Press, 1996). 156-167.

Pease, Donald E. and Robyn Wiegman, eds. *The Futures of American Studies.* (Durham: Duke University Press, 2002).

Pease, Donald. "From American Studies to Cultural Studies: Paradigms and Paradoxes." *European Journal of American Culture* 19:1 (1999), 5-11.

Pease, Donald. "National Narratives, Postnational Narration," *Modern Fiction Studies*, 43.1 (1997), 1-23.

Pedersen, Erik Helmer. "Danish Emigration History," in Steffen Elmer Jørgensen *et al.* eds. *From Scandinavia to America: Proceedings from a Conference held at Gl. Holtegaard*. (Odense: Odense University Press, 1987), 9-27.

Pells, Richard. "American Studies: On the Margins in Europe," *Chronicle of Higher Education*, (August 17, 2001).

Pells, Richard. *Not Like Us: How Europeans Have Loved, Hated, and Transformed American Culture Since WWII*. (New York: Basic Books, 1997).

Porter, Carolyn. "What We Know That We Don't Know: Remapping American Literary Studies." *American Literary History* 6:3 (Fall 1994),467-526.

Qualey, Carlton C. *Norwegian Settlement in the United States*. (Northfield, Minnesota: Norwegian-American Historical Association, 1938).

Quignard, Pascal. *L'occupation américaine*. (Paris: Editions de Seuil, 1994).

Radway, Janice. "What's in a Name?" in Donald Pease and Robyn Wiegman, eds. *The Futures of American Studies*. (Durham, N.C.: Duke University Press, 2002), 45-75.

Radway, Janice. "American Studies, Reader Theory, and the Literary Text: From the Study of Material Objects to the Study of Social Processes," in David E. Nye and Christen Kold Thomsen. *American Studies in Transition*. (Odense: Odense University Press, 1985).

Radway, Janice. "What's in a Name?" Presidential Address to the American Studies Association, 20 November, 1998. *American Quarterly* 51:1 (Winter, 1999, 1-32.

Radway, Janice. *Reading the Romance, Women, Patriarchy, and Popular Literature*. (University of North Carolina Press, 1985).

Rice, John G. "Marriage Behavior and the Persistence of Swedish Settlements in Minnesota," in Nils Hasselmo, ed. *Perspectives on Swedish Immigration, Proceedings of the International Conference on the Swedish Heritage in the Upper Midwest, April 1-3, 1976* (Duluth:

University of Minnesota and the Swedish Pioneer Historical Society, 1978), 136-150.

Roger, Philippe. *The American Enemy: The History of French Anti-Americanism.* (Chicago: The University of Chicago Press, 2005)

Rølvaag, O. E. *Giants in the Earth* (New York: Harper & Row, 1927).

Rönnqvist, Carina. "Scattered Swedes and Single Settlers: On Ethnic Identity Reflected in Nationalistic Sentiments, Gender and Class in 20th-Century Canada," in Lindmark, ed. *Swedishness Reconsidered*, 91-120.

Rosenfeld, Paul. *Port of New York: Essays on Fourteen American Moderns.* (New York: Harcourt, Brace, 1924).

Runblom, Harald, and Lars-Göran Tedebrand. "Future Research in Swedish-American History: Some Perspectives," *Swedish Pioneer Historical Quarterly* 30: 2 (1979), 129-140.

Runblom, Harald. "Svensk emigration och svensk migrationsforskning. Några perspektiv," in Torben Grøngaard Jeppesen, ed. *Danskere og danskheden I USA: Rapporter fra Seminar den 18. September 2000 på Hollufgård.* (Odense: Skrifter fra Odense Bys Museer 8, 2001), 33-40.

Runeby, Nils. *Den nya världen och den gamla: Amerikabild och emigrationsuppfattning i Sverige 1820-1860.* (Stockholm: Svenska Bokförlaget, 1969).

Sarna, Jonathan D. "From Immigrants to Ethnics: Toward a New Theory of 'Ethnicization,'" *Ethnicity* 5 (1978), 370-378.

Scharling, William. "Ind- og udvandring til og fra Danmark 1820-82," *Nationaløkonomisk Tidsskrift* 21 (1883), 409-425.

Schlesinger, Arthur M. "The Significance of Immigration in American History," *American Journal of Sociology* 27, 1 (July 1927), 71-85.

Schultz, April. *Ethnicity on Parade: Inventing the Norwegian-American Through Celebration.* (Amherst: University of Massachusetts Press, 1994).

Semmingsen, Ingrid. "Emigration and the Image of America in Europe," in Henry Steele Commager, ed. *Immigration and American History: Essays in Honor of Theodore C. Blegen.* (Minneapolis: University of Minnesota Press, 1961).

Semmingsen, Ingrid. "Emigration from Scandinavia," *Scandinavian Economic Review* 20 (1972), 45-60.

Semmingsen, Ingrid. "Nordic Research into Emigration," *Scandinavian Journal of History* 3 (1978), 107-129.

Semmingsen, Ingrid. *Veien mot vest, Annen del: Utvandringen fra Norge til Amerika, 1865-1915.* (Oslo: Aschehoug, 1950).

Sibley, Mulford Q. *Political Ideas and Ideologies.* (New York: Harper and Row, 1970).

Silberschmidt, Max, ed. *Amerika-Europa: Freund und Rivale* (Erlenbach/Zürich: Eugen Rentsch, 1970).

Skard, Sigmund. "The American Studies Movement: Problems and Prospects." In *USA in Focus*, 140-73.

Skard, Sigmund. *American Studies in Europe: Their History and Present Organization.* Vols 1-2. (Philadelphia: University of Pennsylvania, 1958).

Skard, Sigmund, ed. *USA in Focus*, (Bergen: Universitetsforlaget, 1966).

Skard, Sigmund. *Trans-Atlantica: Memoirs of a Norwegian Americanist.* (Oslo: Universitetsforlaget for The American Institute, 1978).

Skårdal, Dorothy Burton. *The Divided Heart: Scandinavian Immigrant Experience through Literary Sources.* (Oslo: Universitetsforlaget, 1974).

Skarstedt, Ernst. *Svensk-amerikanska folket i helg och söcken.* (Stockholm: Björck & Börjesson, 1917).

Slotkin, Richard. *Regeneration Through Violence.* (Middletown: Wesleyan University, 1975).

Soike, Lowell J. *Norwegian Americans and the Politics of Dissent, 1880-1924.* (Northfield, Minnesota: Norwegian-American Historical Association, 1991).

Sollors, Werner. *The Invention of Ethnicity.* (New York: Oxford University Press, 1989).

Sørensen, Anthon C. "Danske i amerikansk Landbrug og Mejeri," in P.S. Vig, ed. *Danske i Amerika.* (Minneapolis and Chicago: C. Rasmussen Publishing Company, 1908), 265-326.

Spanos, William. "American Studies in the 'Age of the World Picture'," in Pease and Wiegman, eds. *The Futures of American Studies*, 387-415.

Stearns, Harold. *Civilization in the United States: An Inquiry by Thirty Americans.* (New York: Harcourt, Brace, 1922).

Stephenson, George M. *The Religious Aspects of Swedish Immigration: A Study of Immigrant Churches.* (Minneapolis: University of Minnesota Press, 1932).

Stilling, Niels Peter, and Anne Lisbeth Olsen. *A New Life: Danish Emigration to North America as Described by the Emigrants Themselves in Letters 1842-1946.* (Aalborg: Danes Worldwide Archives, 1994).

Stilling, Niels Peter. "Udvandringen fra Frederiksborg amt 1869-1899," in *Erhvervshistorisk årbog 1978.* (Århus: Universitetsforlaget, 1979), 95-148.

Svalestuen, Andres A. "Professor Ingrid Semmingsen – emigrasjonshistorikeren," in Sivert Langholm and Francis Sejersted, eds. *Vandringer: Festskrift til Ingrid Semmingsen på 70-årsdagen 29. mars 1980.* (Oslo, Aschehoug 1980), 9-42.

Svalestuen, Andres A. *Tinns emigrasjonshistorie 1837-1907.* (Oslo: Universitetsforlaget, 1972).

Takla, Knut. *Det norske folk i De forente stater.* (Oslo: Stenersen, 1913).

Tate, Cecil. *The Search for Method in American Studies.* (Minneapolis: University of Minnesota Press, 1973).

Tedebrand, Lars-Göran. "Sources for the History of Swedish Emigration," in Runblom and Norman, *From Sweden to America*, 76-93.

Tedebrand, Lars-Göran. *Västernorrland och Nordamerika 1875-1913. Utvandring och återinvandring.* (Uppsala: Läromedelsförlagen, 1972).

Thaler, Peter. *Grænsetilfælde: Nationale og etniske identiteter i konflikt og overgang.* (Odense: Syddansk Universitetsforlag, 2004).

Thaler, Peter. *Norwegian Minds – American Dreams: Ethnic Activism among Norwegian-American Intellectuals.* (Newark and London: University of Delaware Press, 1998).

Thistlethwaite, Frank. "Migration from Europe Overseas in the Nineteenth and Twentieth Centuries," in Herbert Moller, ed. *Population Movements in Modern European History.* (New York: Macmillan, 1964), 73-92.

Thomas, Dorothy Swaine. *Social and Economic Aspects of Swedish Population Movements, 1750-1933.* (New York: The Macmillan Company, 1941).

Thomas, F. Richard. *Americans in Denmark: Comparisons of the Two Cultures by Writers, Artists, and Teachers.* (Carbondale: Southern Illinois University Press, 1990).

Thoreau, Henry David. "Slavery in Massachusetts," *Walden and other Writings.* (New York: Modern Library, 1950).

Tilly, Charles, and C. Harold Brown. "On Uprooting, Kinship, and the Auspices of Migration," *International Journal of Comparative Sociology* 8 (1967).

Turner, Frederick Jackson. *The Frontier in American History.* (New York: H. Holt, 1920).

Vecoli, Rudolph J., "*Contadini* in Chicago: A Critique of *The Uprooted*," *Journal of American History* 51 (December, 1964), 404-417.

Wagenleitner, Reinhold. *Coca-Colonization and the Cold War.* (Chapel Hill: University of North Carolina, 1994).

Wagnleitner, Reinhold and Elaine Tyler May, eds. *"Here, There and Everywhere": The Foreign Policies of America Popular Culture.* (Hanover: University Press of New England, 2000).

Walker, Robert H. ed. *American Studies Abroad.* (Westport: Greenwood, 1975).

Wallace, Anthony F. C. *Rockdale.* (New York: W. W. Norton, 1980).

Ward, John William. *Andrew Jackson: Symbol for an Age.* (New York: Oxford University Press, 1955).

Ward, John William. *Red, White, and Blue.* (New York: Oxford University Press, 1969).

Wefald, Jon. *A Voice of Protest: Norwegians in American Politics, 1890-1917.* (Northfield, Minnesota: Norwegian-American University Press, 1971).

Weibull, Jørgen. "The Wisconsin Progressives, 1900-1914," *Mid-America* 47 (July 1965), 191-221.

White, Hayden. *Metahistory: The Historical Imagination in Nineteenth-Century Europe.* (Baltimore: Johns Hopkins University Press, 1973).

Winks, Robin, ed. *Other Voices, Other Views: An International Collection of Essays from the Bicentennial.* (Westport: Greenwood Press, 1978).

Wise, Gene. "Paradigm Dramas in American Studies." *American Quarterly* 31.3 (Fall, 1979), 293-337.

Wise, Gene. *American Historical Explanations: A Strategy for Grounded Inquiry.* (Minneapolis: University of Minnesota, 1980, 2nd edition.)

Wolfe, Alan. "The Difference Between Criticism and Hatred: Anti-American Studies," *The New Republic,* February 10, 2003.

Yetman, Norman R. and David M. Katzman. "Globalization and American Studies." *American Studies* 41:2/3 (2000), 5-11.

Zempel, Solveig. *In Their Own Words: Letters from Norwegian Immigrants* (Minneapolis: University of Minnesota Press, 1991).

Index

The Scandinavian vowels Å and Ø have been indexed with A and O, because non-speakers of these languages will not know that they are placed at the end of the Danish, Norwegian, and Swedish alphabets.

Aaron, Daniel, 30
Adams, Henry, 40
Åkerman, Sune, 141, 143, 145
Ambas Americas, 40
American civilization, 17, 21, 27-28, 35, 109
American Historical Association, 69, 70
American Institute, Berlin, 27
American Literary History, 26, 32,
American literature, 30-31, 44, 60, 65-66, 91, 173-177, 204
American Studies, 42, comparative, 36-40, 43-47, conflicts in, 25-54, 59-79, history of, 26-54, 59-74, 68-83, 108-112, specialization in, 27, 73. *See also* Great Divide, Internationalization, Myth and Symbol School, New Americanists.
American Studies Association, 14, 16, 29, 59, 68-78, 85, 90, 127, 178
American Studies in Scandinavia, 90, 102
American Studies International, 39
American Quarterly, 66, 75, 112
American West, 85
Americanization, 12, 47, 52-54, 96, 100, 125, 132, 136, 149, 179
Amherst College, 202-205
Anderson, Benedict, 151
Anti-Americanism, 11, 19, 90
Argentina, 40-41
Armstrong, Louis, 97
Århus University, 90
Åsard, Erik, 96

Assimilation, 201. *See also* Immigration, Multiculturalism.
Association for Environmental History, 72
Augustana Synod, 132, 151

Baldwin, James, 100, 223
Barth, Fredrik, 151
Barthes, Roland, 65, 213
Baudrillard, Jean, 94
Bergen University, 90
Biography, 65, 207-208
Blanck, Dag, 49, 151, 153
Blegen, Theodore, 48, 129, 132-135, 147, 149, 171, 182
Bodnar, John, 51
Borderland, 115, 120
Boorstin, Daniel, 110
British Association for American Studies, 190
Bryn, Steinar, 96
Brøndal, Jørn, 10, 125
Buell, Laurence, 36-37
Bush, George W., 33

Canadian Association for American Studies, 41-42, 56
Carlsson, Sten, 140
Carter, Dale, 46
Cheffiz, Eric, 37
Chicago, 127
Chisolm, Lawrence, 45
Civil Rights Movement, 60, 201
Clinton, Bill, 96
Cold War, 61-62, 203
Commager, Henry Steele, 128, 204-205

Conzen, Kathleen Neils, 49, 146
Cooke, Alistair, 94
Cooper, James Fennimore, 173
Copenhagen University, 44, 91
Counterculture, 60
Creolization, 74, 98, 104. *See also* Immigration.
Critical Theory, 65
Cunliffe, Marcus, 39-40, 42

Danes Worldwide Archives, 129
Danish Emigration History Society, 157
Danish Heritage Society, 129
Davidson, Cathy, 37
Deconstruction, 36, 65, 80
Degler, Carl N., 138
Denmark, 126, 129-130, 140, 143, 154-155, 216-221
Derrida, Jacques, 65, 213
Duke University, 37

Eastern Europe, 128, 177
Eco, Umberto, 65, 94, 100
Edison, Thomas, 65, 211-213
Emerson, Ralph Waldo, 45, 66
Erickson, Charlotte, 50
Ethnicity Studies, 50, 87. *See also* Immigration.
European Association of American Studies, 14-16, 166, 177, 189-190
Exceptionalism, doctrine of American, 61, 63, 127-128, 130-137
Expatriates, Black, 100
Expatriation, 166-170, 216-223

Finland, 35
Fishkin, Shelly Fisher, 165, 177
Flom, George T., 130
Floto, Inga, 137, 145
Ford, Henry, 207, 208, 210
Foucault, Michel, 64, 213
France, 19, 27, 88
Fridensohn, Doris, 38
Frontier Thesis, 74.
    See Turner, Frederick Jackson
Fulbright Program, 61, 74-75, 91, 93, 99

Galinsky, Hans, 35
Germany, 27, 34-35, 88
Gidley, Mick, 97
Giles, Paul, 37
Gilroy, Paul, 37
Ginsberg, Allen, 206
Gjerde, Jon, 52, 131, 149-150, 154
Globalization, 116
Gordon, Milton M., 138
Gotheborg University, 89
Goudsblom, Johan, 11, 20
Great Divide, 30, 34, 54, 110,112
    See also Marx, Leo.
Greimas, A. J., 211, 213
Gruesz, Kirsten Silva, 37,

Handlin, Oscar, 51, 135-136, 147
Hansen, Marcus Lee, 48, 131, 135, 147, 149, 171
Harvard Univesity, 44, 108, 215
Hays, Samuel P., 138
Henriksson, Markku, 118
Hirst, Paul, 120
History of Technology, 207-208, 215, 221-222
Hobsbawn, Eric, 151
Hofstadter, Richard, 91
Hollinger, David A., 154
Home-making Myths, 17, 129, 178-183, 187
Hvidt, Kristian, 126, 140-141, 145, 154

Iceland, 35
Ickstadt, Heinz, 37, 38
Immigrant Identity, 148-155, 178-187
Immigration, 47-50, 125-163, 166-169, 183
Individualism, 42
Interdisciplinarity, as ideal, 26-
International Association of American Studies, 20, 37
Internationalization, 15, 18, 47, 85-104

James, Henry, 40, 100
Jameson, Fredric, 211
Jay, Gregory, 38
Jeppesen Grøngaard, Torben, 154-155

254   INDEX

Journal of American Ethnic History, 184
Journal of American History, 21

Kaplan, Amy, 32, 36
Kennedy, J. Gerald, 37
Koht, Halvdan, 53
Kulturkunde, 27-28
Kuhn, Thomas, 64, 215
Kouwenhoven, John, 63-64
Kroes, Rob, 10, 11, 14, 53, 85

Landscape, 95
Lauter, Paul, 14, 55
Levi-Strauss, Claude, 63, 209
Liberal consensus, 201
Linguistic Turn, 20, 211
Lipset, Seymour Martin, 87
Lipsitz, George, 32, 36, 78-79
Lovoll, Odd S., 128, 133, 139, 154
Lundén, Rolf, 10, 25, 74, 85

Marcell, David W., 42
Marx, Leo, 30-36, 48, 60, 63, 65-66, 109-111, 204, 215
    See also Great Divide.
Matthiesen, F. O., 60, 78, 110
McCarthyism, 61, 221
McDowell, Tremaine, 43
McNamara, Robert, 203
Melville, Herman, 44, 62, 204
Migration. *See* Immigration.
Miller, Perry, 78, 110
MIT, 215
Moberg, Vilhelm, 140
Modern Language Association, 70
Morpurgu, J. E., 41
Multicultualism, 113-116
Mumford, Lewis, 108
Munch, Peter A., 138
Murdock, Kenneth B., 44-45
Murphey, Murray, 47,
Myrdal, Gunnar, 45, 103
Myth and Symbol School, 25, 29, 31, 61, 63-65, 208, 210

National Ethnic Studies Association, 67, 71

Native Americans, 183-187
Nazis, 28, 34
New Americanists, 25, 33, 36, 76-77, 108, 111-112, 116
New Criticism, 53, 68, 78
New Deal, 60-61
New Sweden colony, 130, 152
New York, 97
Noble, David W., 64, 117, 205
Nordic Association of American Studies, 26, 52, 55-56, 90, 102, 108, 165-166, 179, 190
Nordic Emigration, 141. *See* Immigration.
Norman, Hans, 51
Norway, 126, 133, 137, 143, 147, 170, 187-190
Norwegian-American Historical Association, 129, 133, 182
Norwegian-American literature, 175
Norwegian-American Studies, 129
Nye, David, 46, 59, 85, 199-224

Odén, Birgitta, 137, 144
Odense American Studies International Series, 179
Odense University (renamed University of Southern Denmark), 90, 163, 216, 221
Organization of American Historians, 16, 69-70, 138
Oslo University, 44, 90, 170
Ostergren, Robert C., 49, 160
Øverland, Orm, 10, 17, 165-198

Park, Robert E., 136, 147
Patriot Act, 172
Pearson, Norman Holmes, 173
Pease, Donald, 77-78
Pedersen, Erik Helmer, 141
Pells, Richard, 53
Photography, 97
Poldsaar, Raili, 119
Postmodernism, 111-116
Poststructuralism, 111, 113-115, 146, 209-213
Post-disciplinarity, 34, 56

Radway, Janice, 37, 65-67, 71, 78-79, 81, 111, 113, 116
Return Migration, 155, 163
Robinson, James Harvey, 127
Roger, Philippe, 19
Rölvaag, Ole, 133, 176
Romance, genre, 66
Romanticism, 44
Rosenfeld, Paul, 109
Runblom, Harald, 51

Scandinavia, 85-87
Scandinavian Universities, 92-98
Schlesinger Sr., Arthur M., 128
Schultz, April, 153
Semiotics, 211
Semmingsen, Ingrid, 131, 137, 142-144
Sibley, Mulford, 205
Skard, Sigmund, 17, 25-26, 29, 34, 36, 87-89, 165, 170
Skårdal, Dorothy Burton, 139, 174-175
Slotkin, Richard, 64
Smith, Henry Nash, 110
Society for the History of Technology, 72, 81
Solli, Kristin, 120
State Department, US, 77, 93, 108, 189-190
Stephenson, George M., 48, 132, 135, 149, 171
Stereo Cultural Vision, 46, 85-, 218, 220
Students, US, Scandinavian, 98
Sublime, 95, 222
Sweden, 126, 140, 143-144, 152
Swedish-American Historical Quarterly, 129
Swedish-American Historical Society, 129
Swedish Emigrant Institute, 140
Swierenga, Robert, 50

Tate, Cecil, 64, 209
Teaching abroad, American Studies, 92-98, 216
The Bridge, 129
The 1960s, 69-70, 202-205. *See also* Great Divide.
Thistlethwaite, Frank, 139, 142
Tlostanova, Madina, 117
Tocqueville, Alexis de, 26, 88, 100, 103
Trachtenberg, Alan, 60, 63
Transnational American Studies, 37-39, 43, 53, 55, 120
Turner, Frederick Jackson, 91, 127, 131-132
Twain, Mark, 200

United Kingdom, 41
United States Information Agency/Service, 16, 93, 189-190
University of Amsterdam, 18
University of Minnesota, 48, 68, 73, 79, 117, 134, 179, 205
University of Warwick, 46
Uppsala University, 35, 44, 49, 90, 140-141

Vecoli, Rudolph, 147, 179
Vietnam War, 33, 60, 62, 90, 173, 188-189, 203-205

Walker, Robert H., 39, 42
Wallace, Anthony F. C., 64
Ward, John William, 63, 68-69, 203, 209
Weber, Max, 88, 100
Whitman, Walt, 62, 77, 204
Wise, Gene, 64
Wolfe, Alan, 31, 59, 77, 107
World War I, 27
World War II, 34, 61, 86, 168

Yale University, 45, 172, 174, 184

Contributors

Rob Kroes, since 2005 emeritus professor of American Studies, University of Amsterdam, is an authority on the history of social, cultural, and intellectual life, who has published on virtually every aspect of the United States. He served as President of the European Association of American Studies, and has edited a comprehensive series of American Studies essays, running to more than 60 volumes.

Rolf Lundén, emeritus professor of American Studies, Uppsala University from 2007, has published widely on American Studies, particularly in the relations of literature and culture. He is one of the founders of American Studies in Sweden and the Nordic nations.

David E. Nye, professor of American Studies, SDU-Odense, has been an editor of *American Studies in Scandinavia*. He focuses on technology in American culture, but also writes more generally on US literature and cultural history. In 2005 he received the Leonardo Da Vinci Medal.

Mark Lucarrelli, associate professor of American Studies, University of Oslo, is a specialist in American cultural and environmental history, whose interests also range into American literature and the arts.

Jørn Brøndal, associate professor of American Studies, SDU-Odense, is a specialist in the history of American immigration, race, and ethnicity. His work was recognized by a prize from the Wisconsin Historical Association.

Orm Øverland, since 2006 emeritus professor of American Studies, University of Bergen, has written widely on American literature, immigration, and cultural history. One of the founders of the Nordic Association for American Studies, he long served as editor of *American Studies in Scandinavia*.